# NONPROFIT
# TOUCHDOWN

DR. KITTY BICKFORD, DBS

# NONPROFIT TOUCHDOWN

## WINNING THE 501(C) (3) GAME AGAINST IRS

CHALFANT ECKERT
PUBLISHING

ISBN-13: 978-1-63308-0003 (paperback journal edition)
ISBN-10: 163308005 (paperback journal edition)
ISBN-13: 978-1-63308-001-0 (ebook)
ISBN-10: 1633080013 (ebook)

*Cover Design by* GIDE+ART
*Interior Design by* R'tor John D. Maghuyop

**CHALFANT ECKERT**
PUBLISHING

1028 S Bishop Avenue, Dept. 178
Rolla, MO 65401

www.doyourownnonprofit.com

Printed in the United States of America

*To David Stanley Kulow, Lt. Colonel, USAF, Retired,*

*Who believed in me before I believed in myself*

# TABLE OF CONTENTS

Foreword.................................................................xi

Acknowledgements ................................................xiii

Disclaimer ...........................................................xv

About the Author .................................................xvii

Introduction ..........................................................xxi

## PART I
## PRELIMINARY ORGANIZATIONAL SET UP

**Chapter 1:** Is a 501(c) (3) the Right Choice? ..........................27

**Chapter 2:** Select a Business Name and Reserve
It with the State ......................................................39

**Chapter 3:** Get a Federal Employer Identification
Number (FEIN).....................................................55

**Chapter 4:** Develop a Mission Statement ...............................61

**Chapter 5:** Form a Board of Directors .....................................81

**Chapter 6:** Prepare IRS-Compliant Organizing Document.....97

**Chapter 7:** What to Include in Articles of Incorporation ........105

**Chapter 8:** State Guidelines for Nonprofit Corporations.........113

**Chapter 9:** What to Include In Organizational Bylaws...........167

**Chapter 10:** Develop a Conflict of Interest Policy.....................179

**Chapter 11:** Hold and Document the First Board Meeting.......187

# PART II
# IRS FORM 1023 APPLICATION
# FOR TAX EXEMPT STATUS

**Chapter 12:** Filing IRS Form 1023 Request for Recognition of Exemption ....................................193

**Chapter 13:** Part 1: Identification of Applicant..........................203

**Chapter 14:** Part II: Organizational Structure ...........................209

**Chapter 15:** Part III: Provisions in your Organizing Documents....................................213

**Chapter 16:** Part IV: Narrative Description of Your Activities.........................................217

**Chapter 17:** Part V: Compensation and Other Financial Arrangements With Your Officers, Directors, Trustees, Employees, And Independent Contractors ...............................221

**Chapter 18:** Part VI: Your Members and Other Individuals and Organizations That Receive Benefits from You.....................................229

**Chapter 19:** Part VII: Your History............................................233

**Chapter 20:** Part VIII: Specific Activities ..................................237

**Chapter 21:** Part IX: Financial Data .........................................251

**Chapter 22:** Part X: Public Charity Status .................................265

**Chapter 23:** Part X: Schedules A, B, C, D...................................269

**Chapter 24:** Part X: Schedule E: Organizations Not Filing Form 1023 Within 27 Months of Formation.........289

**Chapter 25:** Part X: Schedules F, G, and H.................................293

**Chapter 26:** Part XI: User Fee Information..................................301

# PART III
# SPECIAL CIRCUMSTANCES

**Chapter 27:** Automatic Revocation of 501(c) (3) Status ...........305

**Chapter 28:** Interactive Online Form i1023 ..............................311

# PART IV
# OPTIONAL FOLLOW UP TASKS

**Chapter 29:** Register for Charitable Fundraising and
Solicitation ............................................................315

**Chapter 30:** Annual Filing Requirements with IRS...................337

**Chapter 31:** Apply for Nonprofit Standard Mail Rates.............343

**Chapter 32:** Get Sales Tax Exemption ......................................345

**Summary**.............................................................................351

**Appendix A**: Actual Approved Nonprofit Applications...............353

**Joint Venture Fundraising** ...........................................................369

# FOREWORD

We are all hesitant to begin something that we know nothing about. We talk ourselves out of even trying. I have seen a lot of people talk themselves out of trying to do something – such as playing a sport – because they don't understand it. Take football for instance. The plays seem difficult, because each position has its own special quality and some appear to be difficult to master. The confusion and reluctance usually stem from a lack of knowledge and understanding. But then they meet a coach who understands their dilemma. This coach sits down with them and explains the game in its simplest form. Once they begin to understand, it becomes clearer and they want to know more.

Then the coach hands them a playbook. This book simplifies the game even more. It gives specific directions of what a player in a specific position is supposed to do to make the machine (the team) work more efficiently. The playbook is simple and specific to each position. Each play is spelled out so there is no confusion.

The coach has removed the confusion to make it simple, fun, and successful. He's the expert. He understands that in order for you to be truly successful you must understand your role as a player. You must know all the ins and outs of each play. The coach's experience makes it possible for him to simplify the game enough for anyone to be successful.

This book, *"Nonprofit Touchdown,"* is your playbook, written by someone who has experienced the challenges involved in setting up a non-profit. With Kitty Bickford's education, experience, and military background, she understands how to simplify things so that people can clearly understand the process.

In *"Nonprofit Touchdown,"* Kitty has done much of the legwork and taken out a lot of the confusion of Who, What, Why, When, Where, and How and replaced the question marks with check marks. In doing so, she simplifies the playbook and the game. This book covers everything you have to do at the state and federal level in easy-to-understand terms and in logical order. This step-by-step book will walk you through the process of how to get started, how to maintain momentum, and how to finish.

In football, the easier you make the playbook, the more the players will understand it, and the more wins you will have. It's the same with this book. It's written in a simple format so more people can understand it and more people can have success.

Now let's get started scoring with the *"Nonprofit Touchdown"*!

Reggie McElroy
NFL FOOTBALL (Retired)
NY Jets, 1982-1989; LA Raiders, 1991-1992;
KC Chiefs, 1993; Minnesota Vikings,
1994; Denver Broncos, 1995-1996
Alternative School Teacher
Rolla Public Schools
Rolla, Missouri

# ACKNOWLEDGEMENTS

I would like to express my gratitude to the many people who stood by me, stayed out of my way, did without me, and helped me get this book finished. I am especially grateful to my husband for keeping me in coffee and listening to me ramble on during my research, not having a clue what I was talking about, but nodding appropriately and smiling just the same. Thank you, my family, for giving me time and space to work when it would have been better for you if I had gone to those soccer games or out to lunch with you.

My editor was amazing. Thanks Norma Jean Lutz (www.normajeanlutz.com). Your kind, quiet spirit and prayers for me were greatly appreciated, and your patience was wonderful. Gleaning from your experience of publishing 50 books was a real treat, I learned a lot from you.

I also want to thank Steve Eggleston, the attorney who tackled my project of creating templates for state and IRS compliant Articles of Incorporation and Bylaws for all 50 states and DC. Having these available for my readers will save them more time than anything else in the 501(c) (3) process. I know it was a lot of work, and I thank you. My readers do too because now they can finish a laborious, time-consuming job in a matter of minutes with full confidence in the legal integrity and substance of their documents. You took the guesswork out. Your Christian character was obvious, your fees were fair, and I enjoyed working with you. (Steve@EggmanGlobal.com)

I am thankful to my friend and colleague, Reggie McElroy, for letting me put his picture on the cover and for all his encouragement. He consistently reminded me that much good would come from this effort and many nonprofits would be started that would make the world a better place.

# DISCLAIMER

While the information contained in this book was prepared with best efforts and in good faith, the publisher and author make no representations or warranties with respect to the accuracy or completeness of the contents herein.

This work (in any electronic or digital form or in any other printed material form) is not intended for use as a source of legal, accounting, tax, or financial advice. If advice concerning legal, accounting, tax, financial, or any other professional advice is needed, the services of a qualified, properly licensed and competent professional should be sought.

The contents of this work reflect the views and opinions of the author. The author and publisher have made their best effort to produce a high quality, informative and helpful course on getting approved for Section 501(c) (3) status by the Internal Revenue Service (IRS). But they make no representation or warranties of any kind with regard to the completeness and accuracy of the contents of the course. Any slights of people and/or organizations are unintentional.

Neither the author nor the publisher accept any liability of any kind for any losses or damages caused or alleged to be caused, directly or indirectly, from using the information contained in this book. Every individual must make his or her own decisions. Although this book describes the experiences of the author, it in no way guarantees similar success for others. Every effort has been made to ensure that this publication is free from errors and/or problems.

# ABOUT THE AUTHOR

## MILITARY CAREER

Dr. Kitty Bickford was born in Holden, West Virginia, but transplanted to a cattle ranch in Cleburne, Texas as a child. She is a Christian woman who spent from 1979 to 1989 on active duty in the United States Air Force, with duty assignments as diverse as Dover Air Force Base, Delaware; the Azore Islands off the coast of Portugal; and a remote assignment to Kunsan, South Korea.

The last five years of her military career were spent as a Master Instructor and On-the-Job Training Advisor for Air Training Command, achieving the noncommissioned officer rank of E-6, Technical Sergeant. (This was at a time when women made up only 14% of the total military personnel. That was up from 7% when Kitty enlisted.)

## SERGEANT JIM BICKFORD

In 1984, tall, silver-haired, crusty reservist Master Sergeant, Jim Bickford, (twenty two years Kitty's senior) came through her office. The Sergeant was upset about having to complete complicated paperwork in triplicate to get carpentry tools for his troops from the supply squadron. He ranted, "Does the buck stop anywhere on this base?" Kitty replied, "Sit down Serge. The buck stops here."

She gave him a cup of coffee, helped him get his toolboxes, and more than thirty years later, they are happily married best friends with four children, fourteen grandchildren (one with God), and two great grandchildren.

## MILITARY COMMENDATIONS

Kitty received two Air Force Commendation Medals, one for technical instruction excellence and the other for excellence in journalism. She was chosen Noncommissioned Officer of the Year for 1987 competing against 94 contenders worldwide. She was also nominated to compete for "12 Outstanding Airmen of America" in 1987. Additionally she received two Superior Achievement awards, two Professional Performer awards, and two Gold Quill Awards for excellence in journalism.

Kitty left the military in 1989 after Jim retired in 1987, but not before completing high school, college, and graduate school. Once she returned to civilian life, she served as Regional Vice President, Primerica Corporation from 1989 -1991, supervising investment counselors and marketing variable contracts such as mutual funds.

## HOME TO MISSOURI

They moved to Rolla, Missouri, to be close to family after being away so many years. There Kitty accepted a position at Boys Town of Missouri as a social worker and group therapist by day, and adjunct professor at Columbia College by night.

Over the years, Kitty and Jim owned various businesses including real estate rental homes and a trucking company. All of their businesses were sold to reduce their workload after Jim suffered a massive stroke that left him a vegetable in a wheelchair in 2001. Over time, God healed Jim, at which time Kitty was able to go back to work.

## TEACHING AND MISSIONARY WORK

She has taught Family and Consumer Science at Rolla Middle School since 2004 and holds lifetime teaching certifications in nine curriculums. She serves on the Board of Directors for Kid Care America/Thrive Student Centers, an afterschool program for at-risk children run by the Assemblies of God church. Jim and Kitty spend their Spring breaks and summers doing mission work from Dillingham, Alaska to Swaziland, Africa.

In 2006, Kitty was selected as ING Corporation's Unsung Hero for Missouri for educational innovation. She has made over 200 microfinance loans to the world's poor through Kiva.org, mostly disadvantaged women. These loans allow women to start their own businesses and become self-sufficient.

She supports missionaries to Zimbabwe, Botswana, Zambia, and Ukraine. She was awarded the 2013 Spirit of Rolla Award in recognition of significant achievement and/or lifetime contribution to the spirit of giving. She holds undergraduate degrees in Educational Administration, Behavioral Science, and Criminal Justice, completed the undergraduate teacher certification program for Missouri, holds a graduate degree in Psychology, has studied Special Education at the doctorate level, and holds a Doctorate in Biblical Studies. She is part of a cohort group through Columbia University looking at the possibilities of Sustainable Development to reduce poverty in third world countries.

# INTRODUCTION

## MY ADOPTED/SPONSORED CHILD

You may be wondering why on earth a grandmother, educator, business woman, ex-military noncommissioned officer would take it upon herself to write a book about setting up a 501(c) (3) tax exempt organization. It all stems from a decision that I made in 2005 to *adopt* (sponsor) a child from a third-world country to provide financial support for that child. The story grows and evolves from that point. No need to relay all the details in this introduction because that would require another entire book. But let me briefly explain what happened.

Once I made the decision, I sent off my application papers, eager to learn about my adopted child. From the outset, I assumed the child would be from India. But when the sponsor package arrived, what a surprise to find a six-year-old boy from Swaziland, Africa, with a name I couldn't pronounce.

## I LEARN ABOUT SWAZILAND

I went online and learned that Swaziland was a tiny country about the size of New Jersey, three quarters surrounded by South Africa, and one quarter by Mozambique. It was one of the few countries that still had a king. The HIV/AIDS pandemic had affected up to 40% of the population, and the average life expectancy was between 31 and 45 years depending on which report I read. In this small country with just over a million people, more than 100,000 children were orphans. Now my heart was even more touched.

## A TRIP TO AFRICA REVEALS THE TRUTH

As I continued to support this child with my finances, I noticed in the organization's literature that they sponsored no children over thirteen years of age. I wondered what would happen to *my* child when he reached that age. This is when I first got the idea of getting on a plane to go visit him. (You have to understand that for a seasoned military traveler like me, this was not as adventurous an undertaking as it first sounds.)

The upshot was that on my visit I discovered the sponsoring organization was not handling the funds with the level of integrity that I expected. Not only that, but I also discovered that the letters I had been receiving from my adopted child were not really from him.

Needless to say, I took immediate action. Upon arriving home I cancelled my sponsorship and began supporting the family one-on-one.

## STARTING OUR OWN 501(C) (3) NONPROFIT ORGANIZATION

Over the months after returning home, God spoke to me about my experiences in Africa. I relived the poverty and struggles I had witnessed from the moment my feet had touched pavement on that continent. I have never been the same, and I have not spent a single day that the plight of the orphans and vulnerable families has not been on my mind and weighed heavily on my heart.

This is when I began to understand that God was leading me to do something about the plight of these people. At first, I wasn't sure what to do, but after much prayer, I knew He wanted me to start our own 501(c) (3) nonprofit to benefit orphans and vulnerable families in Swaziland. This would be an organization that would not be corrupt and would actually do the right thing, an organization that would be effective.

Then came the *sticker shock.* I discovered that it would take up to $7,000 just for the paperwork to set up such a structure. That much money would feed a lot of people in Swaziland. So I set out to do it on my own. After all, how difficult could it be to get the needed paperwork together? I soon learned! It was *extremely difficult!*

There was plenty of segmented, and extremely unorganized, general guidance available, but very little that specifically told me where to begin in Missouri to create a public charity to benefit orphans in another country.

## ACHIEVING THE FINAL GOAL

Little by little I walked through process, stumbling here and hitting brick walls there, until at long last we did achieve the final goal. The IRS approved Pasture Valley Children Missions, www.pasturevalleychildren.com (EIN 35-2468924) on the first try.

I was elated when the determination letter arrived and a fledgling organization was born that would feed hungry children and help pull vulnerable families out of poverty. I praised God for helping me to figure it out and for helping me not to give up when I got confused about what to do next – and had no one to ask.

But the journey wasn't over. Next He spoke to my spirit and said, "Now write a book about your experience so others can do the same thing."

And so I did.

## A GUIDEBOOK – NOT AN ENTERTAINMENT BOOK

By its very nature, this is a book full of methodical, industry specific tables. Remember, this is a guidebook, not a book to entertain. I have here assembled, in one concise place, extensive information that required many months of my time to compile.

Throughout the book you will see the football analogy. This is because at times you will feel you are playing a game – and it's definitely a game that you want to win. This then is your playbook. Herein you will find all the tactics, plays, and strategies needed to make touchdown after touchdown.

The structure of your playbook is designed in such a way that you can literally move from one step to the next, in logical fashion, to apply for your own 501(c) (3) tax exempt organization.

The game of football has its own set of terms and jargon. If you aren't sure what a coffin corner means, or a fumble, or I-formation, or sack, or pick-six, then how will you be able to play the game well? (Or enjoy the game if you are an avid fan and spectator.)

The same is true with applying for your own 501(c) (3) tax exempt organization. Terms that were once foreign to you will be explained in detail in this your playbook so that you can avoid confusion.

Likewise, each football team has different positions such as the lineman, the quarterback, the receivers and so on. In this game of getting your nonprofit status, there are players in the game which are the different offices of the IRS and state agencies that you may have to deal with. Throughout the playbook, I have included the needed contact websites and/or phone numbers of those offices.

In order to play a great game, players often watch videos of other teams in action. From this they learn from example how to execute various plays. This is why I have included an amazing number of examples of other organizations. You can learn a great deal from studying their *plays* so to speak. Why reinvent the wheel, when so many have gone before you – those who have already made their touchdowns and have won their game, and have already received their nonprofit status. (These can be found in *Appendix A: Actual Approved Nonprofit Applications.*)

If you have questions or comments please get in touch with me. I'll help you all I can. Visit www.doyourownnonprofit.com if you need to email me, read my blog, or want fill-in-the-blank state forms to save time.

Meanwhile, here's to your fledgling 501(c) (3) tax exempt organization. And may God bless all your endeavors; and may your touchdowns be many.

Your questions and comments are important to me. Visit www.doyourownnonprofit.com to read the forum and blog, email me, or get fill-in-the-blank state templates to save you time.

# PART I

## PRELIMINARY ORGANIZATIONAL SET UP

# CHAPTER 1

## IS A 501(C) (3) THE RIGHT CHOICE?

*"The game of life is a lot like football. You have to
tackle your problems, block your fears, and score your points when
you get the opportunity."*

—Lewis Grizzard

It is the mission of the Challenged Athletes Foundation® (CAF) to provide opportunities and support to people with physical disabilities so they can pursue active lifestyles through physical fitness and competitive athletics. CAF believes that involvement in sports at any level increases self-esteem, encourages independence and enhances quality of life. (CA)

### YOU NEED AN ATTENTIVE COACH

No football game is complete without a slew of yelling coaches on the sidelines. They stomp, pace, fret, shout, jab their fists in the air, and are almost as entertaining as the game itself. But we all know that game day is not the same as the day-in and day-out hours of grueling hard work that coaches put in to keep their team members at the peak of their playing capacity.

I promise not to yell, but I am stepping up to be your coach in this game. I've played this game before, I've scored a few touchdowns, and I know ways in which the game can be won. I've watched the other teams and I know how they play and I can help you learn from them.

I'm confident in my position and my ability to guide you into your own victory. I have the game plan well in hand and am ready to share it with you. Let's get started!

## BENEFITS OF STARTING A 501(C) (3) TAX EXEMPT ORGANIZATION

So you want to start a nonprofit organization and you don't happen to have hundreds, or thousands of dollars lying around to spend on an attorney to get things going? I'm here to let you know that you're not alone.

I've met many people down through the years who are in the same predicament. Because of that, I've written this book to share the knowledge that I have acquired in walking through the process of setting up a 501(c) (3) without the aid of an attorney.

By reading this book, you will see that much of the legwork has already been done for you. I have provided examples of what completed packages look like and what they include. You are going to discover – to your delight – that the logistical process of starting a 501(c) (3) tax exempt organization is not that complicated.

Many rewards are awaiting those who establish a 501(c) (3) tax exempt organization – some are intangible; some are tangible. Below are a few of the more tangible benefits:

- Tax deductions to contributors
- Limited liability
- Perpetual existence and permanence

- Eligibility for grants
- Tax exempt purchasing power in some states
- Reduced postage
- Discounted internet service provider costs
- Public service announcements on the radio and other media at little or no charge.

## DISADVANTAGES

### Cost

On the flip side of the coin, you will find there are also disadvantages in this process. These include the costs and the time involved to complete the requirements. Your state charges a fee (normally under $125) to register and establish your nonprofit organization. IRS charges either $400 or $850 to accept an application for processing, with no promise of approval. Their charge is contingent upon the submitted budget, even if the budget is an estimate of future finances.

If you also choose to pay an attorney or an accountant to complete the required paperwork, it can range from several hundred to do the minimum up to $7,000 to do everything!

[Good news! If you follow the steps in this book, you eliminate the attorney and accountant fees.]

### Paperwork Nightmare

Another disadvantage is that this process can become a virtual paperwork nightmare. The initial package to IRS with attachments can be dozens of pages. Then – except for churches and organizations that fall under the church umbrella – an annual report must be filed to continue tax exempt status.

### Miscellaneous Stipulations

Over 400,000 nonprofits have recently been automatically revoked by IRS for failure to file *Form 990* reports. This book will cover the reinstatement process for those organizations. In addition, public charities must be funded by a variety of donors beginning the sixth year, not the same foundations and board members year after year as their main means of financial support. There are also limitations and rules on fundraising activities for nonprofits. Failure to comply can result in loss of 501(c) (3) status.

The Internal Revenue Service (IRS) states that for an organization to be tax-exempt, it must be "organized and operated exclusively for exempt purposes set forth in section 501(c) (3)..."

Those exempt purposes include:

- Charitable
- Religious
- Educational
- Scientific
- Literary
- testing for public safety (although contributions are not tax deductible)
- fostering national or international sports competition
- preventing cruelty to children and animals

Tax exempt organizations eligible for 501(c) (3) status are normally nonprofit corporations, but can be cooperative associations; funds; foundations; or community chests that collect money from local people and redistribute it to local people, such as the local United Way. The form of organization is important to qualify for 501(c) (3) status. Individual proprietorships, partnerships, and private foundations do not qualify for 501(c) (3) status.

## IRS DIRECTIVE

Here's how the IRS looks at the status:

> ... the term charitable is used in its generally accepted legal sense and includes relief of the poor, the distressed, or the underprivileged; advancement of religion; advancement of education or science;

*erecting or maintaining public buildings, monuments, or works; lessening the burdens of government; lessening neighborhood tensions; eliminating prejudice and discrimination; defending human and civil rights secured by law; and combating community deterioration and juvenile delinquency.*

## CHURCHES AND RELIGIOUS ENTITIES

Religious nonprofits are harder to pinpoint, but form a class of exemption with some commonalities. If it looks like a church, acts like a church, operates like a church, and feels like a church, then it is probably a church. However, a church must have:

- distinct religious beliefs
- a location to meet
- a schedule of services on a regular basis
- a stable group of people that make up the congregation

Proof of these things may be required to get the exemption. IRS defines church to also include synagogues, temples, and mosques.

In the list below are those that do not have to file the 501(c) (3) application as they are automatically exempt:

- Churches
- Interchurch organizations of the local units of the church
- Conventions or associations of churches
- Integrated auxiliaries of a church (such as a men's or women's organization)
- Religious schools
- Mission societies
- Youth groups

That being said, many churches still choose to file because it assures their donors that contributions qualify for tax deductions. Church auxiliary organizations can fall under the umbrella of the church for 501(c) (3) purposes under certain circumstances. The benefit of being under that umbrella is that there is no requirement to file an annual return with IRS.

Many other religious organizations that are not churches under IRS codes, may still qualify for tax exempt status as religious organizations. These might include:

- Mission organizations
- Speakers' organizations
- Nondenominational ministries
- Ecumenical organizations
- Faith-based social agencies

Each of the above may fulfill the intent of religious exemption and therefore be granted 501(c) (3) status by IRS.

## EDUCATIONAL ORGANIZATIONS

The IRS definition of educational organizations include schools at all levels from elementary to college, as well as trade schools, correspondence schools, and schools that provide education through media such as TV or radio. Some other types of organizations that may not be immediately obvious as educational may qualify:

- Museums
- Zoos
- Planetariums
- Symphony orchestras
- Organizations that conduct public discussion groups, forums, panels, and lectures.

In addition, nonprofit day care centers and youth sports organizations may qualify as educational tax exempt organizations.

## SCIENTIFIC ORGANIZATIONS

Scientific organizations that want 501(c) (3) status must demonstrate that their research is in the public interest. This is done by using the results (including patents, copyrights, processes, or formulas) in a nondiscriminatory way for the public good. The research can be for science education, publication available to the public, curing disease, or to help attract new industry to an area. Research does not include product testing.

## LITERARY ORGANIZATIONS

Literary organizations seeking 501(c) (3) status must be able to show that any sales or publishing they do is related to their tax exempt purpose.

## AMATEUR ATHLETIC ORGANIZATIONS

Amateur Athletic organizations fall into two categories:

1. Those that promote national or international amateur sports competition but do not supply facilities or equipment
2. Those that exclusively develop athletes and/or conduct the national or international amateur sports competition and provide facilities and equipment, even though the membership is local or regional.

## ORGANIZATIONS THAT PREVENT CRUELTY TO CHILDREN AND ANIMALS

Organizations that seek to prevent cruelty to children and animals may:

- Try to protect children forced into labor in dangerous jobs
- Advocate alternatives to child abuse

- Seek humane treatment for laboratory animals
- Assist in animal population control
- Provide shelters for abused animals
- Other attempts to positively impact cruelty to animals or children

## ORGANIZATIONS THAT DO NOT QUALIFY

The following types of organizations DO NOT qualify for 501(c) (3) status:

- Instrumentalities of the United States organized under an act of Congress (like Federal Credit Unions). These are 501(c) (1) organizations.
- Title holding corporations for exempt organizations that collect and pay income from property to exempt organizations. These are 501(c) (2) organizations.
- Civil leagues, social welfare organizations, local associations of employees. These are 501(c) (4) organizations.
- Labor, agriculture, and horticultural organizations. These are 501(c) (5) organizations.
- Business leagues, chambers of commerce, and real estate boards. These are 501(c) (6) organizations.
- Social and recreational clubs. These are 501(c) (7) organizations.
- Fraternal beneficiary societies and associations. These are 501(c) (8) organizations.
- Voluntary employee beneficiary associations. These are 501(c) (9) organizations.
- Domestic fraternal societies, orders, or associations. These are 501(c) (10) organizations.
- Teacher's Retirement Funds. These are 501(c) (11) organizations.
- Local benevolent life insurance associations, mutual ditch or irrigation companies, mutual or cooperative electric or

telephone companies and like organizations. These are 501(c) (12) organizations.

- Cemetery companies. These are 501(c) (13) organizations.
- State chartered credit unions. These are 501(c) (14) organizations.
- Small insurance companies and associations providing insurance to members substantially at cost. These are 501(c) (15) organizations.
- Cooperative organizations to finance crop operations. These are 501(c) (16) organizations.
- Supplemental unemployment benefit trusts. These are 501(c) (17) organizations.
- Employee funded pension trusts created before 1959. These are 501(c) (18) organizations.
- War veterans' organizations. These are 501(c) (19) organizations.
- Black lung benefit trusts. These are 501(c) (21) organizations.
- Withdrawal liability payment funds. These are 501(c) (22) organizations.
- Veterans' organizations created before 1880. These are 501(c) (23) organizations.
- Title holding corporations or trusts with multiple parents. These are 501(c) (25) organizations.
- State sponsored organizations providing health coverage for high-risk individuals. These are 501(c) (26) organizations.
- State-sponsored Worker's Compensation reinsurance organizations. These are 501(c) (27) organizations.
- National Railroad Retirement Investment Trusts. These are 501(c) (28) organizations.
- Religious and apostolic organizations (communal religious communities). These are 501(d) organizations.
- Cooperative hospital service organizations. These are 501(e) organizations.

- Cooperative service organizations of operating educational organizations that perform collective investment services for educational organizations. These are 501(f) organizations.
- Child care organizations. These are 501(k) organizations.
- Charitable risk pools that pool certain insurance risks of 501(c) (3) organizations. These are 501(n) organizations.
- Farmers' cooperative organizations. These are 521(a) organizations.
- Political organizations accepting contributions or making expenditures for political campaigns. These are 527 organizations.

## SEPARATE ENTITY FROM FOUNDERS

Your organization must be set up and organized in such a way that IRS recognizes it as a separate entity from its founders. In other words, the people who start it do not own it. It is not their organization; it is separate and perpetual and will survive even if the founders do not.

For this reason, be careful not to set yourself as an owner of a 501(c) (3) organization. You can start it, you can be on the board, you can be president of the board, you can be an advisor, but you *cannot be an owner*. A tax-exempt organization is NOT owned. It is not operated by one individual, it is normally governed and run by a board of directors, and there are distinct rules about the number and relationships of those on the board (covered in a later chapter).

## NOT FOR PRIVATE INTEREST

Section 501(c) (3) status DOES NOT apply to organizations created for the benefit of private interests or those that do not receive a substantial part of their income from the general public or the government. You cannot get 501(c) (3) status so that you or your family or friends can benefit from the tax exempt status. It must be public to be eligible for 501(c) (3). Your organization also cannot be set up to benefit a specific person or organization. You cannot participate in political campaigns directly or indirectly at any level, but you can have educational meetings, create educational materials, and appear before government bodies. You can encourage people to vote, but cannot specify in any way who to vote for. A substantial portion of the nonprofit organization's assets or their activities cannot be spent on lobbying or other means of influencing legislation. At the time of this writing, for most organizations, the asset usage cutoff for lobbying was 20% of exempt purpose expenditures. You cannot exist to operate a business that is not related to your exempt purpose, and you cannot engage in illegal activities.

Now that you have a general idea of what qualifies an organization or group for a 501(c) (3) status, in the following chapter we will discuss how to choose your group's name and how to reserve that name with your state offices.

# CHAPTER 2

## SELECT A BUSINESS NAME AND RESERVE IT WITH THE STATE

*"Build up your weaknesses until they become your strong points."*
—Knute Rockne

JDCF is a 501(c) (3) public charity and was founded by Covina, CA native and former NFL defensive back, Jason David. Founded on the basis of "Bringing Faith and Courage to Every Corner of the Community," JDCF provides guidance to young boys and girls by offering a free summer Youth Football Camp held annually at Charter Oak High School. After losing a family member to kidney disease in 2007, Jason decided to donate proceeds from his Annual Celebrity Golf Tournament towards increasing the research and awareness of kidney disease to help promote prevention and ultimately find a cure.

## KNOW A FOOTBALL TEAM BY ITS COLORS AND MASCOT

You are faced with a few decisions early on in setting up your nonprofit organization, one of which will be a solid, recognizable name. (Later on perhaps a logo to go along with it.)

In the state of Oklahoma the two rival football teams, Oklahoma State University (OSU) and Oklahoma University (OU), are well known for their colors. One need not even know the names of the colleges to recognize the teams. OSU is bright (*bright*) orange and black. OU is crimson and cream. The flags, banners, bumper stickers, caps, t-shirts and other paraphernalia from each school are recognized at a glance.

This is just one example of how the public recognizes their favorite teams in football. When your nonprofit is still in the planning stages you will want to give a great deal of thought in how to create a name that will clearly define who you are and the mission that you represent.

## FILING ARTICLES OF INCORPORATION

Only trusts, unincorporated associations, or corporations (including limited liability corporations in some instances) are eligible for 501(c)(3) status. Corporations are the most popular entity for nonprofit organizations, and are established by filing articles of organization paperwork with the Secretary of State's office. In most states, the way to form that organization is by filing Articles of Incorporation. Some states require documents by other names, but they all include the same basic information. The filing process will be covered in a subsequent chapter. Limited liability corporations must file Articles of Association, and Trusts file a trust agreement or Declaration of Trust. Don't stress about preparing the documents. I remember trying to figure out the wording and making sure everything was IRS compliant when I started Pasture Valley Children Missions. I do not want you to go through that, so I hired an attorney, Steve Eggleston, J.D., on your behalf to prepare IRS compliant Word and pdf templates for each state. These are legally perfect fill-in-the-blank documents that you complete or alter as needed, print, and mail: done in less than 10 minutes. You are welcome! They are available for a small fee at www.doyourownnonprofit.com

## NAME SELECTION

No two organizations within a state can have the same name. Therefore, before you can start a nonprofit, you must make sure the name you want is available in your state. You may reserve the name you want if desired. If you are in Alabama, it is *required* – except for churches.

Almost all states make it optional to reserve a business name, and a few states do not have name reservation for nonprofit organizations. It is one more step and one more expense. Unless the state requires it or you think someone else may register the same name for a business before you get your organizational paperwork completed, you may just want to skip this step and save the money.

## INCLUDE DESIGNATION

You should also be aware that many states require your name to include a designation at the end to identify the type of entity you have set up, such as Corporation, Inc., LLC, etc. Most nonprofits are established as corporations with the state, which allows them to later seek 501(c) (3) status with IRS. Even if the state does not require a designation at the end of the formal name of the entity, you must select a designation with the state when you file your organizational paperwork.

To save your time, I have provided quick access below for each state. All links worked at the time of publication, but if one no longer works, do an internet search for "Business Entity Search" and the name of the state. That should get you close to the right place to search. If you have additional questions, call the Secretary of State's office for your state and they will steer you in the right direction to get answers.

Below you will find:

- A link to check name availability for your state
- Where to go to reserve a name if you choose to

These links are available live to click on at www.doyourownnonprofit. com

| ST | To Check Availability of Name | Where to go to Reserve the Name |
|---|---|---|
| AL | http://www.sos.alabama. gov/vb/inquiry/inquiry. aspx?area=Business Entity | Name reservations are submitted to the Probate Recording Office in the county where the organization will initially be based. The form is located at: http://www.sos.alabama.gov/ downloads/business/domesti- cEntityNameReservation.pdf |
| AK | http://commerce.alaska.gov/ CBP/Main/CBPLSearch. aspx?mode=Corp | You may reserve the name for 120 days using Form 08-559 available at http://www.commerce.state. ak.us/occ/corp_formsfees.html Scroll down to name reservation. |
| AZ | http://starpas.azcc. gov/scripts/cgiip.exe/ WService=wsbroker1/ eforms.p?form- number=CF0059 | You may reserve the name for 120 days http://star- pas.azcc.gov/scripts/cgiip. exe/WService=wsbroker1/ eforms.p?form- number=CF0059 |

| AR | http://www.sos.arkansas.gov/corps/search_all.php | You may reserve the name for 120 days, but it is established when you file your Articles of Incorporation. This state's on-line Articles of Incorporation filing meets IRS guidelines for 501(c) (3). File form DN-02<br><br>https://www.ark.org/sos/ofs/docs/index.php |
|---|---|---|
| CA | http://www.sos.ca.gov/business/be/name-availability.htm#checking<br><br>You must fill out the form and mail it to:<br><br>Secretary of State<br>Name Availability Unit<br>1500 11th Street, 3rd Floor<br>Sacramento, CA 95814. | You may reserve the name for 60 days. Fill out Name Reservation Request Form found at http://www.sos.ca.gov/business/be/name-availability.htm#reserving |
| CO | https://www.sos.state.co.us/biz/BusinessEntityCriteriaExt.do?resetTransTyp=Y | You may reserve the name for 120 days (120 day renewal available) at http://www.sos.state.co.us/biz/FileDocNameAvailCriteria.do?transTyp=RS<br><br>MUST BE FILED ELECTRONICALLY, no paper forms accepted. |
| CT | http://www.concord-sots.ct.gov/CONCORD/online?sn=PublicInquiry&eid=9740 or call 860-509-6002 | You may reserve a business name using Form CNR-1-1.0 for 120 days. http://www.sots.ct.gov/sots/cwp/view.asp?a=3177&q=392124 |

| | | |
|---|---|---|
| | | Click on Corporation forms, then on Domestic NonStock Application for Reservation of Name. Otherwise, you register your organization name with your Certificate of Incorporation for a NonStock Corporation. |
| DE | https://delecorp.delaware.gov/tin/EntitySearch.jsp or<br><br>https://delecorp.delaware.gov/tin/GINameSearch.jsp | You may reserve the name for 120 days https://delecorp.delaware.gov/tin/EntitySearch.jsp |
| DC | https://corp.dcra.dc.gov/Account.aspx/LogOn?ReturnUrl=%2f | You must register to search for an existing name in DC by setting up an online account at https://corp.dcra.dc.gov/Account.aspx/LogOn?ReturnUrl=%2f<br><br>A business entity name may be reserved for 60 days. |
| FL | http://search.sunbiz.org/Inquiry/CorporationSearch/ByName | Your name is registered with your Non Profit Articles of Incorporation |
| GA | http://corp.sos.state.ga.us/corp/soskb/csearch.asp | Name reservation is not required, but it is available and may cut down on processing time for your organizational paperwork. http://www.sos.georgia.gov/corporations/name_reserve.htm |

| HI | http://hbe.ehawaii. gov/documents/search. html?mobile=N&site_ preference=normal | In Hawaii, you form a business and do all the paperwork online in one process that gives you complete registration including name, and tax payer ID<br><br>https://hbe.ehawaii.gov/BizEx/home.eb |
|---|---|---|
| IA | http://sos.iowa.gov/ search/business/ (S(2gmel52ncv3mri45hlnxsfyz))/ search.aspx | You may reserve the name for 120 days http://sos.iowa. gov/business/FormsAndFees. html#DNC504 |
| ID | http://www.accessi- daho.org/public/sos/corp/ search.html?ScriptForm. startstep=crit | You may reserve the name for up to 4 months http://www.sos. idaho.gov/CORP/reservation. htm |
| IL | http://www.ilsos.gov/ corporatellc/ | You may reserve the name for up to 90 days. Form NFP 104.10<br><br>http://www.cyberdriveillinois. com/departments/business_ser- vices/corp.html and scroll down to Reservation of Name |
| IN | https://secure.in.gov/sos/on- line_corps/name_search.aspx | You may reserve the name for 120 days. State Form 26233 https://secure.in.gov/sos/reg- istration/select_entity_type. aspx?Type=RN |
| KS | https://www.accesskansas.org/ businesscenter/index.html | You may reserve the name for 120 days https://www.kansas. gov/businesscenter/ |

|  |  | Do a name availability search for your business and when it comes up as not found, you can reserve it online for a fee. |
|---|---|---|
| KY | https://app.sos.ky.gov/ftsearch/ | You may reserve the name for 120 days http://www.sos.ky.gov/business/filings/nameavailability/<br><br>and clicking on Application for Reserved Name |
| LA | http://www.sos.la.gov/tabid/819/Default.aspx | You may reserve the name for 120 days http://www.sos.la.gov/Home/Commercial/Corporations/FileOnline/OriginalFilings/tabid/1009/Default.aspx Click on Name Reservation for Corporation or Limited Liability Corporation |
| MA | http://corp.sec.state.ma.us/corp/corpsearch/corp-searchinput.asp | You may reserve the name for 60 days, and renew for 60 days.<br><br>http://www.sec.state.ma.us/cor/corpweb/cornameres/nameres-inf.htm |
| MD | http://sdatcert3.re-siusa.org/UCC-Charter/CharterSearch_f.aspx | Nonprofit name is established when you file Articles of Incorporation for a Tax Exempt Corporation (they charge an extra fee for nonprofit organizations to file). http://www.dat.state.md.us/sdatweb/sdatforms.html#entity |

| | | |
|---|---|---|
| | | Remember not to file the standard state documents, you must add IRS wording to be tax exempt 501(c) (3) |
| ME | https://icrs.informe. org/nei-sos-icrs/ ICRS?MainPage=x | You my reserve the name for 120 days http://www.maine. gov/sos/cec/corp/formsnew/ mnpca1.pdf |
| MI | http://www.dleg.state.mi.us/ bcs_corp/sr_corp.asp | You may reserve a name for 4 months by filing Form CSCL/ CD-540 http://www.dleg.state. mi.us/dms/results.asp?docowne r=BCSC&doccat=Corporation s&offset=25 |
| MN | http://mblsportal.sos.state. mn.us/ | You may reserve the name for one year

http://www.sos.state.mn.us/ index.aspx?page=1094 |
| MO | https://www.sos.mo.gov/Busi- nessEntity/soskb/csearch.asp | You may reserve the name for 60 days, and renew to 180 days. Form BE-1 available at

http://www.sos.mo.gov/busi- ness/corporations/forms.asp |
| MS | https://business.sos.state. ms.us/corp/soskb/CSearch. asp?dtm=590902777777778 | Nonprofits do not have to reserve business name. They file Articles of Incorporation. If you want 501(c) (3) status, DO NOT file the document as written, additional wording needed for 501(c) (3) status. http://www.sos.ms.gov/busi- ness_services_feesForms.aspx |

| MT | https://app.mt.gov/bes/ | You may reserve the name for 120 days, no renewals. http://sos.mt.gov/business/Forms/index.asp and scroll down to 79. |
|----|----|----|
| NE | https://www.nebraska.gov/sos/corp/corpsearch.cgi?nav=search | You may reserve the name for 120 days<br><br>http://www.sos.ne.gov/business/corp_serv/name_procedures.html Scroll down to business and nonprofit link. |
| NV | http://nvsos.gov/sosentitysearch/ | You may reserve the name for 90 days<br><br>http://nvsos.gov/index.aspx?page=139 |
| NH | https://www.sos.nh.gov/corporate/soskb/csearch.asp | Names cannot be reserved for nonprofits in advance of<br><br>Articles of Incorporation. |
| NJ | https://www.njportal.com/DOR/businessrecords/EntityDocs/BusinessStatCopies.aspx | You may reserve the name for 120 days with renewal for additional 120 days by filing Form unrr-1 in triplicate for nonprofits http://www.state.nj.us/treasury/revenue/dcr/geninfo/corpman.shtml#name |
| NM | https://efile.prc.newmexico.gov/Efile/corplookup/Lookdn.aspx | You may reserve the name for 120 days with no renewal by filing Form RS-CS (be sure to read notes at bottom of form for nonprofit code) http://www.nmprc.state.nm.us/corporations/corporation-forms.html |

|  |  | Scroll to bottom for Reservation: Profit/Nonprofit Requirements and Form |
|---|---|---|
| NY | http://www.dos.ny.gov/corps/bus_entity_search.html | You may reserve the name for 60 days with 2 extensions. You get a receipt called "Certification of Reservation" which must be filed when you file your articles of organization.<br><br>http://www.dos.ny.gov/corps/nfpcorp.html and click on fillable application for reservation of name form |
| NC | http://www.secretary.state.nc.us/corporations/CSearch.aspx | You may reserve the name by filing Form BE-03 http://www.secretary.state.nc.us/corporations/forms.aspx?pitemid=5429695&type=businessentity |
| ND | https://apps.nd.gov/sc/busn-srch/busnSearch.htm | You may reserve the name for 12 months (renewable) by Filing SFN 13015<br><br>http://www.nd.gov/sos/nonprofit/registration/corporation/forms.html |
| OH | http://www2.sos.state.oh.us/pls/portal/PORTAL_BS.BS_QRY_BUS_INFORMA-TION1.SHOW_PARMS | You may reserve the name for 180 days Form 534B. http://www.sos.state.oh.us/sos/upload/business/filingforms-feeschedule.asp x?page=251 and scroll way down to Name Reservation. |

| OK | https://www.sos.ok.gov/corp/corpInquiryFind.aspx | You may reserve the name for 60 days by filing SOS Form 0034<br><br>https://www.sos.ok.gov/business/forms.aspx Scroll down to Additional Business Entity Forms |
| --- | --- | --- |
| OR | http://egov.sos.state.or.us/br/pkg_web_name_srch_inq.login | You may reserve the name for 120 days but you have to call and request the form be sent to you (no email). (503) 986-2200. Not available online. |
| PA | https://www.corporations.state.pa.us/corp/soskb/csearch.asp?corpsNav= | You may reserve the name for 120 days by sending a written request (no form available) and $70 fee to:<br><br>Dept. of State, Room 206, 401 North Street, Harrisburg, PA 17120.<br><br>Contact by phone at (717) 787-1057. Website info: http://www.dos.state.pa.us/portal/server.pt/community/corporations/12457/name_availabilities/571895 and scroll to bottom for name reservation info. |
| RI | http://ucc.state.ri.us/CorpSearch/CorpSearchInput.asp | You may reserve the name for 120 days by filing Form 620. Not renewable for nonprofits.<br><br>http://sos.ri.gov/business/filings/corporateforms/domestic-business/ Scroll down to Reservation of Business Entity |

| | | |
|---|---|---|
| SC | http://www.scsos.com/ Search%20Business%20 Filings | You may reserve the name for 120 days. Not renewable. http://www.sos.sc.gov/ Library%20of%20Forms%20 and%20Fees Click on Nonprofit domestic or Nonprofit Foreign, and scroll down to Application to Reserve a Name |
| SD | http://sdsos.gov/Business/ Search.aspx | You may reserve the name for 120 days. Not renewable. http://sdsos.gov/content/viewcontent. aspx?cat=corporations&pg=/ corporations/corporations_ forms.shtm and scroll down to Nonprofit Corporations, click on Reservation of Nonprofit Name for either domestic or foreign corporation. |
| TN | http://tnbear.tn.gov/ECommerce/FilingSearch.aspx | You may reserve the name for 4 months by filing Form ss-4428 http://www.tn.gov/sos/bus_svc/ forms.htm and scroll down to Forms for both For-Profit and Non-Profit Corporations |
| TX | https://ourcpa.cpa.state.tx.us/ coa/ (Taxable Corps) or (512) 463-5555; corpinfo@sos.state. tx.us. | You may reserve the name using Form 501 or by registering the name online at http://www. sos.state.tx.us/corp/sosda/index.shtml |
| UT | https://secure.utah.gov/bes/ action/index | You may reserve the name for 120 days, but need to cancel the registration in order to file the Articles of Incorporation |

| | | |
|---|---|---|
| | | within that 120 days. http://corporations.utah.gov/business/nameinfo.html<br><br>Click on Application for Reservation of Business Name |
| VT | http://corps.sec.state.vt.us/corpbrow.aspx | You may reserve the name for 120 days, renewable twice. Submit form in duplicate.<br><br>http://www.sec.state.vt.us/tutor/dobiz/dobizdoc.htm<br><br>Click on Reserving a Name |
| VA | https://sccefile.scc.virginia.gov/NameAvailability | You may reserve the name for 120 days with renewals as long as you renew within 45 days of expiration. File FORM SCC631/830 http://www.scc.virginia.gov/clk/vanon_corp.aspx<br><br>And scroll down to form. Available in Word and .pdf formats. |
| WA | http://www.sos.wa.gov/corps/ | You may reserve the name for 180 days http://www.sos.wa.gov/corps/registration_forms.aspx<br><br>Scroll down to section on Organizational Maintenance and Procedure Forms |
| WV | http://apps.sos.wv.gov/business/corporations/ | You may reserve the name for 120 days by filing Form NR-1 |

| | | |
|---|---|---|
| | | http://www.sos.wv.gov/business-licensing/Pages/ReservingABusinessName.aspx and click on the link at Complete the Application |
| WI | https://www.wdfi.org/apps/CorpSearch/Search.aspx? | You may reserve the name for 120 days by submitting Form DFI/CORP/1 or a letter to: Department of Financial Institutions Division of Corporate & Consumer Services P O Box 7846 Madison WI 53707-7846 Form available at http://www.wdfi.org/corporations/faqs.htm Scroll down toward the bottom to General Guidelines, to the section called Reserve a Name and click on the Form 1 link. |
| WY | https://wyobiz.wy.gov/Business/FilingSearch.aspx | You may reserve the name for 120 days by filing NP-Name Reservation. Get form at http://soswy.state.wy.us/Forms/FormsFiling.aspx Click on Business Forms, then Nonprofit Corporations, then Wyoming or out of state forms. |

Now that you have the name of your entity settled, your next step will be to acquire the Federal Employer Identification Number. Details follow in the next chapter.

# CHAPTER 3

## GET A FEDERAL EMPLOYER IDENTIFICATION NUMBER (FEIN)

*"I learned that if you want to make it bad enough, no matter how bad it is, you can make it."*

—Gale Sayers

In 1997, Deanna and Brett Favre began the Brett Favre Fourward Foundation. They both wanted their outreach efforts to benefit disadvantaged and disabled children. Over the last ten years, the Foundation donated in excess of $3 million to charities in Wisconsin and Mississippi and signed untold numbers of in-kind items to be used for charity auctions.

### IMPORTANT NUMBER ON THE JERSEY

One of the more important numbers in football is the player's number on his jersey. The numbers appear on the front and back of the jersey and must be eight inches high and four inches wide. This is so that it can be clearly seen as the player rushes down the field. The player on the cover of this book is Reggie McElroy, #68, New York Jets. He also played for the Los Angeles Raiders, Kansas City Chiefs, Minnesota Vikings, and Denver Broncos. He is a personal friend and now a teacher in my school district doing a great job keeping at risk kids from dropping out.

Jersey numbers are so significant to the players that there are instances when a number is actually *retired*, usually after the player has left the team or retires from the sport. Once that number is retired no player is allowed to ever wear that number on their uniform again.

This honor has also been conferred on players who had memorable careers, died prematurely under tragic circumstances, or have had their careers ended by serious injury.

The important identifying number for your nonprofit is the subject of this chapter.

## FEDERAL EMPLOYER IDENTIFICATION NUMBER (FEIN)

The Federal Employer Identification Number (FEIN) number is like a social security number for a business, whether for profit or nonprofit. It is a nine digit number assigned for tax filing and reporting purposes. It can be assigned to:

- Employers
- Sole Proprietors
- Corporations
- Partnerships
- Estates
- Trusts
- Certain Individuals
- And Other Miscellaneous Entities

As confusing as it may seem – with the word *employer* in its name – you do not have to employ anyone to need this number. And to be even more confusing, it goes by other names. It is sometimes referred to as

- Employer Identification Number (EIN),
- Tax Identification Number (TIN)

The FEIN has nothing to do with designating your organization as tax exempt. Rather it identifies it as an *existing recognized business entity*. You must have an FEIN to open a bank account for your nonprofit organization, and to file your articles of organization with the state. Make sure the organization name is exactly the same with IRS as it is with the state, including any required suffix (such as Inc. or Corp.). Suffixes are forbidden in Washington State. They are required in Connecticut, Delaware, Florida (but not "Company" or "Co."), Idaho, Indiana, Kansas, Louisiana, Maryland, Mississippi, Nevada (if you use a person's name), New Jersey (with exceptions), New York (with exceptions), North Carolina, Oklahoma, South Carolina, Vermont, West Virginia, and Wisconsin. If you live in Wyoming, contact the Secretary of State for clarification on your particular nonprofit requirement. All other states give you the choice to use a suffix or not.

Only one FEIN is assigned to an organization and it will never expire, even if it has not been used for a long time. You cannot get a new FEIN for the same organization if you lose the number or forget it. If you have set up a bank account, you can contact the bank and retrieve the number. Or you can contact IRS by calling the Business and Specialty Tax Line at (800) 829-4933 between 7:00 a.m. and 7:00 p.m. local time (Pacific Time for Alaska and Hawaii) Monday through Friday. They will give you the number over the phone if you are an authorized person (such as an officer of the organization).

## THERE ARE THREE WAYS TO GET AN FEIN NUMBER:

1. Fill out and mail or fax IRS Form SS-4. You can get a copy that will fill in online and print at: http://www.irs.gov/uac/

Form-SS-4,-Application-for-Employer-Identification-Number-(EIN)

Print and mail to:

> Internal Revenue Service Center
> ATTN: EIN Operation
> Cincinnati, Ohio 45999

You may fax the completed form to: (859) 669-5760

2.  You can fill out the application online and receive the FEIN number immediately at https://sa2.www4.irs.gov/modiein/individual/index.jsp. You can use the number immediately, but it may take up to two weeks for IRS to get the number electronically published and working in all venues.
3.  Easier yet, call IRS at (800) 829-4933 and tell them what you are starting, give them the information they request, and they will give you the FEIN number over the phone and mail you the FEIN confirmation in about 10 days. I recommend this method because the forms have choices for "other tax exempt organizations" that are confusing and are not 501(c)(3) choices. Be sure to tell the IRS agent that you want to establish a 501(c) (3) organization.

There are different phone numbers for international applicants that are not toll free: (267) 941-1099 or (215) 516-6999.

**IRS NOTE:**

Effective May 21, 2012, to ensure fair and equitable treatment for all taxpayers, the Internal Revenue Service will limit Employer Identification Number (EIN) issuance to one per responsible party* per day. This limitation is applicable to all requests for EINs whether online or by phone, fax or mail.

* *A responsible party is a principal officer of a business if it is a corporation.*

The chances are that you only need one FEIN anyway. If you need a second one, you can simply wait until the following day to apply.

## NO REQUIREMENT THAT YOU *MUST* USE YOUR FEIN

Just because you get an FEIN number does not mean you have to use it, or that the IRS will be looking for a business tax return using that number. Use it when you're ready to conduct business under that number. No requirement says you must use it right away. After all, it may take a while for you to get your organization up and running.

If for some reason you change your mind or things do not work out, you need not ever use it. You are not in trouble with IRS if you get the number and never use it.

## TWO WAYS TO CANCEL AN FEIN ACCOUNT:

1.  If you applied with the intent to set up a 501(c) (3) corporation and you never got around to applying for 501(c) (3) status, you can send a letter to IRS asking them to cancel the FEIN. You must tell them why, give them the FEIN number and the legal name of the organization and mailing address. Send the cancellation to:

    Internal Revenue Service

    > Attn: EO Entity
    > Mail Stop 6273
    > Ogden, UT 84201

    (Or you may fax it to (801) 620-7116).

2.  If you have 501(c) (3) status and chose to terminate the organization, you must notify IRS on the appropriate annual

report, either Form 990, Form 990-N, Form 990-EZ, or Form 990-PF. They will want to know upon your dissolution or termination, if you liquidated assets as per your organizational documents such as Articles of Incorporation or bylaws.

You now have several steps out of the way. The next item on your agenda is to create a strong mission statement. More about that in the next chapter.

# CHAPTER 4

## DEVELOP A MISSION STATEMENT

*"Nobody who ever gave his best regretted it."*
—George Halas

Founded in 1993 by NFL Hall of Famer Steve Young, Forever Young Foundation is focused on passing on hope and resources for the development, strength, and education of children. The Foundation serves children facing significant physical, emotional, and financial challenges by providing them with academic, athletic, and therapeutic opportunities currently unavailable to them. (AZ)

### PLANNING THE GAME PLAYS

A well-played football game is made up of a vast array of *plays*, which are like mental diagrams for every player on the field. When the quarterback calls the play, every player should know exactly what he is referring to. Teams love to give their plays odd names such as Quick Ace, Scat, Hook and Ladder, Flea Flicker, and Buzz. No matter the name, each player knows the reason for the play and exactly how it should be carried out.

In the same way, the mission statement of your nonprofit will let everyone know your purpose and your strategy for carrying out that purpose.

## RELAX – IT'S NOT DIFFICULT

Your organization needs a mission statement. Before you stiffen up and grit your teeth, realize that it's not difficult to write a mission statement. It's the *perception* that it's complicated and difficult that *makes* it complicated and difficult. So relax. If you are the founder(s), you know better than anyone the message you want to convey about your organization.

Your mission statement should tell the world why you exist, and how you are different from other similar organizations. You're on a mission, and your mission statement should reflect your passion. In a sentence or two, what is that mission that motivates you? Your answer should be active, short, inspiring, and cause people to remember you. Erica Olsen states that if your mission statement would make a great T-shirt, it is probably a good one.

## LEARN FROM OTHERS

To help you find the right words to express the mission for your organization, I have located 100 of the top nonprofit organizations in the United States and provided their mission statements for you to study. As you read, notice the statements that define the purpose clearly without fluff or flowery words. Notice the statements that get your attention, inspire you, make you want to know more, or match your pre-existing perception of the organization. Which ones could use some work to be more memorable? Which ones are too vague, broad, puffed up, or general? Which ones are boring?

| United Way | United Way improves lives by mobilizing the caring power of communities around the world to advance the common good. |
| --- | --- |
| Salvation Army | The Salvation Army, an international movement, is an evangelical part of the universal Christian church. Its message is based on the Bible. Its ministry is motivated by the love of God. Its mission is to preach the gospel of Jesus Christ and to meet human needs in His name without discrimination. |
| Catholic Charities USA | Catholic Charities USA aims to reduce poverty, support families, and empower communities in the United States. |
| Feeding America | Feeding America is the nation's leading domestic hunger-relief charity. Our mission is to feed America's hungry through a nationwide network of member food banks and engage our country in the fight to end hunger. |
| American National Red Cross | The American Red Cross prevents and alleviates human suffering in the face of emergencies by mobilizing the power of volunteers and the generosity of donors. |
| Food for the Poor | Our mission is to link the church of the First World with the church of the Third World in a manner that helps both the materially poor and the poor in spirit. |
| American Cancer Society | The American Cancer Society is the nationwide, community-based, voluntary health organization dedicated to eliminating cancer as a major health problem by preventing cancer, saving lives, and diminishing suffering from cancer, |

| | |
|---|---|
| | through research, education, advocacy, and service. |
| World Vision | World Vision is an international partnership of Christians whose mission is to follow our Lord and Savior Jesus Christ in working with the poor and oppressed to promote human transformation, seek justice, and bear witness to the good news of the Kingdom of God. |
| YMCA | The mission of the YMCA is to put Judeo-Christian principles into practice through programs that build healthy spirit, mind, and body for all. |
| Goodwill Industries International | Goodwill works to enhance the dignity and quality of life of individuals and families by strengthening communities, eliminating barriers to opportunity, and helping people in need reach their full potential through learning and the power of work. |
| St. Jude's Children's Research Hospital | The mission of St. Jude Children's Research Hospital is to advance cures, and means of prevention, for pediatric catastrophic diseases through research and treatment. Consistent with the vision of our founder Danny Thomas, no child is denied treatment based on race, religion or a family's ability to pay. |
| AmeriCares Foundation | AmeriCares is a non-profit emergency response and global health organization. In times of epic disaster or daily struggle, we deliver medical and humanitarian aid to people in need worldwide. |
| Boys & Girls Clubs of America | To enable all young people, especially those who need us most, to reach their full potential as productive, caring, responsible citizens. |

| | |
|---|---|
| Habitat For Humanity International | Seeking to put God's love into action, Habitat for Humanity brings people together to build homes, communities and hope. |
| Compassion International | Releasing children from poverty in Jesus' name. In response to the Great Commission, Compassion International exists as an advocate for children, to release them from their spiritual, economic, social and physical poverty and enable them to become responsible and fulfilled Christian adults. |
| Nature Conservancy | The mission of The Nature Conservancy is to conserve the lands and waters on which all life depends. |
| United States Fund for UNICEF | We work for the survival, protection and development of children worldwide through fundraising, advocacy and education. |
| American Heart Association | Building healthier lives, free of cardiovascular diseases and stroke. |
| Campus Crusade for Christ International | Win, build, and send Christ-centered multiplying disciples who launch spiritual movements. |
| Feed the Children | Feed The Children is a Christian, international, nonprofit relief organization with headquarters in Oklahoma City, Oklahoma, that delivers food, medicine, clothing and other necessities to individuals, children and families who lack these essentials due to famine, war, poverty or natural disaster. |
| Boy Scouts of America | To prepare young people to make ethical and moral choices over their lifetimes by instilling in them the values of the Scout Oath and Law. |

| | |
|---|---|
| Samaritan's Purse | Samaritan's Purse is a nondenominational evangelical Christian organization providing spiritual and physical aid to hurting people around the world. Since 1970, Samaritan's Purse has helped meet needs of people who are victims of war, poverty, natural disasters, disease, and famine with the purpose of sharing God's love through His Son, Jesus Christ. The organization serves the Church worldwide to promote the Gospel of the Lord Jesus Christ. |
| Lutheran Services in America | Lutheran Services in America creates opportunities with people in thousands of communities throughout the United States and the Caribbean as an alliance of the Evangelical Lutheran Church in America, The Lutheran Church—Missouri Synod, and their over 300 health and human service organizations. Working neighbor to neighbor through services in health care, aging and disability supports, community development, housing, and child and family strengthening, these organizations together touch the lives of one in 50 Americans each year and have aggregated annual incomes over $18.3 billion. |
| CARE USA | Our mission is to serve individuals and families in the poorest communities in the world. Drawing strength from our global diversity, resources and experience, we promote innovative solutions and are advocates for global responsibility. We facilitate lasting change by:<br><br>• Strengthening capacity for self-help<br>• Providing economic opportunity<br>• Delivering relief in emergencies<br>• Influencing policy decisions at all levels<br>• Addressing discrimination in all its forms |

| | |
|---|---|
| Save the Children Foundation | To inspire breakthroughs in the way the world treats children and to achieve immediate and lasting change in their lives. |
| United Services Organization (USO) | USO lifts the spirits of America's troops and their families. |
| Catholic Relief Services | Catholic Relief Services carries out the commitment of the Bishops of the United States to assist the poor and vulnerable overseas. We are motivated by the Gospel of Jesus Christ to cherish, preserve and uphold the sacredness and dignity of all human life, foster charity and justice, and embody Catholic social and moral teaching as we act to:<br><br>• Promote human development by responding to major emergencies, fighting disease and poverty, and nurturing peaceful and just societies; and,<br>• Serve Catholics in the United States as they live their faith in solidarity with their brothers and sisters around the world.<br><br>As part of the universal mission of the Catholic Church, we work with local, national and international Catholic institutions and structures, as well as other organizations, to assist people on the basis of need, not creed, race or nationality. |
| Memorial Sloan-Kettering Cancer Center | We provide compassionate, evidence-based nursing care to patients and families living with cancer in a healing and innovative environment. |
| Good360 | At Good360, our mission is to fulfill the needs of nonprofits with corporate product donations. |

| | |
|---|---|
| Direct Relief International | Direct Relief International's mission is to improve the health of people living in developing countries and those who are victims of natural disasters, war, and civil unrest. We work to strengthen the indigenous health efforts of our international partners by providing essential material resources–medicines, supplies and equipment. |
| Catholic Medical Mission Board | Founded in 1928 and rooted in the healing ministry of Jesus, Catholic Medical Mission Board works collaboratively to provide quality healthcare programs and services, without discrimination, to people in need around the world. |
| American Jewish Joint Distribution Committee | For 90 years the American Jewish Joint Distribution Committee (JDC) has served as the overseas arm of the American Jewish community. JDC's mission has always been to reach out to Jews in need of urgent help, to provide rescue, relief and reconstruction. |
| Dana-Farber Cancer Institute | The mission of Dana-Farber Cancer Institute is to provide expert, compassionate care to children and adults with cancer while advancing the understanding, diagnosis, treatment, cure, and prevention of cancer and related diseases. |
| Leukemia and Lymphoma Society | Cure leukemia, lymphoma, Hodgkin's disease and myeloma, and improve the quality of life of patients and their families. |
| Population Services International | The mission of PSI is to measurably improve the health of poor and vulnerable people in the developing world, principally through social marketing of family planning and health |

| | products and services, and health communications. Social marketing engages private sector resources and uses private sector techniques to encourage healthy behavior and make markets work for the poor. |
|---|---|
| Mayo Clinic | To inspire hope and contribute to health and well-being by providing the best care to every patient through integrated clinical practice, education and research. |
| Marine Toys for Tots Foundation | The mission of Marine Toys for Tots Foundation is to assist the U. S. Marine Corps in providing a tangible sign of hope to economically disadvantaged children at Christmas. |
| Brother's Brother Foundation | The mission of Brother's Brother Foundation is to promote international health and education through the efficient and effective distribution and provision of donated medical, educational, agricultural and other resources. All BBF programs are designed to fulfill its mission by connecting people's resources with people's needs. |
| Make-A-Wish Foundation of America | We grant the wishes of children with life-threatening medical conditions to enrich the human experience with hope, strength and joy. |
| Susan G. Komen for the Cure | Susan G. Komen for the Cure is fighting every minute of every day to finish what we started and achieve our vision of a world without breast cancer. |
| World Help | World Help is a faith-based humanitarian organization that exists to serve the physical and spiritual needs of people in impoverished communities around the world. |

| Shriners Hospital for Children | Shriners Hospital for Children has a mission to: |
|---|---|
| | Provide the highest quality care to children with neuromusculoskeletal conditions, burn injuries and other special healthcare needs within a compassionate, family-centered and collaborative care environment. |
| | Provide for the education of physicians and other healthcare professionals. |
| | Conduct research to discover new knowledge that improves the quality of care and quality of life of children and families. |
| | This mission is carried out without regard to race, color, creed, sex or sect, disability, national origin or ability of a patient or family to pay. |
| Planned Parenthood Federation of America | The mission of Planned Parenthood is <br><br> • to provide comprehensive reproductive and complementary health care services in settings which preserve and protect the essential privacy and rights of each individual <br> • to advocate public policies which guarantee these rights and ensure access to such services <br> • to provide educational programs which enhance understanding of individual and societal implications of human sexuality <br> • to promote research and the advancement of technology in reproductive health care and encourage understanding of their inherent bioethical, behavioral, and social implications |

| | |
|---|---|
| Operation Blessing International Relief and Development | Our mission is to demonstrate God's love by alleviating human need and suffering in the United States and around the world. |
| Chronic Disease Fund | Chronic Disease Fund is a charitable organization that helps patients with chronic disease, cancer and other life-altering conditions obtain the life-saving medications they need. |
| American Kidney Fund | The mission of the American Kidney Fund is to fight kidney disease through direct financial support to patients in need; health education; and prevention efforts. |
| ChildFund International | • To help deprived, excluded and vulnerable children living in poverty have the capacity to become young adults, parents and leaders who bring lasting and positive change to their communities.<br>• To promote societies whose individuals and institutions participate in valuing, protecting, and advancing the worth and the rights of children |
| Alzheimer's Association | The mission of the Alzheimer's Association is to eliminate Alzheimer's disease through the advancement of research; to provide and enhance care and support for all affected; and to reduce the risk of dementia through the promotion of brain health. |
| Rotary Foundation of Rotary International | To enable Rotarians to advance world understanding, goodwill, and peace through the improvement of health, the support of education, and the alleviation of poverty. |

| Paralyzed Veterans of America | Paralyzed Veterans of America, a congressionally chartered veterans service organization founded in 1946, has developed a unique expertise on a wide variety of issues involving the special needs of our members – veterans of the armed forces who have experienced spinal cord injury or dysfunction. |
|---|---|
| National Multiple Sclerosis Society | We mobilize people and resources to drive research for a cure and to address the challenges of everyone affected by MS. |
| Operation Compassion | Operation Compassion focuses on three priorities: (1) responding to natural disasters nationally and around the world; (2) providing inspiration, information, training and resources to help mobilize churches, individuals and community groups to provide food and basic necessities to the poor and needy; (3) concentrating on international distribution to widows, single mothers and children. |
| Teach for America | Teach for America is growing the movement of leaders who work to ensure that kids growing up in poverty get an excellent education. |
| JDRF | To find a cure for diabetes and its complications through the support of research. |
| March of Dimes Foundation | We help moms have full-term pregnancies and research the problems that threaten the health of babies. |
| Project Hope | Delivering health education, medicines, supplies and volunteers where needed. |
| Big Brothers Big Sisters of America | The mission of Big Brothers Big Sisters of America is to make a positive difference in the |

| | lives of children and youth, primarily through a professionally-supported one-to-one relationship with a caring adult, and to assist them in achieving their highest potential as they grow to become confident, competent and caring individuals. |
|---|---|
| Step Up for Students | Step Up For Students provides legislatively authorized K-12 scholarship programs and related support to give economically disadvantaged families the freedom to choose the best learning options for their children. |
| Christian Aid Ministries | Our primary purpose is to be a trustworthy and efficient channel for Amish, Mennonite, and other conservative Anabaptist groups and individuals to minister to physical and spiritual needs around the world. This is in response to the command, ". . . do good unto all men, especially unto them who are of the household of faith" (Galatians 6:10). |
| Easter Seals | Easter Seals provides services to children and adults with disabilities and other special needs, and support to their families. |
| Doctors Without Borders USA | Every year, Doctors Without Borders/Médecins Sans Frontières (MSF) provides emergency medical care to millions of people caught in crises in more than 60 countries around the world. MSF provides assistance when catastrophic events — such as armed conflict, epidemics, malnutrition, or natural disasters — overwhelm local health systems. MSF also assists people who face discrimination or neglect from their local health systems or when populations are otherwise excluded from health care. |

| | |
|---|---|
| Kingsway Charities | To improve the lives of the sick and suffering worldwide so they will know God's love and compassion by providing life-sustaining resources. |
| Metropolitan Opera Association | The Metropolitan Opera is a vibrant home for the most creative and talented artists, including singers, conductors, composers, orchestra musicians, stage directors, designers, visual artists, choreographers, and dancers from around the world. The Metropolitan Opera Association is described as the most renowned opera association globally. More specifically, nearly every expert cited their HD opera broadcasts as offering a distinct contribution to opera by giving quality access to viewers nationwide. |
| Children's Hospital Boston Archives | The mission of Boston Children's Hospital Archives is to support the goals of Children's by identifying, collecting, preserving and making accessible the non-current records of permanent administrative, legal, fiscal and historical value to hospital community. |
| Christian Broadcasting Network | The mission of CBN and its affiliated organizations is to prepare the United States of America and the nations of the world for the coming of Jesus Christ and the establishment of the Kingdom of God on earth. Our ultimate goal is to achieve a time in history when "the knowledge of the Lord will cover the earth as the waters cover the sea." |
| Public Broadcasting Service | To create content that educates, informs and inspires. |
| UJA/Federation of New York | Through UJA-Federation of New York, you care for people in need, inspire a passion for Jewish |

| | |
|---|---|
| | life and learning, and strengthen communities in New York, in Israel, and around the world. |
| PATH | Empowering children and families to achieve lifelong successes. |
| United Negro College Fund | UNCF's mission is to build a robust and nationally-recognized pipeline of under-represented students who, because of UNCF support, become highly-qualified college graduates; and to ensure that our network of 38 member historically black colleges and universities is a respected model of best practice in moving students to and through college. |
| George W. Bush Foundation | Development of the George W. Bush Presidential Center and the ongoing administration and funding of the foundation's activities including programming of the George W. Bush Institute. |
| Wycliffe Bible Translators | To see a Bible translation program in progress in every language still needing one by 2025. |
| Young Life | Introducing adolescents to Jesus Christ and helping them grow in their faith. |
| Humane Society of the United States | Celebrating Animals, Confronting Cruelty. |
| Smile Train | Our mission is to provide a child born with a cleft the same opportunities in life as a child born without a cleft. |
| Robin Hood Foundation | For more than 20 years, Robin Hood has fought poverty in New York City. |
| American Diabetes Association | To prevent and cure diabetes and to improve the lives of all people affected by diabetes. |

| | |
|---|---|
| Muscular Dystrophy Association | The Muscular Dystrophy Association's mission is to foster and promote the alleviation of the conditions of persons with muscular dystrophy and related neuromuscular disorders through support of basic and applied research seeking the causes of and effective treatments for these diseases. |
| Children International | Children International's mission is to help children living in dire poverty. This is accomplished through the generosity of our contributors by providing children with program benefits and services that meet basic needs, enhance their self-esteem and raise their physical and educational levels in a meaningful, lasting way. |
| Father Flanagan's Boy's Home | Changing the way America cares for children and families by providing and promoting a continuum of care that strengthens body, mind, and spirit. |
| Smithsonian Institution | The increase and diffusion of knowledge. |
| Matthew 25: Ministries | Mission is to fulfill Matthew 25:34-40 of the New Testament by providing nutritional food to the hungry, clean water to the thirsty, clothing to the naked, affordable shelter to the homeless, medical care to the ill, and humanitarian supplies to prisoners. |
| International Rescue Committee | The International Rescue Committee serves refugees and communities victimized by oppression or violent conflict worldwide. |
| Scholarship America | Scholarship America's mission is to mobilize America, through scholarships and educational support, to make postsecondary success possible for all students. |

| | |
|---|---|
| National Cancer Coalition | Dedicated to educating women about the prevention and early detection of cervical cancer and HPV. |
| MAP International | MAP International is a global Christian health organization that partners with people living in conditions of poverty to save lives and develop healthier families and communities. |
| Medical Teams International | To demonstrate the love of Christ to people affected by disaster, conflict and poverty around the world. |
| Junior Achievement USA | We are the passionate people behind a movement that seeks to educate and inspire young people to value free enterprise, business, and economics to improve the quality of their lives. |
| Metropolitan Museum of Art | Collect, preserve, study, exhibit, and stimulate appreciation for and advance knowledge of works of art that collectively represent the broadest spectrum of human achievement at the highest level of quality, all in the service of the public and in accordance with the highest professional standards. |
| Christian Appalachian Project | The Christian Appalachian Project is an inter-denominational, non-profit Christian organization committed to serving people in need in Appalachia by providing physical, spiritual and emotional support through a wide variety of programs and services. |
| The Arc | The Arc promotes and protects the human rights of people with intellectual and developmental disabilities and actively supports their full inclusion and participation in the community throughout their lifetimes. |

| | |
|---|---|
| Houston Food Bank | Leading the fight against hunger. The Houston Food Bank does this by distributing more than 35 million pounds of food each year through a network of nearly 400 hunger relief charities in 18 southeast Texas counties. In addition, Food Bank programs address nutrition education, job training, and social service outreach to people in poverty. |
| Mount Sinai School of Medicine and Hospital | Pursue quality patient care, education, and research and to disseminate this new knowledge as broadly as possible. |
| Combined Jewish Philanthropies | Rooted in compassion and justice and driven by innovation, we care for the vulnerable, forge strong connections with Israel and above all, inspire the next generation to embrace Jewish life and learning. |
| New York Presbyterian Hospital | The Department of Pastoral Care & Education is dedicated to providing and promoting spiritual care, support and hope for patients, families and staff. |
| WGBH Educational Foundation | Our main purpose is help you cope better with the world and in your own life. |
| World Wildlife Federation | For nearly half a century, WWF has been protecting the future of nature. |
| Cystic Fibrosis Foundation | Assure the development of the means to cure and control cystic fibrosis (CF) and to improve the quality of life for those with the disease. |
| Heifer International | To work with communities to end hunger and poverty and care for the Earth. |

| American SPCA (ASPCA) | To provide effective means for the prevention of cruelty to animals throughout the United States. |
|---|---|
| St. Mary's Food Bank Alliance | To promote the elimination of hunger through the gathering and distribution of food while encouraging self-sufficiency through advocacy and education. |

## NOW IT'S YOUR TURN

Now it is time to develop your mission statement. Here are some guidelines to add pizzazz:

1. Keep it short: 6–15 words is normally sufficient.
2. Use active tense: Say, "Feed hungry kids!" instead of "We strive to eliminate hunger in children."
3. Get input from others. This is one task in which a committee might be beneficial but only if the group members share the same enthusiasm and understanding of the organizational goals. If not, be a committee of one and do it yourself.
4. Avoid jargon and formal language. Make it so clear a child could understand what is exciting about what you do. Jargon and formal language do not convey your enthusiasm. If in doubt, ask a kid.
5. Be specific about the population you serve. Chances are you are not going to eradicate AIDS from the planet, but you can provide antiretroviral drugs to Ethiopia's poor. Limit your scope to what you can reasonably expect to accomplish. However, if you plan to expand your reach in time, you may want to use words like *technology* instead of *computers* so that you do not limit yourself down the road. This is a catch-22 area, you don't want to be too broad, and you don't want to be too specific. Use common sense.
6. Make sure your mission statement does not sound theoretical, scholarly, or academic.

7. Leave out words that water down the effectiveness of your organization. Here are a few that you should avoid:

- Try
- Attempt
- Aim
- Help
- Influence
- Endeavor
- Strive
- Undertake

Instead use powerful words like these:

- Prevent
- Abolish
- Confront
- Connect
- Eliminate
- Increase
- Mobilize
- Reduce
- Save
- Solve
- Transform
- Improve

8. Identify the problem you target, and the solution you provide.
9. Use clear, concise, brief, and positive terms to paint a picture of the mission you are on.

You can always change or update your mission statement later if necessary. It doesn't have to be perfect or carved in stone. For now, write it and move on. In the next chapter, you'll learn how to form your board of directors.

# CHAPTER 5

## FORM A BOARD OF DIRECTORS

*"Leaders aren't born, they are made. And they are made just like anything else, through hard work. And that's the price we'll have to pay to achieve that goal, or any goal."*

—Vince Lombardi

OUR MISSION: Inspiring kids to thrive in life through sports by providing resources that get and keep KIDS in the GAME. KIDS in the GAME is an all-volunteer 501(c) (3) nonprofit organization focused on empowering youth to live up to their full potential through positive sports experiences that form active, healthy habits for a lifetime. We provide financial assistance to low-income, underserved youth who cannot afford the increasing costs of playing sports. We raise awareness of the importance of athletics in developing future leaders, with skills and values that transfer from the sports field into the classroom, workplace, family and community. (OR)

### TEAM OWNERS AND MANAGERS

While the public usually sees the coaches as the ones in control of the team, behind the coaches (in pro football) are the owners. Next to the team players, and the coaches, the owners are the most visible persons in the organization. Many owners have a distinct interest in, and love for, the game.

These pro teams are also known as *franchises*. Some franchises such as the Pittsburgh Steelers and the Chicago Bears have been owned for decades by members of one family. The business decisions of the owner can make or break a football team.

Next to the owners, it's the general managers who become the eyes and ears of the owners. Managers must, by the nature of their job, be highly calculating in order to make player trades and free agent acquisitions. They must have a feel for the team and be able to work well with the head coach. (Good in theory, but not always in practice.)

In the same way the board of directors for your nonprofit must have the mission of the organization at heart and be able to make some difficult decisions.

## NOT SHAREHOLDERS, BUT STAKEHOLDERS

Directors make up the governing body of an organization. They are not the managers; management answers to the board of directors. In profit corporations, board members are responsible to the owners, the stockholders. A nonprofit organization is not owned, so board members answer to the following:

- Public
- The government
- Their supporters
- The people the organization serves

For-profit corporations are mostly about the bottom line – the money. However, in a nonprofit atmosphere, board members are not shareholders, they are *stakeholders*. They have a stake in the success of the nonprofit that has little to do with finance.

## QUALIFIED AND WILLING

It is a privilege to be on a nonprofit board of directors, and members should be selected based on qualifications and willingness to serve. They do not need to have great business acumen or experience, but should have good judgment and common sense. The board should be a mix of visionaries and practical souls so that a balance exists, although harmony may not be a 24/7 accomplishment when you put dreamers and realists together. Each person should be matched to the board position that most effectively utilizes their skills and talents. For example, secretary might be the perfect fit for a person with good organizational skills.

## ACCOUNTANT OR ATTORNEY AS BOARD MEMBER?

There are arguments for and against having an accountant or attorney on the board. If you choose to include either, make sure your motives are not so that you can get free expertise. That is unfair to the board member and to the organization. Better to ask them for pro bono or reduced price services and select board members that have a heart for the organization's mission.

## HOW MANY BOARD MEMBERS?

IRS does not specifically establish a set number of board members, but too few or too unqualified can cause delays and questions during the processing phase of your 501(c) (3) application. Relationships are also an important component of board formation. Relatives (by blood or marriage) must hold less than 50% of the vote on a board of directors. As a minimum, three board members who are not related, and if two are related, then five board members are needed to pass IRS scrutiny. There is no maximum number of board members. There should be as many as are needed to govern the organization. In addition, IRS monitors whether board members are independent members who do not benefit financially from the organization while making board decisions.

In Florida, Georgia, Nevada, New Jersey, North Dakota, Pennsylvania, and Utah, officers must be at least 18 years old.

In Minnesota, the majority of the board must be at least 18 years old.

In Michigan, the majority of the quorum (minimum number of members that must be present to transact business, normally a majority of board members) must be at least 18, but board members are allowed at 16 and 17 years old, as long as over half are at least 18.

In many states it is acceptable for one board member to hold more than one office, although it is suspect if the Chairman or President of the Board is also the Chief Financial Officer. Many states (Alabama, Alaska, Washington D.C., New York, Rhode Island, South Dakota, Tennessee, Texas, Vermont, and Washington) prohibit holding positions of President and Secretary concurrently. Only Maine does not allow a person to hold two positions on the board.

In addition to IRS codes, each state has nonprofit business statutes that spell out the minimum number of directors on the board, and in some cases the positions of those directors. Below are the statutes and the board composition guidelines for each state:

| State | 1st line: Statute Numbers 2nd line: Name of State Law | Minimum Board Members | Required Offices Pres VP Sec Treas | | | |
|-------|-------------------------------------------------------|-----------------------|------|---|---|---|
| AL | Title 10A, Chapter 3a<br><br>Chapter 3 A Alabama Non-profit Corporation Act | 3 | x | x | x | x |
| AK | Title 10, Chapter 20<br><br>Chapter 10.20.: Alaska Non-profit Corporation Act | 3 | x | x | x | x |

| | | | | | | |
|---|---|---|---|---|---|---|
| **AZ** | Title 10, Chapters 24-40<br><br>Arizona Nonprofit Corporation Act | 1 | | | x | |
| **AR** | Title 4, Subtitle 3, Chapter 33<br><br>Arkansas Nonprofit Corporation Act,1993 | 3 | | | x | |
| **CA** | California Corp. Code, Title 1, Division 2, Part 2<br><br>Nonprofit Corporation Act of California | 3 | x | | x | x |
| **CO** | Title 7, Articles 121 – 137<br><br>Colorado Revised Nonprofit Corporation Act | 1 | x | | x | x |
| **CT** | Title 33, Chapter 602<br><br>Connecticut Revised Non-stick Corporation Act | 1 | x | | x | x |
| **DE** | Title 8, Chapter 1<br><br>Delaware General Corporation Law  Begin at Section 101 | 1 | | | | |
| **FL** | Title 36, Chapter 617<br><br>Florida Not For Profit Corporation Act (Title XXXVI (Business Organizations) Chapter 617 | 3 | | | x | |

| | | | | | | |
|---|---|---|---|---|---|---|
| **GA** | Title 14, Chapter 3<br><br>Georgia Nonprofit Corporation Code (Title 14, Chapter 3 of the Georgia Code) | 1 | | | x | |
| **HI** | Division 2, Title 23, Chapter 414D<br><br>Hawaii Nonprofit Corporations Act, Chapter 414 D | 3 | | | x | |
| **ID** | Title 30, Chapter 3<br><br>Idaho Nonprofit Corporation Act (Title 30 Chapter 3) | 3 | | | x | |
| **IL** | Chapter 805, Act 105<br><br>General Not For Profit Corporation Act of 1986 of Illinois | 3 | | | x | |
| **IN** | Title 23, Article 17<br><br>Indiana Nonprofit Corporation Act of 1991 | 3 | | | x | |
| **IA** | Title 12, Subtitle 5, Chapter 504<br><br>Revised Iowa Nonprofit Corporation Act, Chapter 504 of the Iowa Code | 1 | | | x | |
| **KS** | Chapter 17, Articles 60-75<br><br>Chapter 17 of the Kansas Statute (Article 60 onward) | 3 | | | x | |

| | | | | | | |
|---|---|---|---|---|---|---|
| **KY** | Title 23, Chapter 273<br><br>Private Corporations and Association Section of the Kentucky Statutes (Title XXIII, Chapter 273) | 3 | | | | |
| **LA** | Title 12, Chapter 2<br><br>Title XII , Chapter 2 of the Revised Statutes of Louisiana | Corp. decides in bylaws | x | | x | x |
| **ME** | Title 13B<br><br>Title 13-B: Maine Nonprofit Corporation Act | 3 | x | | x | x |
| **MD** | Corporations and Associations Code, Titles 1-5<br><br>Corporations And Association Statute of Maryland | 1 | x | x | x | x |
| **MA** | Title 22, Chapter 180<br><br>Title XXII Chapter 180 of the General Law of the Commonwealth of Massachusetts | 3 | x | | x | x |
| **MI** | Chapter 450.2101<br><br>Nonprofit Corporation Act 162 of 1982 | 1 | x | | x | x |
| **MN** | Corporate Code, Chapter 317A<br><br>Chapter 317 A of the Minnesota Statutes | 3 | x | | x | x |

| MS | Title 79, Chapter 11<br><br>Title 79, Chapter 11 of the Corporations, Associations and Partnership Section of the Mississippi Code | Corp. decides in bylaws | | | x | |
| --- | --- | --- | --- | --- | --- | --- |
| MO | Title 23, Chapter 355<br><br>Chapter 355, Nonprofit Corporation Law of Missouri | 3 | | | x | |
| MT | Title 35, Chapter 2<br><br>Title 35, Chapter 2 of the Montana Code Annotated, 2009 | 3 | | | x | |
| NE | Nonprofit Corporations Act, Chapter 21 (Corporations and Other Companies) of the Nebraska Statutes. | 3 | x | x | x | x |
| NV | Title 7, Chapter 82<br><br>Chapter 82 of the Revised Nevada Statutes | 1 | x | | x | x |
| NH | Title 27, Chapter 292<br><br>Chapter 292 of the New Hampshire Revised Statutes | 5 | | | | |
| NJ | Title 15A<br><br>Title 15 A of the New Jersey Statutes | 3 | x | | x | x |
| NM | Chapter 53, Article 8<br><br>New Mexico Ch. 53, Art. 8 Nonprofit Corporation Act | 3 | | | x | |

| | | | | | | |
|---|---|---|---|---|---|---|
| **NY** | N-PLC<br><br>New York Non Profit Corporation Act | 3 | | | | |
| **NC** | Chapter 55A<br><br>Chapter 55A North Carolina Nonprofit Corporation Act | 1 | | x | | |
| **ND** | Title 10, Chapter 10-33<br><br>Chapter 10-33, North Dakota Nonprofit Corporation Act | 3 | x | x | | |
| **OH** | Title 17, Chapter 1702<br><br>Chapter 1702: Nonprofit Corporation Law | 3 | x | x | x | |
| **OK** | Title 18, Chapter 22<br><br>Oklahoma Statutes, Title 18, Corporations | 1 | | x | | |
| **OR** | Title 7, Chapter 65<br><br>Oregon Nonprofit Corporation Act. Chapter 65 | 3 | x | x | | |
| **PA** | Title 15, Part 2, Subchapter C Title 15 Corporations and Unincorporated Associations | 1 | x | | x | x |
| **RI** | Title 7, Chapter 6<br><br>Chapter 7-6, Rhode Island Nonprofit Corporation Act | 3 | x | | x | x |

| | | | | | | |
|---|---|---|---|---|---|---|
| **SC** | Title 33, Chapter 31<br><br>South Carolina Nonprofit Corporation Act | 3 | | | x | |
| **SD** | Title 47, Chapter 22-26<br><br>South Dakota Nonprofit Corporation Act Chapter 22-26 | 3 | x | x | x | x |
| **TN** | Title 48, Chapter 51-68<br><br>Title 48, Corporations and Associations Tennessee Code Annotated | 3 | x | | x | |
| **TX** | Title 2, Chapter 22<br><br>Business Organizations Code, Title 2. Corporations. Chapter 22. Nonprofit Corporations. | 3 | x | | x | |
| **UT** | Title 16, Chapter 6a<br><br>Utah Code — Title 16 — Chapter 06a — Utah Revised Nonprofit Corporation Act | 3 | | | x | |
| **VT** | Title 11b<br><br>Vermont Statutes, Title 11B: Nonprofit Corporations | 3 | | | x | |
| **VA** | Title 13.1, Chapter 10<br><br>Virginia Nonstock Corporation Act | 1 | | | x | |

| | | | | | | | |
|---|---|---|---|---|---|---|---|
| **WA** | Title 24, Chapter 24.03<br><br>Chapter 24.03 RCW Washington Nonprofit Corporation Act | 1 | | x | x | x | x |
| **WV** | Chapter 31E<br><br>Chapter 31E. West Virginia Nonprofit Corporation Act | 3 | | | | x | |
| **WI** | Chapter 181Wisconsin Annotated Code, Chapter181 , Non-stock Corporations | 3 | | | | x | |
| **WY** | Title 17, Chapter 19Wyoming Nonprofit Corporation, Chapter 6 of WY Code | 3 | | | | x | |

## START SMALL

To meet the requirements of IRS and the state, you need at least three board members and at least five members if you are setting up shop in New Hampshire. To start with, you might do well to keep the number of board members to a minimum. It takes less initial paperwork, fewer biographies, and fewer signatures to get everything up and running.

The fewer the board members, the less people IRS will have to scrutinize. You can add more board members after founding the organization. You might want to consider having an odd number of board members so that there is no tie when voting.

## MEMBER TRAITS AND QUALITIES

Regardless of the position held by the board member, there are some defining traits and qualities that are essential to successful governance of a nonprofit organization:

- Ethical behavior and integrity
- No conflicts of interest
- Willingness to speak up and voice an opinion (even if unpopular)
- Inclination to cooperate and compromise when necessary
- Eagerness to invest the time necessary to succeed

Below are basic job descriptions for the positions on the board of directors. You can tailor the job descriptions to whatever your organization needs from the board members. You can call the positions whatever you want, you are not limited to the titles given.

### President (or Chairman) of the Board

Chairman sounds more like a title for a profit corporation, so President is often used for nonprofit corporations. Helpful attributes include:

- Leadership skills
- Earned respect of board members
- Good communication skills
- Ability to make hard calls when difficult decisions must be made
- Willingness to delegate

If you are the founder and you have those qualifications, then consider making yourself the initial President of the Board of Directors. You may be the most qualified person for the job.

A sample job description might be:

*The President of the Board represents the organization as ambassador to the community; presides over the affairs of the board and assists in setting agendas for board meetings; coordinates establishment of committees, assignments, and execution of tasks; steers board selection of an Executive Director; leads strategic planning and fundraising efforts; recruits and trains new board members; and delegates responsibility and authority to accomplish the goals of the organization.*

## Vice President (or Vice Chairman) of the Board

The Vice President is sometimes the successor to the President, a President in Training, or President-elect. The corporate bylaws should reflect whether that is the case. Helpful attributes for Vice President are the same as for the President.

A sample job description might be:

*The Vice President of the Board acts as the President when the President is not available. He or she assists the President in executing duties, and performs other duties as assigned by the Board.*

## Secretary of the Board

The Secretary of the Board is the communication and recordkeeping member of the Board of Directors. He or she should be familiar with the mission and vision of the organization, the Articles of Incorporation, and the bylaws. Helpful attributes include an aptitude for organization, writing abilities, and communication competence.

A sample job description might be:

*The Secretary of the Board maintains records of all Board actions; prepares and distributes meeting minutes; safeguards all corporation records; presides over meetings in the absence of the*

*President and Vice President; and performs other duties as assigned by the Board.*

## Treasurer (or Chief Financial Officer, CFO)

The Treasurer or CFO is the go-to person for financial questions in an organization. He or she must be above reproach in integrity, and maintain transparency in performing the duties of the office. Helpful attributes for Treasurer include critical thinking skills; analytical ability; and willingness to learn financial accounting principles as they relate to nonprofit organizations.

A sample job description might be:

> *The Treasurer coordinates and ensures financial stewardship and financial wellbeing of the organization; manages finances; ensures timely and accurate filing of financial reports to IRS and state agencies; presents annual budget for board approval; reviews annual audits; signs and deposits checks; and performs other duties as assigned by the Board.*

## Board Member or Organizational Director

Not every member of the Board of Directors needs to hold a title to an office. All positions are important and add to the effective governance of a nonprofit organization. Each board member should be a volunteer who is committed to the mission of the organization. This is a person who is willing to make time and actively participate in board meetings, fundraising activities, and public events involving the organization. In addition to investing time, board members should also be willing to invest money. Each member should have a copy of the organization's conflict-of-interest policy, and sign a disclosure form annually.

A sample job description might be:

*Board Members attend regularly scheduled board meetings; actively participate in decision making, considering the best interest of the organization; maintain integrity in use of resources; adhere to the letter and intent of regulatory guidance; establish and carry out planning, policies, fundraising, and budgeting; and evaluate the Executive Director's (if there is one) performance and compensation annually.*

With your board of directors now in place, you are ready to create your IRS-Compliant Organizing Document. Don't get nervous. You'll see that it's not at all difficult!

# CHAPTER 6

## PREPARE IRS-COMPLIANT ORGANIZING DOCUMENT

*"In life, as in football, you won't go far unless you know where the goalposts are."*

—Arnold H. Glasow

Since its beginning in 1986, The Jim Thorpe Association has developed a broad range of civic and charity activities. These are divided into three major categories: Awards & Scholarships, Oklahoma Sports Hall of Fame, and Bright Path Youth Programs.

### A NONPROFIT CALLED THE NFL

Not many people are aware that the NFL itself is an unincorporated nonprofit 501(c) (6) association. This specifically means that the league office is not subject to income tax because it does not make a profit. The NFL is known as a trade association and is made up of, and financed by, the 32 member teams.

This organization is headed up by the commissioner, the secretary, and the treasurer. The secretary and treasurer are both appointed by the commissioner.

It's a sure bet that the paperwork – and all the forms required – that are submitted by the NFL is a much greater load than the one you are about to carry out. So take heart. You can do this!

## THE BIRTH OF AN ORGANIZATION

When a child is born, a vital record of that birth is created in the state in which the child was born – it's called the Birth Certificate. It's recorded by the state and it registers the presence of a new little person. The certificate documents who the parents are, where and when the child was born, and other important information verifying the child's existence. The child is given a name, and in some cases, a suffix (such as Jr. or III) that further identifies the child. The child's origin is declared, such as Caucasian, Hispanic, or Native American. You complete the paperwork and it is sent to the Bureau of Vital Records and a birth certificate is created.

When a nonprofit corporation is born, a vital record of that birth is created in the state in which the organization was born – it's normally called the Articles of Incorporation. It is recorded by the state and it registers the presence of a new organization. This declares who the parents are, where and when the organization was born, and other vital information verifying the organization's existence. The nonprofit is given a name, and in some cases, a suffix (such as Inc. or Corp.) that further identifies the organization. The nonprofit's origin is declared, such as Public Benefit, Mutual Benefit, or Religious. You complete the paperwork and send it in to the Secretary of State and a *business birth certificate* (figuratively speaking) is created.

## A MATTER OF PUBLIC RECORD

A birth certificate is a public record in the sense that if you are related and have a need to know, you can get a copy of a birth certificate. The analogy differs when compared to a nonprofit corporation. Articles of Incorporation (by whatever name they're called in your state) are public records and as such are available to the public. Anyone wishing access is allowed to see, read, and have a copy of your nonprofit's birth certificate. For this reason, it's a good idea to leave out social security numbers and other personal identifiers in the documents you file.

Public charitable foundations, funds, community chests, and some trusts may also be eligible for 501(c) (3) status under certain circumstances, as long as they exist for charitable purposes. Their filing requirements are similar to nonprofit corporations, but their documents have different names, such as Articles of Association instead of Articles of Incorporation. Incorporation provides more legal protection for officers than unincorporated organizations.

## TYPES OF NONPROFITS

To establish this vital record with your Secretary of State and IRS, you must decide the origin or type of organization because it has far-reaching consequences for 501(c) (3) status. There are three basic origins or types of nonprofits:

### Public Benefit

This is normally a charity with a charitable mission, and IRS recognizes this type of organization for 501(c) (3) status. A public benefit corporation cannot be established to help just one organization (such as a particular orphanage) or individual (such as a particular orphan), but must benefit a class of people or group of organizations (such as potentially benefiting any orphan or orphanage in Mexico). You can start small by actually benefiting one or two particular orphanages, but must allow for helping others in the same category or class. If it benefits only one organization or a defined finite group of people who can be identified by name, such as a family, it is a private foundation, not a nonprofit corporation. This does not mean you cannot help an individual or a family, but that you cannot limit your efforts in establishing a nonprofit to specific people or families, you must leave room to grow and add people or families whose names you do not know yet, and who you do not even know need your help right now. There are two caveats: If the organization dissolves, all property and funds must go to another public benefit corporation; and no benefit, private gain, or profit can be given to any member of the nonprofit or their relatives. Benefit must go to the target of your charitable mission.

Public benefit organizations handling less than $5,000 per year are automatically exempt and do not need to file for 501(c) (3) status unless they want contributions to be deductible.

## Mutual Benefit

This type of nonprofit benefits members of a group. It is similar to a club. People pay membership fees or join the group, and assets are distributed among the members if the organization dissolves. IRS does not normally give 501(c) (3) status to mutual benefit organizations because they serve their members, not the public.

## Religious

This type of nonprofit is eligible for 501(c)(3) status and can be a church, or it can be a religious organization established to study or advance religion. If it is a church, it has no requirement to file annual reports declaring income and expenses like other 501(c) (3) organizations must do. There are several requirements for churches that want 501(c) (3) status. They must have a doctrine of beliefs, scheduled services, and a stable congregation, among other requirements. Churches do not have to apply for 501(c) (3) status, but many do because their supporters are assured that contributions are tax deductible.

## FOREIGN VS. DOMESTIC CORPORATION

To conduct nonprofit business in other states, you must first be recognized as a nonprofit entity in your own state by filing origination documents such as *Articles of Incorporation*, which gets you a business birth certificate, figuratively speaking. Then you can apply to the Secretary of State in other states as a *foreign* nonprofit corporation for recognition and approval to conduct nonprofit business in their state. *Foreign* does not mean foreign country, it means from outside the state boundaries, thus not an in-state or *domestic* organization. It normally costs more to register as a foreign nonprofit corporation than a domestic nonprofit in a state. Outsiders usually get charged more.

The way to get recognized is by filling out an application for authorization from the other state or states. This approval is normally given for a fee, and is usually called a *Certificate of Authority*. Each state has its own requirements, fees, and forms. Information for each state is included in this book. Most states require some kind of proof that you are approved and your organization is doing reputable business in your home state. This requirement is usually met by providing a recently certified copy of your state's Certificate of Good Standing, Certificate of Existence, Certificate of Fact (Texas), or similar state document. It is a piece of paper provided by your Secretary of State that you pay to have certified, usually not more than 60 days prior to applying to another state for approval to conduct business. If it gets too old, you have to pay to get another copy certified.

## REQUIREMENT FOR REGISTERED AGENT

To do business as either a domestic or a foreign nonprofit corporation, you must have a *registered agent*. This is a person or business in the state you want to conduct the affairs of your nonprofit. The agent's purpose is to give the Secretary of State a contact person with a street address (as opposed to a post office box) inside state lines who will receive official mail, handle complaints, answer telephone inquiries if they need to call about something, and just generally be the go-to person or company on behalf of your nonprofit.

Your nonprofit cannot be its own registered agent, but you can be a registered agent for your organization in your state if you are willing to be the face and voice behind the corporate name and mission. The registered agent can be a commercial or noncommercial agent. It can be an individual or organization willing to be your representative, or it can be a company for hire who is licensed by the state to represent other organizations.

To find a commercial registered agent, you can do an internet search for registered agent and the state, or you can call the Secretary of State's office and ask for a list of approved registered agents in that state. Some states require the signature of the registered agent stating that they accept appointment to this responsibility, and some do not. If a signature is required, it will be part of the Certificate of Authority or similar application, or (infrequently) require a separate form.

## REQUIRED STATEMENTS FOR IRS 501(C) (3) APPROVAL

The exact wording of your Articles of Incorporation or similar document is not critical except for a few required statements that if missing, will cause your application for 501(c) (3) status to be rejected. If IRS *suggests* something, it is a good idea to follow the suggestion. Here is the IRS suggested wording to meet their required language and statements:

### Benefit Statement:

*No part of the net earnings of the corporation shall inure to the benefit, or be distributable to its members, trustees, officers, or other private persons, except that the corporation shall be authorized and empowered to pay reasonable compensation for services rendered and to make payments and distributions in furtherance of the purposes set forth in previous articles hereof. No substantial part of the activities of the corporation shall be the carrying on of propaganda, or otherwise attempting to influence legislation, and the corporation shall not participate in, or intervene in (including the publishing or distribution of statements) any political campaign on behalf or in opposition to any candidate for public office. Notwithstanding any other provision of these articles, the corporation shall not carry on any other activities not permitted to be carried on (a) by a corporation exempt from federal income tax under section 501(c) (3) of the Internal Revenue Code, or the corresponding section of any future federal tax code, or (b) by a corporation, contributions to which are deductible under section 170(c) (2) of the Internal Revenue Code, or the corresponding section of any future federal tax code.*

## Purpose Statement:

*Said Corporation is organized exclusively for charitable, religious, educational, and scientific purposes, including, for such purposes, the making of distributions to organizations that qualify as exempt organizations under 501(c) (3) of the Internal Revenue Code, or the corresponding section of any future federal tax code.*

## Dissolution Statement:

*Upon the dissolution of the corporation, assets shall be distributed for one or more exempt purposes within the meaning of section 501(c) (3) of the Internal Revenue Code, or corresponding section of any future federal tax code, or shall be distributed to the federal government, or to a state or local government, for a public purpose. Any such assets not so disposed of shall be disposed of by a Court of Competent Jurisdiction of the county in which the principal office of the corporation is then located, exclusively for such purposes or to such organization or organizations as said Court shall determine which are organized and operated exclusively for such purposes.*

Now that you know and understand the concept of the Articles of Incorporation, in the next chapter we'll take a look at what should be included in that document. If you want fill-in-the-blank templates of your state's Articles of Incorporation that contain all required IRS clauses and meet all your state's requirements, they are available for a small fee at www.doyourownnonprofit.com

# CHAPTER 7

## WHAT TO INCLUDE IN ARTICLES OF INCORPORATION

*"One man practicing sportsmanship is far better than 50 preaching it."*

—Knute Rockne

LISC/Chicago was formed in 1980 to organize capital and other resources to support initiatives to stimulate the comprehensive development of healthy, stable neighborhoods and foster their connection to the socioeconomic mainstream of the metropolitan region. Sports-based programming is one of many approaches LISC/Chicago has taken to create healthier urban communities. By engaging youth, creating leadership opportunities and using public spaces for sports activities, their Neighborhood Sports Chicago program (NSC) addresses safety, family strength, school performance, health, positive connections to adults, among others.

## WHAT IS IT ABOUT COLLEGE FOOTBALL?

College football fans are typically the most ardent and the most demonstrative types of sports fans. College allegiance and rivalries run deep – oftentimes dating from many decades into the past.

The two rival teams from Oklahoma were mentioned previously, but then there's Alabama versus Auburn, University of California and Sanford University, and of course Harvard versus Yale (known simply as *the game)*. All these and more add heated excitement to the world of college football.

It's all the color, the pageantry, the tailgate parties, marching bands, pep rallies, and of course the die-hard fans who come from miles around just to attend the games.

Sorry, but I can't promise any excitement about forming your nonprofit corporation, but I can promise you'll be plenty excited when you receive that tax-exempt status when all this paperwork is completed!

## INFORMATION FOR ARTICLES OF INCORPORATION

There is some relatively constant information across states that must be included in the Articles of Incorporation. Virtually every state requires the following:

- Name of the corporation
- Type of corporation: public benefit, mutual benefit, or religious
- Duration (normally perpetual)
- Street address and mailing address of the initial registered office and the name of the initial registered agent
- The required IRS purpose, benefit, and dissolution clauses (see previous chapter)
- Whether the corporation has members (most nonprofits DO NOT have members).
- Who will manage the affairs of the corporation (normally the Board of Directors)

- The number of directors (make sure you include the required positions for your state)
- The term and manner of election of directors (you can say that they will be as provided or described in the Bylaws)
- A statement that the corporation shall have all powers given to a nonprofit corporation as per (the name of the state law provided in chapter 6), and an exempt organization as described in section 501(c) (3) of the Internal Revenue Code of 1986, as amended (or the corresponding provision of any future laws of the State of _____ and Internal Revenue Law).
- That the Articles can be amended by the Board of Directors in the manner provided by the Bylaws (unless you want to include those details in the incorporation documents)
- Articles to protect directors and officers from lawsuits
- A statement that the corporation may purchase general comprehensive liability insurance covering the board members and officers in the performance of their duties
- An affirmation that all information is true and correct, and execution by signature(s) by the incorporator(s) on a specific date

Check your state forms in the following chapter to see what else your state requires in addition to the items listed above.

Following is an example of the approved Articles of Incorporation for Pasture Valley Children Missions, a Missouri Nonprofit Corporation. If you do not want to go to the trouble of writing the Articles of Incorporation (by whatever name they are called in your state), you can go to www.doyourownnonprofit.com and purchase the templates for your state Articles of Incorporation for a small fee. All you have to do is fill in the blanks with your organization's information, print and file. I have included this information several times in this book, not to make sales (the money does not go to me), but to make sure you didn't miss it because you skimmed or skipped chapters. The easier I can make this process for you, the more likely you will actually start a nonprofit that will help the world you live in.

File Number:
N01294481
Date Filed: 02/25/2013
Jason Kander
Secretary of State

# ARTICLES OF INCORPORATION
## OF
## PASTURE VALLEY CHILDREN MISSIONS

A Missouri Nonprofit Corporation

The undersigned, being a natural person of the age of eighteen years or more, for the purpose of forming a corporation under the Missouri Nonprofit Corporation Act, hereby adopts the following Articles of Incorporation:

1.  The name of the corporation is PASTURE VALLEY CHILDREN MISSIONS.

2.  This corporation is a public benefit corporation.

3.  The period of duration of the corporation is perpetual.

4.  The street address of the corporation's initial registered office in Missouri is 11040 SCHRENK CT, ROLLA, MO 65401 (MAILING ADDRESS IS PO BOX 1665, ROLLA, MO 65402), and the name of its initial registered agent at such address is REGINA BICKFORD.

5.  The name and address of the incorporator is REGINA BICKFORD, 11040 SCHRENK CT, ROLLA, MO 65401 (MAILING ADDRESS IS PO BOX 1665, ROLLA, MO 65402).

6.  The corporation is organized, and shall be operated, exclusively for charitable, scientific, literary and educational purposes within the meaning of section 501(c)(3) of the Internal Revenue Code of 1986, as amended (or the corresponding provision of any future United States Internal Revenue Law). No part of the net earnings of the corporation shall inure to the benefit of, or be distributable to, its Trustees, Directors, Officers or other private persons, except that the corporation shall be authorized and empowered to pay reasonable compensation for services rendered and to make payments and distributions in furtherance of the purposes set forth in this Article. The corporation shall not participate in, or intervene in (including the publishing or distribution of statements), any political campaign on behalf of, or in opposition to, any candidate for public office. Except to the extent permitted by section 501(h) of the Internal Revenue Code of 1986, as amended (or the corresponding provision of any future United States Internal Revenue Law), no substantial part of the activities of the corporation shall be the carrying on of propaganda, or otherwise attempting, to influence legislation. Any other provision of these Articles to the contrary notwithstanding, the corporation shall not carry on any other activities not permitted to be carried on (a) by a corporation exempt from the Federal income tax under section 501(c)(3) of the Internal Revenue Code of 1986, as amended (or the corresponding provision of any future United States Internal Revenue Law), (b) by a corporation contributions to which are deductible under section 170(c)(2) of the Internal Revenue Code of 1986, as amended (or the corresponding provision of any future United States Internal Revenue Law), and (c) by a corporation organized under the Missouri Nonprofit Corporation Act as now existing or hereafter amended.

7.  The corporation shall have no Members. The affairs of the corporation shall be managed by its Board of Directors. The number of Directors and their terms shall be as

State of Missouri
Creation - NonProfit 4 Page(s)

3351374.1

T1305616539

provided in the Bylaws, provided that there shall not be less than three Directors. The Directors of the corporation shall be elected in the manner described in the Bylaws.

8.    The corporation shall have all the powers permitted a corporation that is both a nonprofit corporation under the Missouri Nonprofit Corporation Act and an exempt organization described in section 501(c)(3) of the Internal Revenue Code of 1986, as amended (or the corresponding provision of any future laws of the State of Missouri and Internal Revenue Law).

9.    Bylaws of the corporation, consistent with these Articles, shall be adopted by the Board of Directors or the Incorporators, and may be amended in the manner provided in the Bylaws.

10.    These Articles may be amended by the Board of Directors in the manner provided in the Bylaws.

11.    Upon the dissolution of the corporation, the Board of Directors shall, after paying or making provision for the payment of all of the liabilities of the corporation, distribute all the assets of the corporation to one or more organizations then qualified under section 501(c)(3) of the Internal Revenue Code of 1986, as amended (or the corresponding provision of any future United States Internal Revenue Law) selected by the Board of Directors of the corporation. Any of such assets not so disposed of shall be disposed of by the Circuit Court of the city or county in which the principal office of the corporation is then located to such organization or organizations as said court shall determine and as are then qualified as exempt under section 501(c)(3) of the Internal Revenue Code of 1986, as amended (or the corresponding provision of any future United States Internal Revenue Law).

12.

(a)    The provisions of this Article shall be in the nature of a contract between the corporation and each of its Directors and Officers made in consideration of such person's continued service to the corporation. The protection afforded to each Director or Officer by the provisions of this Article shall survive such person's term of office or employment. This Article may not be repealed, nor may the benefits to the Directors and Officers afforded hereby be diminished, except as to liability accruing in respect of acts or omissions occurring after the date of such repeal or modification.

(b)    The corporation shall hold harmless and indemnify each Director and Officer to the fullest extent authorized or permitted by the provisions of Subsections 1 through 6 and 9 through 11 of Section 355.476, Missouri Revised Statutes, as amended (which Section, in its entirety, is hereinafter referred to as the "State Statute") or any other or additional statutory provisions which are hereafter adopted authorizing or permitting such indemnification.

(c)    The corporation may purchase and maintain for the benefit of each Director or Officer, as named insured or additional insured, a policy or policies of general comprehensive liability insurance (covering claims arising out of death, illness or injury or arising out of property loss or damage) and directors' and officers' liability insurance (covering claims arising out of wrongful acts or omissions) in respect of liabilities asserted against and/or incurred by its Directors and Officers in either such capacity or otherwise in the performance of their services for the corporation.

(d)    In addition to the foregoing, and subject only to the exclusions set forth in section (e) of this Article, the corporation shall, to the fullest extent authorized or permitted by the provisions of Subsection 7 of the State Statute, hold harmless and indemnify each Director and Officer: (i) against any and all expenses (including attorneys' fees), judgments, fines and amounts paid in settlement actually and reasonably incurred by such Director or Officer in connection with any threatened, pending or completed action, suit or proceeding, whether civil, criminal, administrative or investigative (including an action by or in the right of the corporation) to which such Director or Officer is, was or at any time became a party, or is threatened to be made a party, by reason of the fact that such Director or Officer is, was or at any time becomes a Director, Officer, employee or agent of the corporation, or is or was serving or at any time serves at the request of the corporation as a Director, Officer, employee or agent of another corporation, partnership, joint venture, trust or other enterprise; and (ii) otherwise to the fullest extent as may be provided to such Director or Officer by the corporation under the non exclusivity provisions of the State Statute.

(e)    No indemnity pursuant to section (d) of this Article shall be paid by the corporation: (i) except to the extent the aggregate of losses to be indemnified thereunder exceeds the amount of such losses for which the Director or Officer is indemnified either pursuant to section (b) of this Article or pursuant to any insurance of the type referred to in section (c) of this Article purchased and maintained by the corporation; (ii) in respect of remuneration paid to such Director or Officer if it shall be determined by a final decision of a court having jurisdiction in the matter that such remuneration was in violation of law; (iii) on account of such Director's or Officer's conduct which is finally adjudged by a court having jurisdiction in the matter to have been knowingly fraudulent, deliberately dishonest or willful misconduct; or (iv) if a final decision by a court having jurisdiction in the matter shall determine that such indemnification is not lawful.

(f)    All agreements and obligations of the corporation contained in this Article shall continue during the period the Director or Officer is a Director or Officer of the corporation (or is or was serving at the request of the corporation as a director, officer, employee or agent of another corporation, partnership, joint venture, trust or other enterprise) and shall continue thereafter so long as the Director or Officer shall be subject to any possible claim or threatened, pending or completed action, suit or proceeding, whether civil, criminal or investigative, by reason of the fact that he or she was a Director or Officer of the corporation or was serving in any other capacity referred to in this Article.

(a)    The corporation will pay, in advance of the final disposition of the action, suit or proceeding, all reasonable expenses of the Director or Officer incurred in defending any civil or criminal action, suit or proceeding against him or her, provided he or she shall have agreed to reimburse the corporation if and to the extent that it shall be ultimately determined that he or she is not entitled to be indemnified by the corporation for such expenses.

In affirmation thereof, the facts stated above are true and correct:
(The undersigned understands that false statements made in this filing are subject to the penalties provided under Section 575.040, RSMo).

Executed this 22nd day of February 2013, by the Incorporator.

*Regina Bickford*

# CHAPTER 8

## STATE GUIDELINES FOR NONPROFIT CORPORATIONS

*"You can learn a line from a win and a book from a defeat."*
—Paul Brown

PLAY IT FORWARD

Play It Forward is a student led organization that engages students in athletics by providing sporting equipment to underserved youth. Started in 2012 by 12-year old Emily Eisner, Play It Forward combines her passion for sports with a desire to help her community all the while encouraging her peers to be active and get involved. The heart and dedication to the mission of Play It Forward led her to establish a 501(c) (3) in early 2013, which has allowed for the depth of the organization to grow. (CA)

### FOOTBALL CONFERENCES AND BOWLS

Which state team plays in what conference is probably one of the more confusing aspects of college football. Most conferences are formed simply to bring together teams on the same competitive level in the same geographical area. Winning a conference championship is a major accomplishment and assists in invitations to bowl games. The bowl games include Fiesta Bowl, Sugar Bowl, Orange Bowl and Rose Bowl.

From these games it is supposedly the Bowl Championship Series (BCS) that then decides the best-of-the-best in college football. However, because of so many varying guidelines that determine eligibility, the system is constantly embroiled in controversy.

You'll find there is no controversy – nor any leeway – when it comes to the state guidelines for completing your Articles of Incorporation.

## STATE GUIDELINES

To save you the time and effort of research, I have included a table of state guidelines below. All these documents and links were up to date at time of publication. If you find a link not working or out of date information, please contact the Secretary of State in your state for current guidelines. I would also appreciate you sending me an email at support@doyourownnonprofit.com letting me know. Please and Thank You!

| State | Name of Document | Guidelines |
|-------|------------------|------------|
| AL | Nonprofit Certificate of Formation (Domestic) -OR- Foreign Corporation (Business or Non-Profit) Application for Registration -and- Certified copy of Articles of Incorporation from original jurisdiction (Foreign) | There is a fillable document, Form DNP Corp Cert of Formation, available at http://www.sos.alabama.gov/downloads/dl3.aspx?trgturl=../downloads/business/sosdf-5.pdf&trgtfile=sosdf-5.pdf but does not cover the IRS 501(c) (3) required language. I suggest you submit your own document which is virtually the same as Articles of Incorporation, but must be titled Non-Profit Certificate of Formation. For domestic organizations, you must attach your name reservation form (except churches). Submit original and 2 copies of your Nonprofit Certificate of Formation application with filing fees to the Office of the Judge of Probate in the county where the corporation's initial registered office is located. There is a Probate Judge fee (varies but minimum fee is $50.00) and a Secretary of State filing fee ($100.00 at time of writing). Processing takes about 15 days (3 day expedited filing available for $100.00 extra). Alabama has a Certificate of Good Standing, but it DOES NOT apply to nonprofits. You can get a Certificate of Existence for nonprofits however. For foreign organizations, file Foreign Corporation (Business or Non-Profit) |

|  |  | Application for Registration along with a copy of your Articles of Incorporation or similar form certified by the Secretary of State from your originating state. The filing fee is $150.00 and an additional $100.00 for expedited service.<br><br>Mail forms to:<br><br>Secretary of State<br>Business Services<br>P.O. Box 5616<br>Montgomery, AL 36103-5616<br><br>For questions, call Secretary of State, Business Division at (334) 242-5324.<br><br>You can also fax the application to (334) 240-3138. |
|---|---|---|
| **AK** | Articles of Incorporation<br><br>(Domestic)<br><br>*-OR-*<br><br>Certificate of Authority,<br><br>Foreign Nonprofit Corporation<br><br>*-and-*<br><br>Contact Information Sheet<br><br>(Foreign) | There is a fillable document (Form 08-405) available online at https://www.commerce.state.ak.us/CBP/Corporation/startpage.aspx?file=CRFIL&entity=NPRO&isforeign=N but does not include IRS 501(c) (3) required language. Suggest you file your own Articles of Incorporation instead of using the template.<br><br>You must include a six digit NAICS business code. Most appropriate codes for nonprofits are located on the last page of the application, Form 08-405. You must be at least 19 years old to be an incorporator on the application.<br><br>Domestic corporations mail documents to:<br><br>State of Alaska |

| | | |
|---|---|---|
| | | Corporations Section<br>PO Box 110808<br>Juneau AK 99801<br><br>Filing fee at time of writing was $50.00. Standard Processing 10-15 days.<br><br>For Foreign corporations, submit Certificate of Authority, Foreign Nonprofit Corporation, Form 08-452, and Contact Information Sheet, Form 08-561available at http://commerce.alaska.gov/occ/pub_corp/08-452.pdf Filing fee is $50.00.<br><br>Foreign corporations mail documents to:<br><br>State of Alaska<br>Corporations Section<br>PO Box 110806<br>Juneau AK 99801<br><br>For questions, contact Secretary of State at (907) 465-2550 in Juneau, or (907) 269-8160 in Anchorage. |
| **AZ** | Cover Sheet<br><br>*-and-*<br><br>Articles of Incorporation-Nonprofit<br><br>*-and-*<br><br>Certificate of Disclosure<br><br>*-and-* | There are four forms you must submit to become a nonprofit in Arizona, and five if you are foreign corporation. None of them are hard, some are not much more than a signature. So relax and just do one thing at a time.<br><br>Arizona state links are notorious for not working, so to get to the forms you need, do an internet search for "Arizona Corporation Commission Forms Index" and it should take you to http://www.azcc.gov/Divisions/Corporations/forms/formsindex.asp |

| | Statutory Agent Acceptance Form  *-and-*  Application for Authority to Conduct Affairs in Arizona (Foreign Corporations Only) | Under Corporate Forms, you will need:<br><br>• Domestic and Foreign Corporations submit Certificate of Disclosure, Form C003.001<br>• Domestic Corporations submit Articles of Incorporation-Nonprofit, Form C011.001, but it does not include IRS 501(c) (3) required language, so I suggest you file your own document.<br>• Domestic and Foreign corporations submit Statutory Agent Acceptance, Form M002.001<br>• Foreign corporations submit a certified copy of the Articles of Incorporation or similar organizing documents and certified copies of all amendments from your originating jurisdiction. You also need a certified copy of Certificate of Existence or Certificate of Good Standing. All certified copies must be less than 60 days old, so you may have to order new certified copies.<br>• Under Miscellaneous Forms toward the bottom, you will need:<br>• Domestic and Foreign corporations, submit Cover Sheet, Form CFCVLR<br><br>Send completed forms to:<br><br>Arizona Corporation Commission<br>Corporate Filings Section<br>1300 W. Washington St<br>Phoenix, AZ 85007 |

| | | Filing fees at time of writing:<br><br>• Domestic Articles of Incorporation-Nonprofit: $40 (add $35 to expedite)<br>• Certificate of Disclosure: Free (add $35 to expedite)<br>• Statutory Agent Acceptance: Free (add $35 to expedite is submitted separate)<br>• Cover Sheet: Free<br>• Application to Conduct Affairs in Arizona (foreign corporations only): $175 (add $35 to expedite)<br>• Processing time is 3 weeks - 2 months, depending on whether expedited.<br><br>For questions, contact the Arizona Corporate Commission at (602) 542-3026 or inside Arizona at (800) 345-5819. |
|---|---|---|
| **AR** | Articles of Incorporation<br><br>(Domestic)<br><br>*-OR-*<br><br>Application for Certificate of Authority<br><br>*-and-*<br><br>Certificate of Existence | You hit the jackpot if you live in Arkansas. It is one of very few state that gives you a choice of templates that contain the correct language so that if you plan to obtain 501(c) (3) status, you can do it easily. However, the form is not fillable online. Go to http://www.sos.arkansas.gov/BCS/Pages/articlesIncorporationDNP.aspx and select *Form 2, Articles of Incorporation – Domestic Nonprofit 501(c) (3) Compliant Language.* This is Form NPD-01-501. If the link does not work, do an internet search for "Arkansas Secretary of State, Nonprofit Articles of Incorporation" |

| (Foreign) | You can print and fill out this form online or use your own template, either is acceptable.

Foreign corporations file an Application for Certificate of Authority, Form F-01. It can be filed online, by mail, or in person. The form is available at http://www.sos.arkansas.gov/BCS/Pages/foreign.aspx Scroll down to Foreign Corporation. You will also need a Certificate of Existence (or similar document) dated within 30 days of filing with Arkansas, or a certified copy of amendment as filed in your state of incorporation dated within 60 days of filing with Arkansas. If filing online, you must fax or email this certificate or copy or amendments one to seven days prior to online filing. Fax to (501) 682-3437 or email to arkansascorporations@live.com If you do not, your application will be rejected.

Mail documents to:

Arkansas Secretary of State
Business and Commercial Services
1401 West Capitol Avenue
Ste. 250 Victory Building
Little Rock, AR 72201

Filing fees are $50.00 (domestic), and $300.00 (foreign). Processing time is 24 hours online, 2 - 5 days by mail, or while you wait if you go in person.

For questions, contact Business and Commercial Services at (501)682-3409 or toll free at (888) 233-0325. |

| CA | Articles of Incorporation <br><br> *-and-* <br><br> Statement of Information (within 90 days of filing Articles of Incorporation) <br><br> *-OR-* <br><br> Statement and Designation by <br><br> Foreign Corporation <br><br> *-and-*Certificate of Good Standing <br><br> (Foreign) | Articles of Incorporation online fillable forms are located at http://www.sos.ca.gov/business/be/forms.htm#corp <br><br> You must choose which one applies to you: <br><br> Mutual Benefit (Form ARTS-MU) <br> Public Benefit (Form ARTS-PB), or <br> Religious (Form ARTS-RE) <br><br> Required IRS language for 501(c) (3) status is not included in the templates, so I suggest you use your own form. <br><br> Foreign corporations file Statement and Designation by Foreign Corporation, Form S&DC-STK/NP, located at http://www.sos.ca.gov/business/corp/pdf/foreign/s&dc-sn.pdf You must also submit a certified Certificate of Good Standing from your original state. It must be less than 6 months old and state you are a nonprofit organization on it. <br><br> Mail documents to: <br><br> Secretary of State <br> Business Entities <br> P.O. Box 944260 <br> Sacramento, CA 94244-2600 <br><br> Drop off Articles of Incorporation at: <br><br> Secretary of State <br> 1500 11th Street., 3rd Floor <br> Sacramento, CA 95814 <br><br> Fee is $30.00 for domestic and foreign. Add $15.00 if you drop off the form instead of mail. Add $5.00 if you want |

| | | |
|---|---|---|
| | | a certified copy of your filing document (recommended).<br><br>Statement of Information (Form SI-100) must be filed online within 90 days of incorporating. Fillable form is available online and can be filed online at https://businessfilings.sos.ca.gov/<br><br>Filing fee is $20.00. Add $5.00 to receive certified copy (recommended).<br><br>For questions, call Business Programs/ Business Entities at (916) 657-5448. |
| **CO** | Articles of Incorporation<br><br>(Domestic)<br><br>*-OR-*<br><br>Statement of Foreign Entity Authority<br><br>(Foreign) | You must fill out the state's online template at http://www.sos.state.co.us/pubs/business/forms_main.html On the left, click on Forms; or in the center, click on Nonprofit Corporations-Nonprofit; or on the right, click on Nonprofit Corporations. Under Nonprofit Corporations, click on online filing link. This template does not contain the required IRS 501(c) (3) language, so you must provide it as an attachment when you get to item 7 of the online form.<br><br>Domestic filing fee is $50.00.<br><br>Foreign corporations must file online a Statement of Foreign Entity Authority. The entity ID number is left blank for first time registration and will be assigned after the filing is complete. The online template is available at http://www.sos.state.co.us/pubs/business/forms_main.html Click on or scroll down to Foreign Entities.<br><br>Foreign filing fee is $100.00.<br><br>For questions, contact Business |

| | | |
|---|---|---|
| | | Organizations at 303-894-2200 & press 2, or email business@sos.state.co.us |
| **CT** | Certificate of Formation<br><br>(religious)<br><br>-*OR*-<br><br>Certificate of Incorporation -*and*- Organization and First Report<br><br>(nonprofit) | You do not have to use the state forms to incorporate in Connecticut. They do not contain the required wording for IRS approval of 501(c) (3) status, so you will need to add that language, or use your own form.<br><br>You must choose the right form based on what you are setting up. If it is a church or religious society, you may use Certificate of Formation-New Religious Corporation Form CICR-1-1.0 located at http://www.sots.ct.gov/sots/lib/sots/commercialrecording/allforms/cert_of_formation_-_religious_corp_or_society.pdf Filing fee is $50.00. Three or more people must agree to form this organization and sign the form. If you choose the option of forming as a voluntary association instead of getting corporation status right away, you must later file Certificate of Incorporation of Existing Religious Society http://www.sots.ct.gov/sots/lib/sots/commercialrecording/allforms/cert_of_incorp_-_existing_religious_soc.pdf and pay an additional $50.00. If you want to get done in one process, select the Religious Corporation option on the Certificate of Formation.<br><br>If you are forming other than a religious corporation, you need to file a Certificate of Incorporation-Nonstock (filing fee is $50.00) http://www.sots.ct.gov/sots/lib/sots/commercialrecording/allforms/cert_of_inc_-_nonstock_corp.pdf (Form CIN-1-1.0) *and* Organization and First |

| | | |
|---|---|---|
| | | Report form (filing fee is $150.00) http://www.sots.ct.gov/sots/lib/sots/commercial-recording/allforms/corp-organization.pdf (Form COS-1-1.0). These forms are filed simultaneously.<br><br>Mail form(s) to:<br><br>Commercial Recording Division<br>Secretary of the State<br>PO Box 150470<br>Hartford, CT 06115-0470<br><br>For questions, contact the Secretary of State's office at (860) 509-6001. |
| **DE** | Certificate of Incorporation for Exempt Corporation<br><br>(Domestic)<br><br>*-OR-*<br><br>Qualification<br><br>of Foreign Corporation<br><br>*-and-*<br><br>Certificate of Existence<br><br>(Foreign) | File Delaware Certificate of Incorporation for Exempt Corporation. A fillable form is located at http://corp.delaware.gov/Inc_Exempt.pdf however, it does not contain the required language for IRS approval of 501(c) (3) status, so you may want to file your own form. Domestic filing fee is $89 plus $9 per page after the first page.<br><br>Foreign corporations file Qualification of Foreign Corporation form located at http://corp.delaware.gov/forqual09.pdf along with a Certificate of Existence dated within 6 months prior to filing with Delaware.<br><br>Foreign filing fee is $245.00.<br><br>Expedited service is available in Delaware. One hour service is $1,000.00, 2 hour service is $500.00, and same day is $100.00 and is $50.00. |

| | | |
|---|---|---|
| | | One copy of your document will be returned to you, but if you want a certified copy, it is $50.00 more. <br><br> For questions, contact: <br><br> Delaware Division of Corporations <br> 401 Federal Street – Suite 4 <br> Dover, DE 19901 <br><br> For questions, call (302) 739-3073. Fax: (302) 739-3812 |
| **DC** | Articles of Incorporation for Domestic Nonprofit Corporation <br><br> (Form DNP-1) <br><br> *-OR-* <br><br> Foreign Registration Statement <br><br> (Form FN-1) | Online fillable form available at http://dc.gov/DC/DCRA/Publication%20Files/DCRA/Corporations/Domestic%20Nonprofit%20Corporation/Articles%20of%20Incorporation%20of%20Domestic%20Nonprofit%20Corporation%20DNP-1.pdf but does not contain IRS required language. You can add it under *Miscellaneous Provisions* section, or submit your own document. If you file online, you may use credit card to pay. <br><br> For foreign (out of state) registration, online form is available at http://dc.gov/DC/DCRA/For+Business/Corporate+Registration/Foreign+Registration+Statement+FN-1 <br><br> Filing fee is $80.00. Checks payable to <br><br> "D.C. Treasurer" <br><br> Mail your Articles of Incorporation to: <br><br> Department of Consumer and Regulatory Affairs |

| | | |
|---|---|---|
| | | Corporations Division<br>PO Box 92300<br>Washington, DC 20090<br><br>For questions, call (202) 442-4400. |
| **FL** | Articles of Incorporation<br><br>*-and-*<br><br>Cover letter | DO NOT FILE THE ONLINE Articles of Incorporation. They contain only the minimum required state language for non-profit organizations, not the required IRS 501(c) (3) language for purpose and disso-lution of the corporation. Instead, prepare your own Articles of Incorporation. The basic form and cover letter are located at http://form.sunbiz.org/pdf/cr2e006.pdf<br><br>Total fees are $87.50 and include filing fee ($35.00), designation of registered agent ($35.00), certified copy of Articles of Incorporation ($8.75 for up to 8 pages, then $1.00 for each additional page, op-tional), and a Certificate of Status ($8.75, optional).<br><br>Mail original and one copy of Articles of Incorporation, with the cover letter to:<br><br>Department of State<br>Division of Corporations<br>P. O. Box 6327<br>Tallahassee, FL 32314<br><br>For questions, call (850) 245-6052. |
| **GA** | Articles of Incorporation<br><br>*-and-*<br><br>Transmittal | You prepare your own Articles of Incor-poration, making sure they contain eve-rything required in O.C.G.A. 14-3-202 (nonprofit). You can also file online by using this website: http://sos.georgia.gov/corporations/new_entity_notice.htm but it |

| Form 227 | does not cover the mandatory IRS 501(c)(3) language. |
|---|---|
| -and- | |
| | Transmittal form is located at http://www.sos.ga.gov/Corporations/Entity%20conversion/form227%20%20profit%20and%20nonprofit%20transmittal.pdf |
| Notice of Incorporation | |
| -or- | |
| Notice of Intent to Incorporate | Filing fee is $100.00 and it takes about 12 days to process. |
| | publish for 2 consecutive weeks. The fee is standard in Georgia and set by law: $40.00. You do not submit proof of publication to the state, but keep a copy for your records. |
| | Mail forms to: |
| | Office of Secretary of State<br>Corporations Division<br>313 West Tower<br>2 Martin Luther King, Jr. Drive<br>Atlanta, Georgia 30334-1530 |
| | For questions, call (404) 656-2817. |
| | NOTE: Georgia requires every new domestic corporation, profit or nonprofit, to file a Notice of Incorporation or Notice of Intent to Incorporate with a major newspaper (referred to as "the official legal organ of the county") in the county in which the organization will be initially located. (Call your county courthouse to find out which newspaper to publish the notice in.) This must be done within one business day after filing Articles of Incorporation. It has to be run once a week for two consecutive weeks. Send it in the form of a letter to the publisher giving |

| | | |
|---|---|---|
| | | notice that the articles of incorporation have been filed, and include the name of the organization, the registered agent, and the office address, and instructions to |
| **HI** | Articles of Incorporation | File Articles of Incorporation (Form DNP-1) found at http://hawaii.gov/dcca/ breg/registration/forms/dnp-1-pdf.pdf but does not include mandatory IRS 501(c) (3) language. Suggest you file your own form.<br><br>Form can be typewritten or printed in black ink.<br><br>Filing fee is $25.00. Certified copies are $10.00 each (optional). Expedite fee is $25.00 (optional). Make checks payable to Department of Commerce and Consumer Affairs.<br><br>Mail form to:<br><br>Department of Commerce and Consumer Affairs<br>PO Box 40<br>Honolulu, HI 96810<br><br>For questions, call (808) 586-2744 (Administration) or (808) 586-2727 (Documents registration). |
| **ID** | Articles of Incorporation (Non-Profit) | You file Articles of Incorporation, an online form is located at http://www.sos. idaho.gov/corp/acro4/arts_inc_np.pdf You may fill in the required IRS 501(c) (3) language on this form for purpose and dissolution or create your own document. |

| | | |
|---|---|---|
| | | Filing fee is $30.00 (add $20.00 to expedite).<br><br>Mail form to:<br><br>Office of the Secretary of State<br>450 N 4th Street<br>PO Box 83720<br>Boise ID 83720-0080<br><br>For questions, call (208) 334-2301. |
| **IL** | Articles of Incorporation–Not For Profit | DO NOT USE ONLINE FORM! You cannot include IRS 501(c) (3) language on that form. You must file your own form. Submit 2 identical copies.<br><br>Filing fee is $50.00. Expedite fee is $25.00 (optional). Payment Processing fee is $2.75.<br><br>Mail form to whichever is appropriate:<br><br>Secretary of State<br>Department of Business Services<br>Corporations Division<br>350 Howlett Building<br>Springfield, IL 62756<br><br>-or-<br><br>Secretary of State<br>Department of Business Services<br>Corporations Division<br>69 W. Washington, Ste. 1240<br>Chicago, IL 60602<br><br>For questions, call (217) 782-6961 (Springfield), or (312) 793-3380. |

| IN | Articles of Incorporation<br><br>*-OR-*<br><br>Application for Certificate of Authority<br><br>*-and-*<br><br>Nonprofit Application for Sales Tax Exemption | Submit original and one copy of Articles of Incorporation, or you can use Articles of Incorporation for a Nonprofit Corporation, State Form 4162 (Domestic Corporation), or Application for Certificate of Authority of a Foreign Nonprofit Corporation to Transact Business in the State of Indiana, State Form 37035 (Foreign) can be found online at http://www.in.gov/sos/business/2426.htm If you use the state forms, you must add the required language for purpose and dissolution to make the organization 501(c) (3) eligible.<br><br>Secretary of State's Office<br>Corporations Division<br>302 West Washington St., Rm. E018<br>Indianapolis, IN 46204<br><br>Filing fee is $30.00<br><br>For questions, call (317) 232-6576<br><br>www.IN.gov/sos/business/corporations.html<br><br>You must also register with the Indiana Department of Revenue by filing Form NP-20A (state form 51064), Nonprofit Application for Sales Tax Exemption, within 120 days of formation. There is no fee to file, and you will be given an Indiana Taxpayer Identification Number for sales tax exemption. You can get a copy at http://www.in.gov/dor/3506.htm If by then you have your determination letter from IRS as a 501(c) (3) corporation, send a copy. If not, just file the form. It gives |

| | | |
|---|---|---|
| | | nonprofits the right to buy with no sales tax, and sell up to 30 days (in some cases year round) without collecting sales tax (except for social organizations).<br><br>Send form to:<br><br>Department of Revenue<br>100 N. Senate Ave.<br>Indianapolis, IN 46204<br><br>Nonprofit Organizations phone number is (317) 232-2188. |
| IA | Articles of Incorporation<br><br>(Domestic)<br><br>*-OR-*<br><br>Application for Certificate of Authority (Foreign) | File Articles of Incorporation and receive back Certificate of Acknowledgement from the Secretary of State. There is no form, you create your own. It must contain the requirements listed at http://sos.iowa.gov/nonprofits/MinCodeReq.html<br><br>Foreign corporations desiring to do business in Iowa file Application for Certificate of Authority, Form 635_0110A<br><br>Filing fee is $20.00 (domestic) or $25.00 (foreign).<br><br>Mail Articles of Incorporation or Application for Certificate of Authority to:<br><br>Secretary of State<br>Business Services Division<br>Lucas Building, 1st Floor<br>Des Moines, IA 50319<br><br>For questions, call (515) 281-5204. |

| KS | Not-For-Profit Corporation Articles of Incorporation<br><br>-OR-<br><br>Foreign Not-For-Profit Corporation Application | Kansas has Form CN 51-02, Not-For-Profit Corporation Articles of Incorporation, however there is not room on the form to include the required IRS 501(c)(3) required language, so I suggest you file your own document. Foreign corporations should file FN 51-17, Foreign Not-For-Profit Corporation Application. Foreign corporations must send in an original Certificate of Good Standing or Existence from the jurisdiction or state of origin.<br><br>Filing fees are $20 for domestic and $115 for foreign.<br><br>Mail document to:<br><br>Kansas Office of Secretary of State<br>Memorial Hall, 1st Floor<br>120 S.W. 10th Avenue<br>Topeka, KS 66612-1594<br><br>For questions, call (785) 296-4564. |
| KY | Articles of Incorporation Non-Profit Corporation (Domestic)<br><br>-OR-<br><br>Certificate of Authority (Foreign Business Entity)<br><br>(Foreign) | Kentucky's domestic Articles of Incorporation, Form NAI, do not meet IRS 501(c)(3) required language, so submit your own. Their form is located at http://www.sos.ky.gov/nr/rdonlyres/09135178-87e2-4b63-9930-bc12e26dec7d/0/naiarticlesofincorporationnonprofitcorporation.pdf for reference, but should not be used as your filing document. Foreign nonprofits should file Certificate of Authority (Foreign Business Entity), Form FBE. |

| | | The form is located at http://www.sos. ky.gov/NR/rdonlyres/287CBE00-84BD-4A2A-9C92-379593D5F22D/0/FBECertificateofAuthorization_ForeignBusinessEntity.pdf |
| --- | --- | --- |
| | | Filing fee for a domestic nonprofit is a whopping $8.00 in Kentucky. Make check payable to: Kentucky State Treasurer. Foreign filing fee is $90.00. |
| | | Mail Articles of Incorporation or foreign form to: |
| | | Division of Business Filings<br>Business Filings<br>PO Box 718<br>Frankfort, KY 40602 |
| | | For questions, call (502) 564-3490. |
| LA | Transmittal Information for all Business Filings Cover Sheet<br><br>*-and-*<br><br>Articles of Incorporation- Louisiana Nonprofit<br><br>(Domestic)<br><br>*-OR-*<br><br>Application for | Transmittal Information cover sheet is located at http://www.sos.la.gov/Portals/0/395ArticlesofIncorporationLouisianaNon-Profit.pdf<br><br>Use the first page, but the Nonprofit Articles of Incorporation-Louisiana Nonprofit (Form SS395A) do not contain IRS 501(c)(3) required language, so you must submit your own document. Notice that the registered agent must sign an affidavit of acknowledgement and acceptance and it must be notarized.<br><br>Foreign corporations should file Application for Authority to Transact Business in Louisiana, Form SS326, |

|  |  |  |
|---|---|---|
|  | Authority to Transact Business in Louisiana<br><br>(Foreign) | located at http://www.sos.la.gov/Portals/ 0/326ApplicationofForeignCorporation forCertificateofAuthority.pdf<br><br>Filing fee is $60.00 (domestic) and $100.00 (foreign). Make check payable to: Secretary of State.<br><br>Send documents to:<br><br>Commercial Division<br>PO Box 94125<br>Baton Rouge, LA 70804-9125<br><br>For questions, call (225) 925-4704. |
| **ME** | Cover Sheet<br><br>*-and-*<br><br>Articles of Incorporation<br><br>*-OR-*<br><br>Foreign<br><br>Nonprofit Corporation Application for Authority to Carry on Activities | Domestic Nonprofit Corporation Articles of Incorporation, Form MNPCA-6 can be found at http://www.maine.gov/sos/cec/ corp/formsnew/mnpca6.pdf<br><br>You can include the IRS 501(c) (3) language for purpose on the form, and attach the required dissolution language as an attachment to the form, or complete your own document. In either case, use the required cover sheet at the end of the document linked above.<br><br>Foreign nonprofits must file Application for Authority to Carry On Activities, Form MNPCA-12, located at http://www. maine.gov/sos/cec/corp/formsnew/mn-pca12.pdf<br><br>Filing fees are $40.00 (domestic) and $45.00 (foreign). |

| | | |
|---|---|---|
| | | Mail forms to: <br><br> Secretary of State <br> Division of Corporations, UCC and Commissions <br> 101 State House Station <br> Augusta, ME 04333-0101 <br><br> For questions, call (207) 624-7752. |
| **MD** | Articles of Incorporation <br><br> For a Tax-Exempt Nonstock Corporation <br><br> (Domestic) <br><br> *-OR-* <br><br> Articles of Incorporation for Tax-Exempt Religious Corporations <br><br> (Domestic) <br><br> *-OR-* <br><br> Foreign Corporation Qualification and Certificate of Good Standing | Articles of Incorporation for a Tax-Exempt Nonstock Corporation, is located at http://www.dat.state.md.us/sdatweb/ex_corp_form.pdf and contains all IRS 501(c) (3) required language. Articles of Incorporation for Tax-Exempt Religious Corporations is located at http://www.dat.state.md.us/sdatweb/rel_form.pdf and does contain IRS 501(c) (3) required language. Must be typed and printed in black ink only. <br><br> Filing fee is $170.00 for Tax-Exempt Nonstock Corporation. (The fee to file Articles of Incorporation in $100.00 plus a $20.00 organization and capitalization fee and a $50.00 assessment for the Maryland Not-For-Profit Development Center Program Fund for a total of $170.00). Fee for Articles of Incorporation for Tax-Exempt Religious Corporations is $120.00. Expedite fee is $50.00 for 7 day processing, otherwise 7 - 8 weeks processing time. Make check payable to: SDAT (State Department of Assessment and Taxation). <br><br> For foreign nonprofit corporations, you file |

| | | |
|---|---|---|
| | | a Foreign Corporation Qualification form located at http://www.dat.state.md.us/sdatweb/forcp.pdf and attach a copy of your Certificate of Good Standing from your state. You must have a Maryland Registered Agent. Filing fee is $170.00, $50.00 to expedite, plus $5.00 for return mail processing fee to get a copy of the filing.<br><br>Mail forms to:<br><br>State Department of Assessments and Taxation<br>Charter Division<br>301 W. Preston Street, 8th Floor<br>Baltimore, MD 21201-2395<br><br>Fax completed forms with MasterCard of Visa credit card payment information to 410-333-7097. Fax request will be charged the additional expedited service fee.<br><br>For questions, call (410) 767-1350 or toll free (888) 246-5941. |
| **MA** | Articles of Organization<br><br>-*OR*-<br><br>Foreign Corporation Certificate of Registration and Certificate of Existence or Good Standing | Articles of Organization, Form 180art, is available at http://www.sec.state.ma.us/cor/corpdf/180art.pdf It does not contain IRS 501(c) (3) required language, but there is room to insert the required clauses, and you can attach an additional sheet http://www.sec.state.ma.us/cor/corpdf/attach-ment.pdf if needed. You can file online, just be sure to include IRS required clauses in the filing. A copy of your filing is available online after processing. You may want to file your own document. |

| | | |
|---|---|---|
| | | Foreign corporations may file a Certificate of Registration located at http://www.sec.state.ma.us/cor/corpdf/c156d-s1503950c11348.pdf along with a Certificate of Existence or Good Standing from the jurisdiction originally incorporated. If you need to attach any documents, use the attachment sheet located at http://www.sec.state.ma.us/cor/corpdf/attachment.pdf <br><br> You can file online for either domestic or foreign organization by registering at https://corp.sec.state.ma.us/corp/loginsystem/login_form.asp?FilingMethod=I <br><br> Filing fees are $35.00 (domestic) and $400 (foreign). Make checks payable to Commonwealth of Massachusetts. <br><br> Send documents to: <br><br> Secretary of the Commonwealth <br> Corporations Division <br> One Ashburton Place, 17th floor <br> Boston, MA 02108-1512 <br><br> For questions, call (617) 727-9640. |
| **MI** | Articles of Incorporation (Domestic) <br><br> *-OR-* <br><br> Application For Certificate of Authority to Transact Business | Articles of Incorporation for Use by Domestic Nonprofit Corporations, Form BCS/CD-502, can be found at http://www.michigan.gov/documents/CIS_Form_502_2457_7.pdf but does not include IRS 501(c) (3) required language. Suggest you create your own document. <br><br> Foreign corporations must file Application For Certificate of Authority to Transact |

| | | |
|---|---|---|
| | or Conduct Affairs in Michigan<br><br>and current Certificate of Good Standing and Articles of Incorporation<br><br>(Foreign) | Business or Conduct Affairs in Michigan, Form BCS/CD-560 located at http://www.michigan.gov/documents/CIS_Form_560_2448_7.pdf You must attach a current Certificate of Good Standing from your original jurisdiction not older than 30 days prior to filing. Also include your original Articles of Incorporation from your home state, and any amendments to them.<br><br>Filing fee is $20.00, domestic or foreign.<br><br>Send document to:<br><br>Michigan Department of Labor & Economic Growth<br>Bureau of Commercial Services<br>Corporation Division7150 Harris Drive<br>P.O. Box 30054<br>Lansing, MI 48909<br><br>For questions, call (517) 241-6470. |
| MN | Articles of Incorporation<br><br>(Domestic)<br><br>-OR-<br><br>Certificate of Authority<br><br>(Foreign) | Articles of Incorporation for a MN Corporation is available at http://www.sos.state.mn.us/index.aspx?page=1086 (Minnesota Nonprofit Corporation/Articles of Incorporation) online filing or to fill out and mail in. This form does not contain the IRS 501(c) (3) required language, so you may want to file your own document. Keep the signed original and submit a photocopy.<br><br>Filing fee (domestic) is $90.00 online or in person, $70.00 by mail. |

| | | |
|---|---|---|
| | | Foreign Corporation or Cooperative/Certificate of Authority to Transact Business in Minnesota is available at http://www.sos.state.mn.us/index.aspx?page=1087<br><br>Filing fee (foreign) is $70.00 express on-line or in person, $50.00 by mail.<br><br>Send documents to or file in person at:<br><br>Minnesota Secretary of State - Business Services Retirement Systems of Minnesota Building<br>60 Empire Drive, Suite 100<br>St Paul, MN 55103<br><br>For questions, call (877) 551-6767 or in Metro Area, call (651) 296-2803. |
| **MS** | Articles of Incorporation<br><br>(Domestic)<br><br>*-OR-*<br><br>Certificate of Authority<br><br>(Foreign) | Articles of Incorporation (Form F0001) is available at http://www.sos.ms.gov/links/business/fees/corporations/F0001.pdf but does not contain the IRS 501(c) (3) required language. You can add the required clauses under "Other Provisions" as an additional separate attachment. You may want to file your own document.<br><br>Application for Certificate of Authority (Form F0002) is available at http://www.sos.ms.gov/links/business/fees/corporations/F0002.pdf You must enclose an original Certificate of Existence from your home state dated not more than 60 days prior to filing.<br><br>Filing fee is $50.00 (domestic), and |

| | | |
|---|---|---|
| | | $100.00 (foreign) payable to Mississippi Secretary of State. Send documents to: Secretary of State PO Box 136 Jackson, MS 39215-1020 For questions, call (601) 359-1633. |
| **MO** | Articles of Incorporation (Domestic) *-OR-* Certificate of Authority (Foreign) | Articles of Incorporation available at http://www.sos.mo.gov/forms/corp/corp52.pdf (Form Corp 52), but does not contain the IRS 501(c) (3) required language. The required clauses are stated in the instructions but does not fit in the fillable online form. You may want to file your own document. Application for Certificate of Authority of a Foreign Nonprofit (Form Corp 55A) is available at http://www.sos.mo.gov/forms/corp/corp55a.pdf You must attach a certified copy of your state's Certificate of Good Standing or Certificate of Existence less than 60 days old. Filing fee is $25.00 domestic or foreign, payable to Secretary of State. Send documents to: Secretary of State Attn: Corporations Division PO Box 778 Jefferson City, MO 65102 For questions, call (866) 223-6535 or (573) |

| | | |
|---|---|---|
| | | 751-4153. For help at branch offices, call (816) 889-2925 in Kansas City, (417) 895-6330 in Springfield, or (314) 340-7490 in St. Louis. |
| **MT** | Articles of Incorporation (Domestic) *-OR-* Certificate of Authority (Foreign) | Articles of Incorporation for Domestic Nonprofit Corporation is available at http://sos.mt.gov/business/forms/Nonprofit/Domestic/54-Domestic_Nonprofit_Corporation_Articles_of_Incorporation.pdf (Form 54). The actual form does not contain the IRS 501(c) (3) required language, but is available at http://sos.mt.gov/Business/Forms/General/501C3.pdf and can be typed onto a separate attachment and submitted as part of the Articles of Incorporation. You must submit a copy with original signatures. Certificate of Authority for a Foreign Nonprofit Corporation is available at http://sos.mt.gov/business/Forms/Nonprofit/Foreign/64-Foreign_Nonprofit_Corporation_Certificate_of_Authority.pdf (Form 64). Enclose a Certificate of Existence from your home jurisdiction within 6 months of this application. Filing fee is $20.00 domestic or foreign. Twenty four hour priority handling available for an additional $20.00 and one hour service expedited service is available for an additional $100.00. Do not staple payment to forms. |

| | | |
|---|---|---|
| | | Send documents to:<br><br>Secretary of State<br>PO Box 202801<br>Helena, MT 59620-2801<br><br>For questions, call Business Services Division at (406) 444-3665. |
| **NE** | Articles of Incorporation<br><br>(Domestic)<br><br>*-OR-*<br><br>Certificate of Authority (Foreign) | There is no form for Articles of Incorporation in Nebraska, so you must file your own document. Send original and one copy.<br><br>Application for Certificate of Authority to Transact Business (Non-Profit Corporations is available at http://www.sos.ne.gov/business/corp_serv/pdf/19_148.pdf Submit 2 copies of the application and a Certificate of Good Standing less than 60 days old. After filing is complete and approved, a notice of incorporation must be published in a legal, local newspaper of general circulation for three consecutive weeks.<br><br>Filing fee is $10.00 plus $5.00 per page (domestic), and $25.00 (foreign), plus $5.00 for each additional page. (Foreign starts with page 3 because the application is 2 pages long).<br><br>Nebraska has eDelivery, an online filing system that speeds up the process of filing. Details are available at https://www.nebraska.gov/apps-sos-edocs/ There is an extra fee that depends on the document and number of pages. |

| | | |
|---|---|---|
| | | You can also use Nebraska One Stop Business Registration Information System at https://www.nebraska.gov/osbr/index.cgi<br><br>Send documents to:<br><br>Secretary of State<br>Corporation Division<br>Room 1301<br>State Capital Building<br>Lincoln, NE 68509<br>For questions, call (402) 471-4079. |
| **NV** | Articles of Incorporation<br><br>(Domestic)<br><br>*-OR-*<br><br>Qualification to do Business in Nevada<br><br>(Foreign) | Nonprofit Articles of Incorporation is available at https://nvsos.gov/Modules/ShowDocument.aspx?documentid=808 but does not contain the IRS 501(c) (3) required language. It can be added by attachment of a separate sheet or you can file your own document. Scroll through the whole document to find cover sheet (or you can provide your own) and expedite forms.<br><br>Qualification to do Business in Nevada is available at http://www.nvsos.gov/Modules/ShowDocument.aspx?documentid=609<br><br>File with a Certificate of Existence from your home jurisdiction and a file stamped copy of the most recently filed corporate document in your home jurisdiction indicating how much stock or that you are a nonprofit, nonstock corporation.<br><br>Filing fee is $50.00 (domestic or foreign |

| | | |
|---|---|---|
| | | Nonstock corporation) or regular corporate fees if filing a nonprofit stock corporation. Expedite fee is $125.00 (24 hour and can be picked up), but you can get 2 hour service for an additional $500.00 or 1 hour service for an additional $1,000.00. Unless you specify pick up or give FedEx authorization, expedited packages are returned by First Class mail, but a fax or email can be sent to confirm expedited service processing before mailing back to you if requested at the time you file. You may also place a telephone order and pay by credit card at (775) 684 5708.<br><br>Send documents to:<br><br>Secretary of State<br>204 North Carson Street, Suite 4<br>Carson City, Nevada 89701-4520<br><br>Expedited filings can be processed through satellite office if you are near Las Vegas:<br><br>Secretary of State – Las Vegas<br>Commercial Recordings Division<br>555 East Washington Ave, Suite 5200<br>Las Vegas NV 89101<br><br>For questions, call (775) 684 5708 or (702) 486-2880 Las Vegas. |
| **NH** | Articles of Agreement of a New Hampshire Nonprofit Corporation<br><br>(Domestic) | Articles of Agreement of a New Hampshire Nonprofit Corporation is available at http://www.sos.nh.gov/corporate/PDF/Form_NP-1_V-1.0.pdf (Form NP-1), but does not contain the IRS 501(c) (3) required language. There is sufficient room to add that language to the |

| | | |
|---|---|---|
| | *-OR-*<br><br>Application for Registration of a Foreign Nonprofit Corporation<br><br>*-AND-*<br><br>Register of Charitable Trusts Application for Registration<br><br>(Foreign) | form, or you can file your own document. At the time of or before you file your IRS 501(c) (3) package, you must also fill out Register of Charitable Trusts Application for Registration (Form NHCT-1). It is available at http://www.doj.nh.gov/charitable-trusts/documents/nhct-1-application.pdf<br><br>Application for Registration of a Foreign Nonprofit Corporation (Form FNP-1) is available at http://www.sos.nh.gov/corporate/PDF/Form_FNP-1_V-1.0.pdf<br><br>Foreign nonprofits must also file Charitable Trusts Application for Registration (NHCT-1) available at http://www.doj.nh.gov/charitable-trusts/documents/nhct-1-application.pdf You will need to attach some of your governing documents to the application as requested in the application.<br><br>Filing fee is $25 (domestic and foreign) and $25 for the Charitable Trusts application.<br><br>Send documents to:<br><br>Corporation Division<br>Department of State<br>107 North Main Street<br>Concord NH 03301-4989<br><br>For questions, call (603) 271-3246. |
| **NJ** | Public Records Filing for New Business Entities | Public Records Filing for New Business Entities is available at http://www.state.nj.us/treasury/revenue/pdforms/pubrec.pdf but does not contain the IRS 501(c) |

| | | |
|---|---|---|
| | *-or-*<br><br>Articles of<br>Incorporation<br><br>(Domestic)<br><br>**-OR-**<br><br>Public Records<br>Filing for New<br>Business Entity<br><br>(Foreign) | (3) required language. Domestic corporations have the option of filing Articles of Incorporation using your own document.<br><br>Religious nonprofits filing "Title 16" incorporation (reduced filing fee and no annual report required.)<br><br>Filing fee is $75.00 (domestic or foreign) Make payment to: Treasurer, State of New Jersey.<br><br>Religious nonprofits filing under Title 16 instead of Title 15a have a $5.00 filing fee and no annual report required. The Center for Nonprofits in New Brunswick, NJ provides this guide: http://www.nj.gov/njbusiness/pdfs/ThinkingOfForming_2010.pdf , and discusses religious nonprofits starting on page 15. You also might want to call them at (732) 227-0800 and discuss your options.<br><br>Send documents to:<br><br>State of New Jersey<br>Division of Revenue, Corporate Filing Unit<br>PO Box 308<br>Trenton, NJ 08646<br><br>Or overnight to:<br><br>State of New Jersey<br>Division of Revenue<br>33 West State St., 5th Floor<br>Trenton, NJ 08608-1214<br><br>For questions, call (609) 292-9292. |

| NM | Articles of Incorporation (Domestic) -OR- Application for Certificate of Authority (Foreign) -AND- Document Delivery Instructions -AND- Statement of Registered Agent | Document Delivery Instructions, Articles of Incorporation, and Statement of Registered Agent (Form D-STMNT) are available at http://www.nmprc.state.nm.us/corporations/pdf/charter/dnp.pdf but the Articles of Incorporation do not contain IRS 501(c) (3) required language, so you might want to submit your own document. Document Delivery Instructions, Application for Certificate of Authority, and Statement of Registered Agent (Form D-STMNT) are available at http://www.nmprc.state.nm.us/corporations/pdf/charter/fnp.pdf Filing fee is $25.00 (domestic and foreign). Submit original and one copy. To certify your return copy, add $10.00. Make checks payable to New Mexico Public Regulation Commission (NMPRC). Send documents to: Public Regulation Commission Corporations Bureau Chartered Documents Division PO Box 1269 Santa Fe, NM 87504-1269 For questions, call (505)827-4508 or (505) 827-4511. |
|---|---|---|
| NY | Certificate of Incorporation (Domestic) -OR- | Certificate of Incorporation (Form DOS1511-f-l) is available at http://www.dos.ny.gov/forms/corporations/1511-f-l.pdf but does not include the IRS 501(c) (3) required language, but there is a box |

| | | |
|---|---|---|
| | Application for Authority<br><br>(Foreign) | provided to add IRS required statements. Instructions for this form are located at http://www.dos.ny.gov/forms/corporations/1555-f-l-a.pdf You will be asked what type of nonprofit you are organizing. You want "Type B" which covers all 501(c) (3) purposes. You may want to file your own document.<br><br>Note: Religious corporations file a Certificate of Incorporation with the County Clerk in the County they live in as per Religious Corporations Laws, Article 3. It must be acknowledged or proved by a the right official at county level, and the County Clerk can direct you to the right person to sign it in your county.<br><br>Application for Authority is available at http://www.dos.ny.gov/forms/corporations/1555-f-l-a.pdf Attach a Certificate of Good Standing/Existence.<br><br>Filing fee is $75.00 (domestic) and $135.00 (foreign). Expedited handling is $25 for 24 hour, $75 for same day, or $150.00 for 2 hour service. Make checks payable to Department of State.<br><br>Send documents to:<br><br>Department of State<br>Division of Corporations<br>State Records and Uniform Commercial Code<br>99 Washington Avenue, Suite 600<br>Albany, New York 12231<br><br>For questions, call Corporate Information at (518) 473-2492. |

| NC | Articles of Incorporation (Domestic) *-OR-* Certificate of Authority (Foreign) | Articles of Incorporation For Nonprofit (Form N-01) is available at http://www.secretary.state.nc.us/corporations/Forms.aspx?PItemId=5429733 The document in Word form can be used to add the IRS 501(c) (3) required language for dissolution under item 8, and the required language for purpose would need to be added under item 9. You may want to file your own document. Application for Certificate of Authority for Nonprofit Corporation (Form N-09) is available at http://www.secretary.state.nc.us/corporations/Forms.aspx?PItemId=5429733 File original and one copy. Filing fee is $60.00 (domestic) and $125.00 (foreign). Send documents to: Secretary of State Corporations Division PO Box 29622 Raleigh, NC 27626-0622 For questions, call (919) 807-2000. |
| ND | Articles of Incorporation (Domestic) *-OR-* Certificate of Authority (Foreign) | North Dakota Nonprofit Corporation Articles of Incorporation (Form SNF 13003) is available at http://www.nd.gov/eforms/Doc/sfn13003.pdf but does not contain IRS 501(c) (3) required language. It can be added to the form in items 4 and 5, or you can submit your own document. Certificate of Authority Foreign Corporation Application (Form SNF |

| | | |
|---|---|---|
| | | 13100) is available at http://www.nd.gov/ eforms/Doc/sfn13100.pdf Must attach a current Certificate of Good Standing/Existence from home state jurisdiction. |
| | | Filing fee is $40.00 (domestic) and $50.00 (foreign). You may pay by credit card by filling out Credit Card Payment Authorization (SNF 51578) contained a the end of the forms. |
| | | Send documents to: |
| | | Business Registration Unit<br>Secretary of State<br>State of North Dakota<br>600 E Boulevard Ave., Dept. 108<br>Bismarck, ND 58505-0500 |
| | | You may fax documents to (701) 328-2992, but does not expedite filing time. |
| | | For questions, call (701) 328-2904 or toll free at (800) 352-0867 (extension 328-2904). |
| **OH** | Initial Articles of Incorporation<br><br>-*and*-<br><br>Initial Appointment of Statutory Agent<br><br>(Domestic)<br><br>-*OR*-<br><br>Foreign Nonprofit | Initial Articles of Incorporation and Initial Appointment of Statutory Agent (Form 532) are available at http://www.sos.state.oh.us/sos/upload/business/forms/532.pdf but the Articles of Incorporation do not include IRS 501(c) (3) required language, so you might want to submit your own document and just use the Statutory Agent part of the form (page 3 of 3). Instructions are included at the bottom of the form. |

| | Application for License (Foreign) | Foreign Nonprofit Application for License (Form 530b) is available at http://www.sos.state.oh.us/sos/upload/business/forms/530b.pdf<br><br>Attach a Certificate of Good Standing/Existence/Subsistence from original state jurisdiction. DO NOT include a social security or Tax ID number on this form, it will be rejected.<br><br>Filing fee is $125.00 (domestic or foreign).<br><br>Expedited 2 day processing service is an additional $100.00.<br><br>Send documents to:<br><br>Secretary of State<br>PO Box 670<br>Columbus, OH 43216<br>Send expedited documents to:<br>Secretary of State<br>PO Box 1390<br>Columbus, OH 43216<br><br>For questions, call (614) 466-3910 or toll free (877) 767-3453. |
|---|---|---|
| **OK** | Articles of Incorporation (Domestic) -*OR*- Certificate of Qualification (Foreign) | Articles of Incorporation (SOS Forms 0008 and 0009 combined) are available at https://www.sos.ok.gov/forms/FM0008. PDF but does not contain IRS 501(c) (3) required language, so you may want to submit your own document.<br><br>Certificate of Qualification Foreign Corporation (SOS Forms 0012 and 0013 combined) are available at https://www.sos.ok.gov/forms/FM0012.PDF |

| | | |
|---|---|---|
| | | Attach a Certificate of Good Standing, Certificate of Existence, or Certificate of Fact (Texas) not more than 60 days old.<br><br>Filing fee is $25.00 (domestic) and $300.00 (foreign), and expedited one day service is an additional $25.00. May file in person, online, fax, or mail. Fax number is (405) 521-3771.<br><br>Send documents to:<br><br>Secretary of State<br>2300 N. Lincoln Blvd.<br>Room 101, State Capitol,<br>Oklahoma City, Oklahoma 73105-4897<br><br>For questions call (405) 521-3912 (domestic) or (405) 522-2520. |
| **OR** | Articles of Incorporation<br><br>(Domestic)<br><br>*-OR-*<br><br>Application for Authority to Transact Business<br><br>(Foreign) | Articles of Incorporation Nonprofit (Form 30) is available at http://filinginoregon. com/pages/forms/business/np_articles.pdf but does not contain the IRS 501(c) (3) required language. The required wording is at the end of the instructions, but does not fit on the lines provided, so you might want to submit your own document.<br><br>Application for Authority to Transact Business - Nonprofit (Form 60) is available at<br><br>http://www.filinginoregon.com/pages/ forms/business/fnp_authority.pdf<br><br>Attached a Certificate of Existence not more than 60 days old, or registry number for Oregon to check status online. |

| | | |
|---|---|---|
| | | Filing fee is $50.00 (domestic or foreign) payable to Corporate Division.<br><br>Send documents to:<br><br>Secretary of State - Corporate Division<br>255 Capitol St. NE, Suite 151<br>Salem, OR 97310-1327<br><br>For questions, call (503) 986-2200. |
| **PA** | Articles of Incorporation<br><br>(Domestic)<br><br>*-OR-*<br><br>Application for Certificate of Authority<br><br>(Foreign)<br><br>*-AND-*<br><br>Docketing Statement | Articles of Incorporation - Nonprofit (Form DSCB:15-5306/7102B-2) is available at http://www.portal.state.pa.us/portal/server.pt/community/corporation_bureau/12457/pennsylvania_nonprofit_corporations/571889 It does not contain the IRS 501(c) (3) required language, but you can add it as a separate sheet or provide your own document.<br><br>Application for Certificate of Authority (Form DSCB:15-4124/6124-2) is available at http://www.portal.state.pa.us/portal/server.pt/community/corporations/12457/foreign_business_corporations/571872<br><br>Both domestic and foreign filings must also attach a Docketing Statement (Form DSCB:15-134A) available at http://www.portal.state.pa.us/portal/server.pt/community/corporation_bureau/12457/pennsylvania_nonprofit_corporations/571889<br><br>Filing fee is $125.00 (domestic) payable to Commonwealth of Pennsylvania, and $250.00 (foreign) payable to Department of State. |

| | | |
|---|---|---|
| | | NOTE: Publication of either the intent to file or the actual filing of Articles of Incorporation or if a foreign corporation, its intention to apply or its application for a Certificate of Authority must be made in two newspapers of general circulation, one a legal journal, if possible. A list of legal journals in Pennsylvania is available at http://www.portal.state.pa.us/portal/server.pt/community/corporations/12457/x_geographical_listing_of_legal_publications/571893 You must keep a record of publication and file it with your meeting minutes. |
| | | NOTE: No Certificate of Incorporation or Certificate of Authority are issued for nonprofits in Pennsylvania. The Secretary of the Commonwealth (about the same as the Secretary of State in other states) signs and dates the Articles of Incorporation or Certificate of Authority and that indicates filing is complete. |
| | | Send documents to: |
| | | Department of State<br>Bureau of Corporations and Charitable Organizations<br>PO Box 8722<br>Harrisburg, PA 17105-8722 |
| | | For questions, call (717) 787-1057. |
| **RI** | Articles of Incorporation<br><br>(Domestic)<br><br>*-OR-* | Nonprofit Corporation Articles of Incorporation (Form 200) is available at http://sos.ri.gov/documents/business/forms/200.pdf but does not contain IRS 501(c) (3) required language. There are |

| | | |
|---|---|---|
| | Certificate of Authority (Foreign) | some lines available to type in statements, but they are not sufficient to put all the required IRS language in. You may want to submit your own document.<br><br>Application for Certificate of Authority by a Foreign Non-Profit Corporation (Form 250) is available at http://sos.ri.gov/documents/business/forms/250.pdf Attach certified copies of Articles of Incorporation and any amendments. These copies must be less than 60 days old.<br><br>Filing fee is $35.00 (domestic) and $50.00 (foreign) payable to Rhode Island Secretary of State.<br><br>Send documents to:<br><br>Office of the Secretary of State<br>Division of Business Services<br>148 W. River Street<br>Providence, RI 02904-2615<br><br>For questions, call (401) 222-3040. |
| **SC** | Articles of Incorporation (Domestic) *-OR-* Certificate of Authority (Foreign) | Articles of Incorporation, Nonprofit Corporation - Domestic (Form NP – Domestic - Articles of Incorporation) is available at http://www.sos.sc.gov/forms/Non%20 Profits/ArticlesofIncorporationNPDomestic.pdf but does not include all IRS 501(c) (3) required language. It does have a dissolution clause that IRS will accept, but there is no room for the purpose clause. However, there is an attachment available with all IRS required language at |

| | | |
|---|---|---|
| | | http://www.sos.sc.gov/forms/Non%20 Profits/501c3%20Attachment.pdf You can also submit your own document. Submit original plus one copy.<br><br>Application by a Foreign Nonprofit Corporation for a Certificate of Authority to Transact Business in the State of South Carolina (no form number) is available at http://www.sos.sc.gov/forms/Non%20 Profits/Foreign/Application%20for%20 a%20Certificate%20of%20Authority.pdf Attach a certified copy of the Certificate of Good Standing/Existence.<br><br>Filing fee is $25.00 (domestic), or $10.00 (foreign), payable to SC Secretary of State.<br><br>Send documents and a self-addressed stamped legal size return envelope to:<br><br>South Carolina Secretary of State's Office<br>Attn: Corporate Filings<br>1205 Pendleton Street, Suite 525<br>Columbia, SC 29201<br><br>For questions, call (803) 734-2158. |
| **SD** | Articles of Incorporation<br><br>(Domestic)<br><br>-*OR*-<br><br>Certificate of Authority<br><br>(Foreign) | Articles of Incorporation Domestic Nonprofit Corporation (Form NonprofitArticlesofincorporation) is available at http://sdsos.gov/content/html/corporations/corporationpdfs/nonprofitarticlesofincorporation20110101.pdf but does not contain IRS 501(c) (3) required language. However, there is sufficient room provided to type in the required statements. You may also submit your own document. |

| | | |
|---|---|---|
| | | Nonstock Application for Certificate of Authority Foreign Nonprofit Corporation (Form Nonstockcertificateofauthority) is available at http://sdsos.gov/content/html/corporations/corporationpdfs/nonprofit-nonstockcertificateofauthority20110101.pdf Attach a Certificate of Good Standing/Existence not more than 90 days old.<br><br>Filing fee is $30.00 (domestic), and $125.00 (foreign), payable to Secretary of State. Expedite fee is $50.00 but a waste of money because most applications are processed in just a few days anyway.<br><br>Send original and one photocopy of documents to:<br><br>South Dakota Secretary of State<br>500 East Capitol Suite 204<br>Pierre, SD 57501<br><br>For questions, call (605) 773-4845. |
| **TN** | Nonprofit Charter<br><br>(Domestic)<br><br>*-OR-*<br><br>Certificate of Authority<br><br>(Foreign) | Charter Nonprofit Corporation (Form SS-4418) is available at http://www.tn.gov/sos/forms/ss-4418.pdf but does not include the IRS 501(c) (3) required language, so you might want to submit your own document. The information contained in a Tennessee is essentially the same as Articles of Incorporation in other states. They just call it a charter.<br><br>Application for Certificate of Authority Nonprofit Corporation (Form SS-4432) is |

| | | |
|---|---|---|
| | | available at http://www.tn.gov/sos/forms/ ss-4432.pdf Attach a Certificate of Good Standing/Existence not more than 60 days old.<br><br>Filing fee is $100.00 (domestic), free for domestic school organizations, and $600.00 (foreign) payable to Tennessee Secretary of State.<br><br>Send documents to:<br><br>Secretary of State's Office<br>ATTN: Corporate Filings<br>312 Rosa L. Parks Ave.<br>6th Fl. - Snodgrass Towers<br>Nashville, TN 37243-1102<br><br>Forms can be faxed to 615-532-9870.<br><br>For questions, call (615) 741-2286. |
| **TX** | Certificate of Formation<br><br>(domestic)<br><br>*-OR-*<br><br>Application for Registration<br><br>(Foreign) | Certificate of Formation for a Nonprofit Corporation (Form 202) is available at http://www.sos.state.tx.us/corp/forms_boc.shtml but does not include IRS 501(c)(3) required language. You can add it in the blanks provided or submit your own document.<br><br>Nonprofit Corporation Application for Registration (Form 302) is available at http://www.sos.state.tx.us/corp/forms_boc.shtml<br><br>Filing fee is $25.00 (domestic or foreign) payable to Secretary of State. Expedite fee is $25.00. |

| | | |
|---|---|---|
| | | Send original and copy of documents to: <br><br> Secretary of State <br> PO Box 13697 <br> Austin, TX 78711-3697 <br><br> Forms can be faxed to (512) 463-5709 along with Form 807, available at https://webservices.sos.state.tx.us/forms/payment.pdf <br><br> Forms can be delivered to: <br><br> James Earl Rudder Office Building <br> 1019 Brazos <br> Austin, TX 78701 <br><br> For questions, call (512) 463-5555. |
| UT | Articles of Incorporation <br><br> (domestic) <br><br> **-OR-** <br><br> Certificate of Authority <br><br> (Foreign) | Articles of Incorporation form is available by clicking on the link on the right of the page at http://corporations.utah.gov/business/dnp.html but does not contain IRS 501(c) (3) required language. You may want to submit your own document. file two original copies. <br><br> Application for Certificate of Authority to Conduct Affairs for a Foreign Corporation is available by clicking the link on the right of the page at http://corporations.utah.gov/business/fnp.html <br><br> Filing fee is $30.00 (domestic or foreign) payable to State of Utah. <br><br> Send documents to: <br><br> State of Utah |

| | | |
|---|---|---|
| | | Division of Corporations & Commercial Code<br>Box 146705<br>Salt Lake City, UT 84114-6705<br><br>Walk in applications accepted at:<br><br>160 East 300 South, Main Floor<br>Salt Lake City, UT<br><br>For questions, call (801) 530-6438. Fax: (801) 530-6438 |
| **VT** | Articles of Incorporation<br><br>(Domestic)<br><br>*-OR-*<br><br>Certificate of Authority<br><br>(Foreign) | Articles of Incorporation Form Nonprofits and cooperatives is available at http://www.sec.state.vt.us/corps/forms/nparts.htm but do not contain all the IRS 501(c) (3) required language. You may want to submit your own document.<br><br>Application for Certificate of Authority is available at http://www.sec.state.vt.us/corps/forms/fcauth.htm Attach Certificate of Good Standing/Existence no more than 30 days old.<br><br>Filing fee is $75.00 (domestic) and $100.00 (foreign).<br><br>Send original and one copy of documents, along with self addressed stamped return envelope to:<br><br>Secretary of State<br><br>128 State Street<br>Drawer 09<br>Montpelier, VT 05633-1101.<br><br>For questions, call (802) 828-2386. |

| VA | Articles of Incorporation (Domestic) *-OR-* Certificate of Authority (Foreign) | Articles of Incorporation of a Virginia Nonstock Corporation (Form scc819) is useless for a nonprofit that seeks IRS 501(c) (3) status. None of the required language is on the form, and no attachments are allowed. Therefore, you must submit your own form. |
|---|---|---|

Application for a Certificate of Authority to Transact Business in Virginia is available at http://www.scc.virginia.gov/publicforms/249/scc759.pdf Attach certified copy of Articles of Incorporation and amendments. There must be a statement on the certified copy that it is "true and correct" or something similar from the home state jurisdiction, and it must dated within the last 12 months. Virginia does not accept Certificate of Good Standing/Existence.

Filing fees are $75.00 for domestic or foreign. (Charter fee $50.00 and filing fee $25.00) payable to State Corporation Commission.

Expedited service is $200.00 same day, $100.00 next day. These documents are Schedule A documents. To expedite, use Form SCC21.2 available at http://www.scc.virginia.gov/publicforms/488/scc212.pdf

Send documents to:

Clerk of the State Corporation Commission
PO Box 1197
Richmond, Virginia 23218-1197

| | | |
|---|---|---|
| | | Walk in filing at:<br><br>1300 E. Main Street<br>Tyler Building, 1st Floor<br>Richmond, VA 23219<br><br>For questions, call (804) 371-9733 or toll free (866) 722-2551. |
| **WA** | Articles of Incorporation<br><br>(Domestic)<br><br>*-OR-*<br><br>Certificate of Authority<br><br>(Foreign) | Articles of Incorporation (Form NonProfit Corporation - Incorporation) is available at<br><br>http://www.sos.wa.gov/_assets/corps/NonProfitArticles2010.pdf but does not contain IRS 501(c) (3) required language. It can be added as attachments or you can file your own document. DO NOT refer to or attach bylaws in the Articles of Incorporation.<br><br>Foreign Nonprofit Corporation Certificate of Authority (Form Foreign NonProfit Corporation - Certificate) is available at http://www.sos.wa.gov/_assets/corps/ForeignNonProfitCertificate2010.pdf<br><br>Attach Certificate of Good Standing/Existence less than 60 days old. DO NOT attach or refer to bylaws.<br><br>Filing fee is $30.00 (domestic or foreign). Expedite fee is $50.00. Write EXPEDITE on the outside of the envelope.<br><br>Send documents to:<br><br>Secretary of State<br>Corporations Division |

| | | |
|---|---|---|
| | | 801 Capitol Way S<br>PO Box 40234<br>Olympia WA 98504-0234<br><br>For questions, call (360) 725-0377. |
| **WV** | Articles of Incorporation<br><br>(Domestic)<br><br>*-OR-*<br><br>Certificate of Authority<br><br>(Foreign) | Articles of Incorporation (Form CD-1) is available at http://www.sos.wv.gov/business-licensing/forms/Documents/Corporation/cd-1.pdf but does not contain IRS 501(c) (3) required language. You may want to submit your own document.<br><br>Certificate of Authority (Form CF-1) is available at http://www.sos.wv.gov/business-licensing/forms/Documents/Corporation/cf-1.pdf Attach a Certificate of Good Standing/Existence dated during the current tax year.<br><br>Filing fee is $25.00 (domestic), $50.00 (foreign), plus $15.00 for certified copy, payable to West Virginia Secretary of State.<br><br>Send two original documents (if you want one returned) to:<br><br>Secretary of State<br>Corporations Division<br>1900 Kanawha Blvd E<br>Bldg. 1, Suite 157-K<br>Charleston, WV 25305<br><br>For questions, call (304) 558-8000. |
| **WI** | Articles of Incorporation<br><br>(Domestic) | Articles of Incorporation - Nonstock Corporation (Form DFI/CORP/102) is available at http://www.wi-aresraces.org/501c3/form102_f.pdf but does not |

| | |
|---|---|
| *-OR-*<br><br>Certificate of Authority<br><br>(Foreign) | contain IRS 501(c) (3) required language. You might want to file your own document. No certificate of incorporation is issued. "FILED" endorsement is stamped on the document by the Department of Financial Institutions, and that is the proof of acceptance.<br><br>Foreign Nonstock Corporation - Certificate of Authority Application (Form DFI/ CORP/121) is available at http://www. wdfi.org/_resources/indexed/site/corporations/Form121R11-2012.pdf<br><br>Attach Certificate of Status/Good Standing/Existence not more than 60 days old.<br><br>Filing fee is $35.00 (domestic) and $45.00 (foreign), payable to Department of Financial Institutions. Expedited service available for additional $25.00. Clearly mark documents "FOR EXPEDITED SERVICE."<br><br>Send original and one exact copy of documents to:<br><br>Department of Financial Institutions<br>P O Box 7846<br>Madison, WI, 53707-7846<br><br>For Express Mail:<br><br>Department of Financial Institutions<br>Division of Corporate & Consumer Services<br>201 W. Washington Ave – Suite 300<br>Madison WI 53703 |

| | | |
|---|---|---|
| | | For questions, call Division of Corporate & Consumer Services at (608) 261-7577. |
| **WY** | Articles of In- corporation (Domestic) *-OR-* Certificate of Authority | Nonprofit Articles of Incorporation (Form NP-ArticlesIncorporation) is available at http://soswy.state.wy.us/Forms/Business/ NP/NP-ArticlesIncorporation.pdf but does not contain IRS 501(c) (3) required language. You might want to submit your own document. Attach a Registered Agent Consent (Form RAConsent) located on the last page of the Articles of Incorpora- tion link. Foreign Nonprofit Corporation Applica- tion for Certificate of Authority (Form FNP-CertificateAuthority) is available at http://soswy.state.wy.us/Forms/Business/ FNP/FNP-CertificateAuthority.pdf Attach certified copy of Certificate of Good Standing/Existence not more than 60 days old. For domestic and foreign, Attach a Regis- tered Agent Consent (Form RAConsent) located on the last page of the links above. Filing fee is $25.00 (domestic and foreign), payable to Wyoming Secretary of State. Processing is 3 - 5 days and no expedited service is available. Send one original and one exact photocopy of documents to: |

|  |  | Wyoming Secretary of State<br>State Capitol Bldg., Room 110<br>200 West 24th St<br>Cheyenne, WY 82002<br><br>For questions, call (307) 777-7311. |
|--|--|--|

# CHAPTER 9

## WHAT TO INCLUDE IN ORGANIZATIONAL BYLAWS

*"Show me a good and gracious loser and I'll show you a failure."*

—Knute Rockne

Red Rock Sports offers adult sports leagues and outdoor activities in Golden/Lakewood, CO and leverages the participants in these leagues as our platform to provide charitable activities for orphans, at-risk youth, physically and mentally disabled, and homeless individuals in the Denver community.

### STANDARD FOOTBALL POSITIONS

In the game of football each team has eleven players on the field and every player has a specific *position*. Each team has three "platoons" of players, the offense (the team with the ball, who is trying to score), the defense (the team trying to prevent the other team from scoring, and to take the ball from them), and the special teams (who play in kicking situations). Within those platoons, various specific positions exist depending on what the player's main job is.

When looking at your nonprofit organization, it is as if you are creating your own winning team to go out and do good things in the world. Because you are the incorporator, you may feel that you are playing every position on the field. But very soon, as your organization begins to grow, you will have a strong team of players.

Each player must know the rules and what is expected so that they can follow them. Your nonprofit corporation bylaws establish the "rules of the game" in which business is conducted.

## CREATING THE CONSTITUTION

Another way to understand the significance of bylaws is to think of them as the organization's constitution. You cannot put everything in the Constitution, only the really important stuff. A good rule of thumb is to put as little in the bylaws as possible. Once it is written and approved, it's the way things are done. If you ever want to change something, you have to amend the bylaws, just as you would have to amend the Constitution. Keep trivial aspects that are subject to change (such as the day of the week board meetings are held) out of the bylaws. Be sure to attach any changes to the bylaws directly to the master copy as soon as changes are made.

It is not uncommon to make a change, put it in the meeting minutes, but then forget which meeting the change was made, and it is never attached to the master copy of the bylaws. The solution is to assign the responsibility to update the bylaws to one of the board positions. If you keep it simple, there will not be many changes to keep up with.

## BYLAW CONTENTS

So exactly what do you put in the bylaws? It depends on which state you live in, but there are some general items addressed in virtually all nonprofit bylaws:

1. Name of the organization and the mission.
2. How many board members (minimum established by the state) and what constitutes a quorum? (Normally a majority of members be present.)
3. Qualifications of board members.
4. How officers and board members will be elected or appointed and how long they will serve. If you want them to be able to serve more than one term, you need to say so in the bylaws. Also address limitations on personal liability. What are the procedures for removing a board member if necessary?
5. Duties of Board Members
6. Procedures for calling and conducting meetings, including special and emergency board meetings; and when regular meetings will be held (suggest monthly, bi-monthly, or quarterly, nothing more specific so that you have flexibility to make changes).

   In this era of electronics, will you allow board meetings by email, teleconferencing, electronic conferencing software such as Skype, etc.? Each state has its own laws about what is acceptable, and not all states have caught up to technology. To find out if you can conduct meetings by other methods than meeting in a room face to face, contact your state Attorney General to find out the rules for your state.
7. How will conflicts of interest be handled? I suggest you reference a Conflict of Interest Policy so that if you ever change procedures, you can more easily update a conflict of interest policy than make formal changes to bylaws.
8. How funds will be accounted for and disbursed.

9. If the nonprofit has members, what are the rights of membership? (Most nonprofits do not have members).
10. How committees can be convened and dissolved.
11. How can bylaws be changed (for example, by majority vote of the board)?
12. Choose an accounting or fiscal year. This should fit with the normal flow of your organizations activities. Education related activities might need a different fiscal year than an animal shelter.
13. Authorize bank signatories.

If you do not want to write bylaws from scratch, you can purchase fill-in-the-blank templates at www.doyourownnonprofit.com for a small fee. I hired an attorney on your behalf to draw them up so that they are legal in your state and with IRS. All you have to do is fill in the blanks with your organization's information, make changes if you want to, and print. I do not present these for my profit (I will take nothing from the sales), but for your convenience to save time and headache. The easier I can make it for you, the better I have done my job with this book.

The following pages contain an example of actual bylaws from Pasture Valley Children Missions. You can use it for a guide and feel free to borrow any wording you want to use.

# BYLAWS
## OF
## PASTURE VALLEY CHILDREN MISSIONS

A Missouri Nonprofit Corporation

## ARTICLE I: OFFICES

The corporation may have offices at such places as the Board of Directors may from time to time determine or the business of the corporation may require.

## ARTICLE II: DIRECTORS

1.    The affairs of the corporation shall be managed by the Board of Directors. The number of Directors to constitute the Board of Directors shall be determined by the Board of Directors, provided, however, that there shall always be at least three Directors. Directors shall be elected at the annual meeting of the Directors to serve for a term of three years or until his or her successor shall have been elected and qualified. Nothing herein shall prohibit a director from serving consecutive terms. Directors may be removed, with or without cause, by the vote of at least two-thirds of all the Directors at a meeting of the Directors called expressly for that purpose. Any vacancy created by such removal shall be filled for the unexpired term in respect of such vacancy by majority vote of the Directors present at such special meeting or, in the absence of such action at such special meeting, by resolution of the Board of Directors.

2.    The Directors may keep the books of the corporation at the principal business office of the corporation in this state or at such other place as they may from time to time determine and as may be permitted by law.

3.    If the office of a Director becomes vacant for any reason, other than by removal of the Director in the manner described in paragraph 1 hereof, the remaining Directors shall choose a successor or successors which successor(s) shall hold office for the unexpired term in respect of which such vacancy occurred or until the next election of Directors.

Adopted on _____

## ARTICLE III: COMPENSATION OF DIRECTORS

Directors, as such, shall not receive any stated salary for their services, but by resolution of the Board, expenses of attendance, if any, may be allowed for attendance at each regular or special meeting of the Board; provided that nothing herein contained shall be construed to preclude any Director from serving the corporation in any other capacity and receiving compensation or reimbursement of expenses therefor.

## ARTICLE IV: MEETINGS OF THE BOARD

1.     The annual meeting of the Board shall be held at such time and place as shall be determined by the Board.  Regular meetings of the Board may be held without notice at such time and place as shall from time to time be determined by the Board.

2.     Special meetings of the Board may be called by the President, the Secretary, or 25 percent of the Directors on not less than two days' notice to each Director, either personally or by first class mail, telegram, telephone or facsimile.

3.     A Director's attendance at or participation in a meeting waives any required notice of the meeting unless the Director upon arriving at the meeting or prior to the vote on a matter not noticed in conformity with the law, the Articles or Bylaws, objects to lack of notice and does not vote for or assent to the objected to action.  Neither the business to be transacted at, nor the purpose of, any regular or special meeting of the Board of Directors need be specified in any notice or waiver of notice of such meeting.

4.     At all meetings of the Board, a majority of all the Directors in office shall be necessary and sufficient to constitute a quorum for the transaction of business, and the act of a majority of the Directors present at any meeting at which there is a quorum shall be the act of the Board of Directors, unless the action is one upon which, by express provision of the statutes, the Articles of Incorporation, or these Bylaws, a different vote is required, in which case such express

2

provision shall govern and control. If a quorum shall not be present at any meeting of Directors, the Directors present thereat may adjourn the meeting, from time to time, without notice other than announcement at the meeting, until a quorum shall be present.

5.      Members of the Board of Directors may participate in a meeting of the Board by means of a conference telephone or similar communications equipment whereby all persons participating in the meeting can hear each other, and participation in a meeting in this manner shall constitute presence in person at the meeting.

6.      Action required or permitted by law to be taken at a Board of Directors' meeting may be taken without a meeting if the action is taken by all members of the Board. The action shall be evidenced by one or more written consents describing the action taken, signed by each Director, and included in the minutes filed with the corporate records reflecting the action taken. Such action shall be effective when the last Director signs the consent, unless the consent specifies a different effective date.

## ARTICLE V: COMMITTEES

1.      The Board of Directors, by a resolution adopted by a majority of the Directors in office, may designate an Executive Committee, which shall consist of at least two Directors of the corporation. The Executive Committee shall have and exercise the authority of the Board of Directors between meetings of the Board of Directors.

2.      The Board of Directors, by a resolution adopted by a majority of the Directors in office, may designate one or more other Board committees, each of which shall consist of at least two Directors. Such committees shall, to the extent provided in such resolution, have and exercise the authority of the Board of Directors.

3.      At all meetings of committees, a majority of the members of the committee shall be necessary and sufficient to constitute a quorum for the transaction of business, and the act

3

of a majority of the members of the committee present at any meeting at which there is a quorum shall be the act of the committee, unless the action is one upon which, by express provision of the statutes, the articles of incorporation, these bylaws, or a resolution of the Board of Directors, a different vote is required, in which case such express provision shall govern and control. Provisions in these bylaws pertaining to meetings of the Board shall also apply to a committee or committees of the Board.

## ARTICLE VI: NOTICES

1.     Whenever, under the provisions of the statutes, the Articles of Incorporation, or these Bylaws, notice is required to be given to any Director, such notice may be given orally or in writing. Notice may be communicated in person; by any form of wire or wireless communication such as telephone or telegraph; by mail or private carrier; by electronic mail; or if the preceding forms of personal notice are impracticable, by a newspaper of general circulation in the area where published; or other form of public broadcast communication such as radio, or television.

2.     Whenever any notice is required to be given, a waiver thereof in writing signed by the person or persons entitled to said notice, whether before or after the time stated therein, and filed with the minutes or corporate records, shall be deemed equivalent thereto.

## ARTICLE VII: OFFICERS

1.     The officers of the corporation shall consist of a President, a Secretary, Treasurer, and such other officers as may be elected by the Board of Directors. The Board of Directors may also elect a Chairman of the Board, one or more Executive Vice Presidents, one or more Vice Presidents who may be identified as "Senior" or "First" or by other appropriate title, one or more Assistant Secretaries and Assistant Treasurers, and such other officers and agents as it shall deem necessary, who shall exercise such powers and perform such duties as shall be determined

4

from time to time by the Board of Directors. The compensation of all officers, if any, shall be fixed by the Board of Directors.

2. The officers of the corporation shall hold their offices for a term of one year, or for such other term not exceeding three years as shall be determined from time to time by the Board of Directors. Officers may be reelected to successive terms. Any officers may be removed at any time by the Board of Directors. An officer may resign at any time by delivering notice to the corporation. A resignation is effective when the notice is delivered unless the notice specifies a future effective date. If the office of any officers becomes vacant for any reason, the vacancy may be filled by the Board of Directors.

## ARTICLE VIII: PRESIDENT

1. The President shall be the chief executive officer of the corporation and shall preside at all meetings of the Directors at which he or she is present. He or she shall perform such duties as the Board of Directors may prescribe and shall see that all orders and resolutions of the Board are carried into effect.

2. The President shall execute bonds, mortgages and other contracts except where permitted by law to be otherwise signed and executed, and except where the signing and execution thereof shall be expressly delegated by the Board of Directors to some other officer or agent of the corporation.

## ARTICLE IX: CHAIRMAN OF THE BOARD

The Chairman of the Board, if any, shall preside at all meetings of the Directors at which he or she is present, and shall perform such other duties as the Board of Directors or these Bylaws may prescribe.

## ARTICLE X: EXECUTIVE AND SENIOR VICE PRESIDENTS

The Executive and Senior Vice Presidents, if any, in the order of their seniority shall, in the absence or disability of the President, perform the duties and exercise the powers of the President, and shall perform such other duties as the Board of Directors may prescribe.

## ARTICLE XI: OTHER VICE PRESIDENTS

Other Vice Presidents, if any, in the order of their seniority shall, in the absence or disability of the President and any Executive Vice Presidents, perform the duties and exercise the powers of the President, and shall perform such other duties as the Board of Directors may prescribe.

## ARTICLE XII: SECRETARY AND ASSISTANT SECRETARIES

1.      The Secretary shall keep or cause to be kept a record of all meetings of the Board of Directors and shall record all votes and the minutes of all proceedings in a book to be kept for that purpose. He or she shall give, or cause to be given, notice of all special meetings of the Board of Directors, and shall perform such other duties as may be prescribed by the Board of Directors or President, under whose supervision he or she shall be. He or she shall be responsible for authenticating the records of the corporation.

2.      The Assistant Secretaries, if any, in order of their seniority shall, in the absence or disability of the Secretary, perform the duties and exercise the powers of the secretary and shall perform such other duties as the Board of Directors may prescribe.

## ARTICLE XIII: TREASURER AND ASSISTANT TREASURERS

1.      The Treasurer shall have the custody of the corporate funds and securities, shall keep full and accurate accounts of receipts and disbursements in books belonging to the corporation, shall deposit all moneys and other valuable effects in the name and to the credit of the

Adopted on _____

corporation in such depositories as may be designated by the Board of Directors and shall perform such other duties as the Board of Directors may prescribe.

  2.  The Treasurer shall disburse the funds of the corporation as may be ordered by the Board, taking proper vouchers for such disbursements, and shall render to the President and Directors, at the regular meetings of the Board, or whenever they may require it, an account of all his or her transactions as Treasurer and of the financial condition of the corporation.

  3.  If required by the Board of Directors, the Treasurer shall give the corporation a bond in such sum and with such surety or sureties as shall be satisfactory to the Board for the faithful performance of the duties of his or her office and for the restoration to the corporation, in case of his or her death, resignation, retirement or removal from office, of all books, papers, vouchers, money and other property of whatever kind in his or her possession or under his or her control belonging to the corporation.

  4.  The Assistant Treasurers, if any, in the order of their seniority shall, in the absence or disability of the Treasurer, perform the duties and exercise the powers of the Treasurer and shall perform such other duties as the Board of Directors may prescribe.

## ARTICLE XIV: EXECUTIVE DIRECTOR

An Executive Director may be designated by the Board of Directors. He or she shall not be an officer of the corporation, and he or she shall exercise such authority and perform such duties as the Board of Directors may from time to time assign to him or her.

## ARTICLE XV: CHECKS

All checks or demands for money and notes of the corporation shall be signed by such officer or officers or such other person or persons as the Board of Directors may from time to time designate.

## ARTICLE XVI: FISCAL YEAR

The fiscal year of the corporation shall begin the first day of January in each year.

## ARTICLE XVII: SEAL

The corporation shall not have a seal.

## ARTICLE XVIII: ALTERATION, AMENDMENT OR REPEAL OF BYLAWS

These bylaws may be altered, amended or repealed at any regular or special meeting of the Directors by the affirmative vote of a majority of all the Directors in office.

## ARTICLE XIX: RECORDS

1.      The corporation shall keep as permanent records minutes of all meetings of its Board of Directors, a record of all actions taken by the Directors without a meeting, and a record of all actions taken by committees of the Board of Directors.

2.      The corporation shall maintain appropriate accounting records. A copy of the following records shall be kept at the corporation's principal office: the Articles of Incorporation and all amendments to them currently in effect, these Bylaws and all amendments to them currently in effect, a list of the names and business or home addresses of the current Directors and officers, the most recent annual report delivered to the Secretary of State, and appropriate financial statements of all income and expenses.

Adopted on _____

# CHAPTER 10

## DEVELOP A CONFLICT OF INTEREST POLICY

*"Don't give up at half time. Concentrate on winning the second half."*

—Paul Bear Bryant

Up2Us is a national coalition of Sports-Based Youth Development (SBYD) organizations. Since 2008, Up2Us has been leading the movement to use sports to address critical issues facing youth–issues like childhood obesity, poor health and nutrition, academic failure and antisocial behavior. (NY)

### BIG MONEY AND MEDIA EQUALS CONFLICT OF INTEREST IN FOOTBALL

As with any big sporting events, a great deal of money is at stake in the game of football. This is true not only in the NFL, but on the college level as well.

It's not uncommon to see names in the headlines of commissioners, media biggies, and even coaches embroiled in conflict of interest scandals. These are people who want to "have their cake and eat it too," by making decisions that line their pockets as opposed to what's best for the team and the game of football. Sad to say, integrity and honesty are not always at the top of the list of character traits for those in high-level positions.

The same will be true for your organization. You will want to be extremely careful in this area. This chapter will help you in taking those conflict-of-interest precautions.

## SET PERSONAL INTERESTS ASIDE

IRS is concerned about conflicts of interest within 501(c) (3) corporations. A conflict of interest occurs when someone in a responsible position within a nonprofit has competing interests and is faced with making choices that could benefit themselves (or friends and family members) to the detriment of the organization. Board members and directors of a nonprofit have a first duty to promote the best interest of the organization. They must lay their personal interests aside when conducting the business of the nonprofit. Should a conflict of interest arise, it should be disclosed immediately.

On the next page you will find a sample conflict of interest policy from IRS containing the minimum requirements. This one is for a health care organization but can be tailored to your needs. In addition, IRS wants board members and directors to fill out an annual Conflict of Interest disclosure statement which should be kept on file with the corporation's other important documents. A fill-in-the-blank template and the Annual Conflict of Interest Statement are free with select organizational document packages available at www.doyourownnonprofit.com

# IRS SAMPLE CONFLICT OF INTEREST POLICY

## ARTICLE I

### PURPOSE

The purpose of the conflict of interest policy is to protect this tax-exempt organization's (Organization) interest when it is contemplating entering into a transaction or arrangement that might benefit the private interest of an officer or director of the Organization or might result in a possible excess benefit transaction. This policy is intended to supplement but not replace any applicable state and federal laws governing conflict of interest applicable to nonprofit and charitable organizations.

## ARTICLE II

### DEFINITIONS

#### 1. INTERESTED PERSON

Any director, principal officer, or member of a committee with governing board delegated powers, who has a direct or indirect financial interest, as defined below, is an interested person.

If a person is an interested person with respect to any entity in the health care system of which the organization is a part, he or she is an interested person with respect to all entities in the health care system.

## 2. FINANCIAL INTEREST

A person has a financial interest if the person has, directly or indirectly, through business, investment, or family:

a.  An ownership or investment interest in any entity with which the Organization has a transaction or arrangement,
b.  A compensation arrangement with the Organization or with any entity or individual with which the Organization has a transaction or arrangement, or
c.  A potential ownership or investment interest in, or compensation arrangement with, any entity or individual with which the Organization is negotiating a transaction or arrangement.

Compensation includes direct and indirect remuneration as well as gifts or favors that are not insubstantial. A financial interest is not necessarily a conflict of interest. Under Article III, Section 2, a person who has a financial interest may have a conflict of interest only if the appropriate governing board or committee decides that a conflict of interest exists.

# ARTICLE III

## PROCEDURES

### 1. DUTY TO DISCLOSE

In connection with any actual or possible conflict of interest, an interested person must disclose the existence of the financial interest and be given the opportunity to disclose all material facts to the directors and members of committees with governing board delegated powers considering the proposed transaction or arrangement.

## 2. DETERMINING WHETHER A CONFLICT OF INTEREST EXISTS

After disclosure of the financial interest and all material facts, and after any discussion with the interested person, he/she shall leave the governing board or committee meeting while the determination of a conflict of interest is discussed and voted upon. The remaining board or committee members shall decide if a conflict of interest exists.

## 3. PROCEDURES FOR ADDRESSING THE CONFLICT OF INTEREST

a. An interested person may make a presentation at the governing board or committee meeting, but after the presentation, he/she shall leave the meeting during the discussion of, and the vote on, the transaction or arrangement involving the possible conflict of interest.

b. The chairperson of the governing board or committee shall, if appropriate, appoint a disinterested person or committee to investigate alternatives to the proposed transaction or arrangement.

c. After exercising due diligence, the governing board or committee shall determine whether the Organization can obtain with reasonable efforts a more advantageous transaction or arrangement from a person or entity that would not give rise to a conflict of interest.

d. If a more advantageous transaction or arrangement is not reasonably possible under circumstances not producing a conflict of interest, the governing board or committee shall determine by a majority vote of the disinterested directors whether the transaction or arrangement is in the Organization's best interest, for its own benefit, and whether it is fair and reasonable. In conformity with the above determination it shall make its decision as to whether to enter into the transaction or arrangement.

## 4. VIOLATIONS OF THE CONFLICTS OF INTEREST POLICY

a. If the governing board or committee has reasonable cause to believe a member has failed to disclose actual or possible conflicts of interest, it shall inform the member of the basis for such belief and afford the member an opportunity to explain the alleged failure to disclose.

b. If, after hearing the member's response and after making further investigation as warranted by the circumstances, the governing board or committee determines the member has failed to disclose an actual or possible conflict of interest, it shall take appropriate disciplinary and corrective action.

# ARTICLE IV

## RECORDS OF PROCEEDINGS

The minutes of the governing board and all committees with board delegated powers shall contain:

a. The names of the persons who disclosed or otherwise were found to have a financial interest in connection with an actual or possible conflict of interest, the nature of the financial interest, any action taken to determine whether a conflict of interest was present, and the governing board's or committee's decision as to whether a conflict of interest in fact existed.

b. The names of the persons who were present for discussions and votes relating to the transaction or arrangement, the content of the discussion, including any alternatives to the proposed transaction or arrangement, and a record of any votes taken in connection with the proceedings.

# ARTICLE V

## COMPENSATION

a. A voting member of the governing board who receives compensation, directly or indirectly, from the Organization for services is precluded from voting on matters pertaining to that member's compensation.

b. A voting member of any committee whose jurisdiction includes compensation matters and who receives compensation, directly or indirectly, from the Organization for services is precluded from voting on matters pertaining to that member's compensation.

c. No voting member of the governing board or any committee whose jurisdiction includes compensation matters and who receives compensation, directly or indirectly, from the Organization, either individually or collectively, is prohibited from providing information to any committee regarding compensation.

# ARTICLE VI

## ANNUAL STATEMENTS

Each director, principal officer and member of a committee with governing board delegated powers shall annually sign a statement which affirms such person:

a. Has received a copy of the conflicts of interest policy,

b. Has read and understands the policy,

c. Has agreed to comply with the policy, and

d. Understands the Organization is charitable and in order to maintain its federal tax exemption it must engage primarily in activities which accomplish one or more of its tax-exempt purposes.

# ARTICLE VII

## PERIODIC REVIEWS

To ensure the Organization operates in a manner consistent with charitable purposes and does not engage in activities that could jeopardize its tax-exempt status, periodic reviews shall be conducted. The periodic reviews shall, at a minimum, include the following subjects:

a.  Whether compensation arrangements and benefits are reasonable, based on competent survey information and the result of arm's length bargaining.
b.  Whether partnerships, joint ventures, and arrangements with management organizations conform to the Organization's written policies, are properly recorded, reflect reasonable investment or payments for goods and services, further charitable purposes and do not result in inurnment, impermissible private benefit or in an excess benefit transaction.

# ARTICLE VIII

## USE OF OUTSIDE EXPERTS

When conducting the periodic reviews as provided for in Article VII, the Organization may, but need not, use outside advisors. If outside experts are used, their use shall not relieve the governing board of its responsibility for ensuring periodic reviews are conducted.

Now that the conflict of interest matters are take care of, it's time to lay out plans for the first board of directors meeting.

# CHAPTER 11

## HOLD AND DOCUMENT THE FIRST BOARD MEETING

*"You miss 100% of the shots you don't take."*

—Wayne Gretzky

Coach Vince Lombardi is known as a maker of champions. His spirit, enthusiasm and commitment to excellence have touched countless lives – on and off the field. Five National Football League championships are not easily forgotten. But more than a coach, Vince Lombardi was a human being who, on September 3, 1970, lost his most victorious battle when he died of colon cancer. He was fifty-seven. Vince Lombardi's death started a process that has changed the lives of thousands of cancer survivors and the lives of those who still face the fight... In 1971, the first annual Vince Lombardi Memorial Golf Classic was held in Wisconsin with the support of Mrs. Marie Lombardi, members of North Hills Country Club and other civic-minded individuals. The purpose of the Golf Classic was to raise money for cancer research and education in memory of Coach Lombardi.

## COACHES AND MEETINGS

Sitting around in endless meetings is not what most fans think of when thinking of the life of a football coach. However, that is exactly how many of their hours are spent. Meetings with staff members, meetings with team owners, meetings with managers and scouts, meetings with the team players (both in groups and individually), and the list goes on.

College coaches meet regularly with the school's athletic director and administrators going over such things as the financial budgets and player eligibility. Hours are spent lining out every play and analyzing and dissecting each one. Additional hours are spent watching videos to help players break down a single play into the minutest details.

In the same way, your board members will be required to attend a number of meetings throughout the year in order to keep the organization running smoothly. How these meetings are conducted could mean the success or failure of your nonprofit.

## MINUTES ARE LEGAL DOCUMENTS

Did you know that IRS and auditors consider board meeting minutes as legal documents that will hold up in court? Many people believe that if it's not in the meeting minutes, it didn't occur, because the meeting minutes are the formal record of the business conducted and the decisions made by an organization.

There is no set format for meeting minutes and each organization should decide how the meeting minutes should look. When secretaries of the board change, the format often changes as well to suit the new secretary. As long as the required information is recorded, the format is not critical. Copies of meeting minutes from previous meetings should be given to board members for review and approval. All meeting minutes should be filed in a safe accessible place.

## WHAT SHOULD BE INCLUDED

There are some things that should be included in every set of meeting minutes:

1. Name of the organization
2. Date and time of the meeting
3. Who ran the meeting?
4. Who was there and who was absent
5. What was voted on and whether anyone abstained from voting
6. All motions made
7. When the meeting ended
8. Who prepared the meeting minutes.

Personal opinions and heated arguments or discussions should not be included. Minutes should cover the business of the organization, not document disagreements among members. Also do not include in-depth details of reports. It's better to simply attach the reports to the minutes.

## FIRST BOARD MEETING

If you are about to conduct your first board meeting, you want to include the business of setting up the organization and getting it running. Your meeting minutes should include the following:

1. Who is on the initial board of directors?
2. How you will elect or appoint board members in the future
3. Approve application for an FEIN number (if not already done)
4. Approve development of Articles of Incorporation (if not already done)
5. Adopt the organization's bylaws
6. Approve applying for 501(c) (3) status with IRS
7. Approve setting up banking accounts and decide how funds will be handled

8.  Approve the Conflict of Interest policy
9.  Determine fiscal accounting year

At this meeting, most of the preliminary matters have been taken care of. A template of the first board meeting minutes is included free with select organizational document packages available at www.doyourownnonprofit.com

It's now time to learn about the forms needed to attain your 501(c)(3) status.

# PART II

## IRS FORM 1023 APPLICATION FOR TAX EXEMPT STATUS

# CHAPTER 12

## FILING IRS FORM 1023 REQUEST FOR RECOGNITION OF EXEMPTION

*"Success is not forever and failure isn't fatal."*
—Don Shula

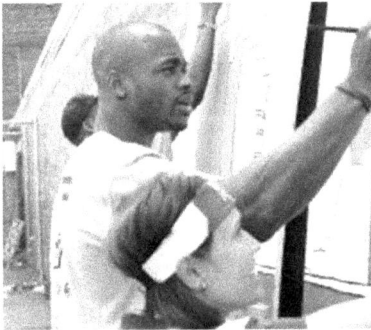

Adrian Peterson established the All Day Foundation in 2008 to raise awareness and funds for programs that inspire hope and build a better future for at-risk children, with a special focus on girls' empowerment. The All Day Foundation partners with non-profits to make an impact in three primary areas: Girls' Empowerment; Children & Families; AD Hometown Programs (TX)

## THE BASIC GAMEBOOK OF PLAYS

Enough of the introductory information – we've now arrived at the actual gamebook for gaining your nonprofit status. It is called the *IRS Form 1023*. In the next chapters, in the role of your head coach, I will be breaking down each play into easy-to-follow steps. Through these guidelines, you will be able to maneuver out there on the playing field and take your team to a great victory.

Let's go!

## WHERE TO BEGIN

If you have completed all the requirements in the previous chapters, you're ready to complete the IRS Form 1023, Request for Recognition of Exemption under Section 501(c) (3) of the Internal Revenue Code. You can get a copy of the form to fill out online and print at http://www.irs.gov/pub/irs-pdf/f1023.pdf. Or you can go to www.irs.gov and search for Form 1023.

The IRS has touted coming out with Form i1023 which can be completed and filed online, but experienced delays for several years. They did come out with a beta version that I was given the opportunity to review, test drive, and give feedback to IRS in September, 2013. The final version they came out with is a zip file that is downloaded to your computer. It cannot be filed online. You can download it at http://www.stayexempt.irs.gov/StartingOut.aspx as well take a mini-course on IRS rules for nonprofit status.

The interactive version is very similar to the link for Form 1023 except that for each question, there is a pop-up explanation of what to put in the box. Although being able to eventually file online **may** be less expensive and speed up processing, the actual form provides only minimal guidance on what goes in each box. It merely copies what is in the instruction book for the Form 1023. The narratives and financials still must be developed from scratch just as the paper version or the fill and print online version.

The interactive Form i1023 starts by asking if you have the preliminary steps completed that must be done before you file for federal tax exempt status. It asks if you have your FEIN, organizing documents, and bylaws. If you do not, it just tells you that they must be complete before you can file. Throughout the application, there are icons to click on for more information. Some of them are helpful and even lead you to the correct publications to read for further guidance. Others simply repeat the instructions for the box. For example, the address box icon gives you instructions to put a post office box number in it if you have a post office box, which is relatively self-explanatory.

## WHAT TO EXPECT

It takes several months to hear back from IRS after filing. If you provide complete information on your application, and any required accompanying schedules, you'll probably hear back from them within 3 months. However eight weeks is more likely.

If your application contains everything IRS needs to know, a determination letter will be issued. If not, you will receive requests for additional clarification or information. Needing more information can significantly delay approval. Once the application is approved, it will be effective as of the original date of the application you sent in.

You can get expedited handling if you request it for a compelling reason. Good compelling reasons might include:

- Pending grants that will not be made without 501(c) (3) status;
- Your organization is created to provide relief to victims of disasters such as recent floods, hurricanes, tsunamis, or tornadoes
- Your application has been delayed because of problems at IRS due to no fault of your organization

IRS estimates that it takes over 100 hours for a novice to complete the 501(c) (3) process. Hopefully this book will cut down those hours by more than half. But get ready to dig in, and describe your organization completely to IRS so that a quick determination can be made without required follow up from IRS. If you put in the work upfront to do it right the first time, you'll not have to deal with ongoing correspondence and paperwork from IRS. Also if you use examples from the narratives in Appendix A, you can cut that time down to one or two day's effort instead of two weeks or more.

## DISCLOSURE

Here's an interesting tip that most people do not know. You are allowed to see a copy of the Form 1023 for most nonprofit organizations that have been approved after July 15, 1987. You can be charged a fair price for making copies. Not all organizations know they are required to disclose their applications. You can ask for a copy of the paperwork and quote the IRS guidance located at http://www.irs.gov/Charities- &-Non-Profits/Public-Disclosure-and-Availability-of-Exempt- Organizations-Returns-and-Applications:-Documents-Subject-to- Public-Disclosure which states (as of April 28, 2013):

> An exempt organization must make available for public inspection its exemption application. An exemption application includes the Form 1023 (for organizations recognized as exempt under Internal Revenue Code section 501(c) (3)), Form 1024 (for organizations recognized as exempt under most other paragraphs of section 501(c)), or the letter submitted under the paragraphs for which no form is prescribed, together with supporting documents and any letter or document issued by the IRS concerning the application. A political organization exempt from taxation under section 527(a) must make available for public inspection and copying its notice of status, Form 8871.
>
> In addition, an exempt organization must make available for public inspection and copying its annual return. Such returns include Form 990, *Return of Organization Exempt from Income Tax*; Form 990-EZ, *Short Form Return of Organization Exempt*

*from Income Tax*; Form 990-PF, *Return of Private Foundation*; Form 990-BL, *Information and Initial Excise Tax Return for Black Lung Benefit Trusts and Certain Related Persons*; and the Form 1065, *U.S. Partnership Return of Income.*

A section 501(c) (3) organization must make available for public inspection and copying any Form 990-T *Exempt Organization Business Income Tax Return*, filed after August 17, 2006. Returns must be available for a three-year period beginning with the due date of the return (including any extension of time for filing). For this purpose, the *return* includes any schedules, attachments, or supporting documents that relate to the imposition of tax on the unrelated business income of the charitable organization. For more information, go to http://www.irs.gov/Charities-&-Non-Profits/Charitable-Organizations/Public-Inspection-and-Disclosure-of-Form-990-T.

An exempt organization is not required to disclose Schedule K-1 of Form 1065 or Schedule A of Form 990-BL. With the exception of private foundations, an exempt organization is not required to disclose the name and address of any contributor to the organization.

A political organization exempt from taxation under section 527(a) must make available for inspection and copying its report of contributions and expenditures on Form 8872, *Political Organization Report of Contributions and Expenditures.* However, such organization is not required to make available its return on Form 1120-POL, *U.S. Income Tax Return for Certain Political Organizations.*

Many organizations meet the disclosure requirements by putting their public documents online. Some of those websites for approved nonprofits are contained in Appendix A to this book so you can look at actual paperwork and get a feel for what goes in each section and in the narrative of Form 1023. Seeing how others have handled the paperwork should remove some of the anxious feeling you might have about this part of the process.

**NOTE:** On July 1, 2014, IRS added Form 1023-EZ, *Streamlined Application for Recognition of Exemption under Section 501(c) (3) of the Internal Revenue Code,* for smaller organizations to simplify filing. It must be filed online, the cost is $400, and you must complete the Eligibility Checklist (which is 5 pages but not difficult). This is great news for small nonprofits because the Form 1023-EZ is only 3 pages compared to the Form 1023, which is 26 pages. Eligibility worksheet is located at http://www.irs.gov/pub/irs-pdf/i1023ez.pdf after the instructions. There are many restrictions on use of this new form and many types of nonprofits are not eligible.

To be eligible to use the Form 1023-EZ, you must meet ALL these requirements:

1. Less than $50,000 gross receipts for the past three years and projected for the next three years
2. Less than $250,000 in assets
3. Formed in the U. S. and have a U. S. mailing address (or U. S. territory)
4. Must not be a successor to, or controlled by, an entity suspended under section 501(p) terrorist organization
5. Cannot be a limited liability corporation (LLC)
6. Cannot be successor to a for-profit entity
7. Must not have been previously revoked for failing to file Form 990-series for 3 years and applying for retroactive reinstatement
8. Must not be a church, convention, or association of churches
9. Must not be a school, college, university, or cooperative service organization for an educational institution
10. Must not be a hospital, medical research organization, or cooperative hospital service organization
11. Must not be a qualified charitable risk pool
12. Must not be a supporting organization to other nonprofits
13. Must not be credit counseling or consumer credit services

14. Cannot invest 5% or more of your total assets in securities or funds that are not publicly traded
15. Not participate, or intend to participate, in partnerships (including entities treated as partnerships for federal tax purposes) in which you share profits and losses with partners other than section 501(c)(3) organizations
16. Cannot sell carbon credits or carbon offsets
17. Must not be an HMO
18. Cannot engage in Accountable Care Organization (ACO) activities
19. Cannot maintain donor advised funds
20. Cannot be testing for public safety
21. Must not be a private operating foundation

The remaining chapters of the book contain instructions for filling out Form 1023. If you are eligible to use the streamlined Form 1023-EZ, those instructions can help you fill out the streamlined form.

Here is a rundown of the sections of Form 1023-EZ with comments to help you answer the questions:

**Part I:** Identification of Applicant. The new form combines Part I and Part V of Form 1023, but eliminates many questions. It is much faster to fill out than the long form.

**Part II:** Organizational Structure. Most organizations will be corporations and the organizing document is the Articles of Incorporation. You must be able to check the boxes in questions 5, 6, and 7 for approval. If you used the document templates in earlier chapters, you have no problem checking these boxes.

**Part III:**

Question 1: NTEE Code is a 3 character code that describes your activities. A list of NTEE codes can be found on pages

18 – 20 of the Form 1023-EZ instructions, which are located online at http://www.irs.gov/pub/irs-pdf/i1023ez.pdf

Question 2: Most organizations are charitable. Remember that you are not eligible to use Form 1023-EZ if you are a school or church organization, or test for public safety.

Question 3: You must be able to check the box attesting that you will not violate the rules.

Question 4: Best if you can answer "no." Stops questions, delays, and filing Form 5768.

Question 5: Remember your organization's gross receipts are less than $50,000 to qualify to use this form, so compensation paid, if any, should be proportionate.

Question 6: Reimbursing employee business expenses does not count when considering this question.

Question 7: It is perfectly fine to conduct activities and provide grants and assistance to individuals and organizations outside the United States, as long as it is for tax exempt purposes.

Question 8: Tricky question. If you answer "yes," your application may be delayed pending further inquiry from IRS.

Question 9: If you answer "yes," you must fill out an additional tax return at the end of the year, Form 990-T for the unrelated business income.

Question 10: Bingo and other gaming activities have many restrictions and safeguards from the state and federal government. Could delay your application if IRS needs more information. For more information, see Publication 3079, Tax-Exempt Organizations and Gaming.

Question 11: If you provide disaster relief, mark "yes," and see Publication 3833, Disaster Relief: Providing Assistance through Charitable Organizations.

**Part IV:** Foundation Classification. Most organizations will check 1a.

**Part V:** If you use this application, your effective date will not be retroactive to the day you were revoked. When you check the box, you are saying you did not fail to file intentionally, and that you have made changes to keep it from happening again. There are 3 conditions you must meet to use this form for reinstatement: It must be the first time you were revoked, you must have been eligible to file Form 990-N (electronic postcard return) or Form 990-EZ (short form return), and you must file within 15 months of being revoked.

Go to www.pay.gov and register. Enter 1023-EZ in the search box, and complete the form. You can set up a deduction from your bank account or use a credit card to pay the application fee.

If you cannot use the Form 1023-EZ, you will need to use the long form, Form 1023. Instructions for completing that form start in the next chapter.

# CHAPTER 13

## PART 1: IDENTIFICATION OF APPLICANT

*"Setting a goal is not the main thing. It is deciding how you will go about achieving it and staying with that plan."*

—Tom Landry

Skip Program provides education, opportunities, and promotes inclusion. At-risk youth, children living in impoverished conditions, and children diagnosed with disabilities are not afforded enough opportunities to live a healthy lifestyle or learn vital skills. Skip Program strives to equal the playing field by providing opportunities to participate in sports and community activities and by providing sports programs combined with educational programming and community projects, teaching vital skills for a successful future. (PA)

### TAKE IT ONE STEP AT A TIME

You are now at the point where you will begin filling out the actual application. No need to be overwhelmed – simply take it one step at a time and you will get through this.

*NOTE: If you are unsure of what to put in any section of the Form 1023, call IRS Tax Exempt and Government Entities Customer Account Services at (877) 829-5500. Better to ask now than to delay the approval of your application for months.*

Start by pulling up the online application at http://www.irs.gov/pub/irs-pdf/f1023.pdf

A good rule of thumb is to work on the application in sections, save it to your computer, and then come back and add to it later. I strongly suggest that you print a copy of all completed sections as you finish them. This is just in case your computer malfunctions, or for some reason the online document does not save your answers the way it should. That way you will not have come up with the answers again. (Work smart – take all necessary precautions.)

Below I have listed exactly what is needed for each specific line in the application:

## LINE 1: FULL NAME OF ORGANIZATION (EXACTLY AS IT APPEARS IN YOUR ORGANIZING DOCUMENT)

Enter your organization's name from Articles of Incorporation or similar document, including amendments.

## LINE 2: C/O NAME

If you want a specific person to be the go-to person for correspondence, put in an *in-care-of* name here. If you are the founder and are using your personal address, you can use your name. You can also leave it blank.

## LINE 3: MAILING ADDRESS

This will be the address you want correspondence sent to. A post office box is fine if that is where you get your mail. (For overseas addresses, list information in this order: city, province or state, and fully-spelled-out country, followed by the customary postal code for the country.)

## LINE 4: EMPLOYER IDENTIFICATION NUMBER (EIN)

Enter the FEIN given to you by IRS. It is 9-digits long. The first 2 digits, a dash, and the last 7 digits. For example, the EIN for Pasture Valley Children Missions (a nonprofit I founded) is 35-2468924. If you do not have an FEIN number, go back to Chapter 4 and follow the directions. You can get a number over the phone from IRS. IRS no longer accepts applications for organizations without FEIN numbers.

## LINE 5: MONTH THE ANNUAL ACCOUNTING PERIOD ENDS (01-12)

Your accounting year should end at a logical point. For example, a school organization may end in June 30 or July 31. Most other organizations will have a December 31 accounting period end. Put the month in which you plan to end your annual accounting period. The last day of the accounting period will be the last day of the month you select. Also check your bylaws to verify the accounting period. Depending on the month you select, your first accounting period may be less than one calendar year. For example, if you start your nonprofit in May and your accounting year ends in December, you will only have a seven month accounting period the first year. This is not a problem.

## LINE 6A: PRIMARY CONTACT

Who do you want IRS to talk with if they need to discuss your application, organizational documents, bylaws, or other such matters? This person can be an officer, director, or any other person you designate to discuss your organization's rules and procedures. It can also be you. Another option is to designate an authorized representative, attorney, or accountant to represent you by filing an IRS *Form 2848, Power of*

*Attorney and Declaration of Representative* with your application. You can get that form online at http://www.irs.gov/pub/irs-pdf/f2848.pdf

## LINE 6B: PHONE

What is the contact person's phone number? Include the area code.

## LINE 6C: FAX (OPTIONAL)

Enter fax number if you have one.

## LINE 7

If you have authorized an attorney or accountant to talk with IRS on your behalf, check "Yes" and attach IRS Form 2848. If your contact is you or a member of your organization in some facet, check "No."

## LINE 8

Is there anyone outside your organization that you have paid or promised to pay to:

- Help you fill out your Form 1023?
- Help you establish your organization?
- Set up fundraising programs?
- Handle tax matters?
- Prepare financials?
- Handle other organizational matters?

If you mark "Yes," you must provide the person's name, the name and address of the firm they represent, how much you paid or are going to pay, and exactly what the person has done or is doing. If not, then mark "No."

## LINE 9A: ORGANIZATION'S WEBSITE

If you have a website, list it here. The information you have on your actual website must match the information you include in this application. If you do not have a website, put in N/A. Also, if any other websites have your information on them or are maintained on your behalf, list them.

## LINE 9B: EMAIL (OPTIONAL)

If you want educational materials sent to you by IRS, give an email address if you have one. They will not contact you with confidential information by email, but will use U.S. Postal Service or fax. You do not have to include an email address.

## LINE 10

This item has to do with whether you will be required to file an annual information return using some version of Form 990. If you are a church, certain church affiliated organizations, or certain affiliates of government units, you are not required to file a Form 990. Include an explanation in the narrative section of why you do not think you need to file one of the versions of Form 990. Private foundations must file a Form 990-PF regardless of gross receipts. For small budget organizations, you can do your information return online quickly.

As long as you keep good records, it is not difficult to comply with the Form 990 requirement, especially if you set up your books using the same categories as are contained on the Form 990. Many grant-making organizations check to see that you are filing a Form 990 before they will accept or approve your application for a grant.

Failure to file a required Form 990 return for three years (in whatever version you must use) results in automatic revocation of 501(c) (3) status. When this occurs, you have 15 months to file your application all over again (and pay the fees again) to get your status back retroactive to the date of revocation.

If you file after 15 months from being revoked, you lose tax exempt status for the time you were revoked and the donations made to your organization during the time of revocation are not tax deductible to your donors.

## LINE 11

What date is on Articles of Incorporation? That is the date you use. If you choose to use an earlier date because you have been conducting business longer, you can request an earlier date. Just be aware that you must file for 501(c) (3) status within 27 months of beginning operations.

## LINE 12

Was your organization formed in another country outside the U.S.? Organizations formed in United States territories or possessions, Indian tribal or Alaska Native governments, or Washington, D.C. are considered domestic, not foreign. If you check "Yes," you must list the foreign country your organization was formed in. Otherwise, check "No."

Now that wasn't too painful, was it? In the next chapter you'll fill out all the information needed regarding your organizational structure.

# CHAPTER 14

## PART II: ORGANIZATIONAL STRUCTURE

*"Success is no accident. It is hard work, perseverance, learning, studying, sacrifice and most of all, love of what you are doing or learning to do."*

—Pele

**BEATING HOMELESSNESS THROUGH FOOTBALL** The Homeless World Cup is an annual, international football tournament, uniting teams of people who are homeless and excluded to take a once in a lifetime opportunity to represent their country and change their lives forever. It has triggered and supports grass roots football projects in over 60 nations working with over 25,000 homeless and excluded people throughout the year. (UK)

This section of the application has to do with your organizational structure. Your organization must be a corporation (including a limited liability company), or a trust in order to be eligible for 501(c) (3) status. In this section, you must select your form of organization and attach your organizing documents to the application.

## LINE 1: CORPORATION

IRS defines a corporation as:

> *"An entity organized under a Federal or state statute, or a statute of a federally recognized Indian tribal or Alaskan native government."*

This is the most popular and frequent organizational structure for 501(c) (3) status. You document your corporate status by filing Articles of Incorporation with your state. (See Chapter 7) The state gives you back a certification of filing that includes the date you became a corporate entity. You must include an exact copy of your filed document with the Form 1023, as well as any amendments to the original document.

If you do not have an exact copy, you can contact your Secretary of State for another copy (recommended), or you can include a substitute copy either handwritten, typed, or printed, or otherwise reproduced. If you substitute, you must include a statement signed by a corporate officer that it is a complete and correct copy of the actual organizing document. You could use this declaration:

> "I, _____ (name), _____ (office you hold), declare under penalty of law that this is a complete and correct copy of the articles of incorporation and that it contains all the powers, principles, purposes, functions, and other provisions by which we currently govern ourselves."

## LINE 2: LIMITED LIABILITY CORPORATION

Not all Limited Liability Corporations or Companies are eligible for 501(c) (3) status. To qualify, all the membership of an LLC must be other 501(c) (3) agencies. LLC companies made up of individuals are not eligible for tax exempt status. LLCs are owned by members;

nonprofit organizations are not owned, they are separate entities. This structure of organization is confusing, contradictory, and brings problems you may not want to try to solve. If you are contemplating LLC structure, contact an attorney for further guidance to avoid laborious paperwork with IRS and extended timeframes for approval or rejection of your application.

## LINE 3: UNINCORPORATED ASSOCIATION

An unincorporated association must have a written agreement laying out the purpose of the association. There must be at least two members. According to IRS instructions, "the articles of organization of an unincorporated association must include the name of your organization, your purpose, the date the document was adopted, and the signatures of at least two individuals." Date of adoption is important to IRS. You must file for tax exempt status within 27 months of inception.

## LINE 4A: TRUST

A trust can be established by a will or by a trust agreement or declaration of trust. If created by a will, a copy of the death certificate and a copy of pertinent parts of the will must be attached to the application. A trust involves three groups of people:

- The donor(s)
- The trustee(s)
- The beneficiaries

Trustees can be sued on behalf of the trust. Not all trust instruments and structures are eligible for 501(c) (3) status.

## LINE4B: HAVE YOU BEEN FUNDED?

For a trust to exist, it must be funded with money or real or personal property to be legal.

## LINE 5: BYLAWS

If you have bylaws, attach them. IRS does not require them, but if you do not have them, some of their questions about how you function as an organization will not be answered. In that case, they may not approve your application without further information. This could delay your application for many months. Be safe, send the bylaws and eliminate the delay.

# CHAPTER 15

## PART III: PROVISIONS IN YOUR ORGANIZING DOCUMENTS

*"The difference between a successful person and others is not a lack of strength, not a lack of knowledge, but rather a lack of will."*

—Vince Lombardi

**GOALS | Haiti**

GOALS uses soccer in Haiti to engage youth in community work that improves their quality of life, their health, the environment, and local leadership. Ongoing programs include after-school soccer clubs, educational seminars (language, health, sanitation and disease prevention, technology) and community service and community-identified development projects, scholarship opportunities, peer-mentored homework help and quarterly mobile medical clinics. All participants are provided with a meal and clean drinking water daily. (FL)

### LINE 1: LOCATION OF PURPOSE CLAUSE

Your organizing document must contain a purpose clause that is consistent with IRS requirements. This question wants to know exactly where it is located in your Articles of Incorporation or Association, or Declaration of Trust. Here is the example of an acceptable purpose clause contained in the IRS instructions for completing Form 1023:

*"The organization is organized exclusively for charitable, religious, educational, and scientific purposes under section 501(c) (3) of the Internal Revenue Code, or corresponding section of any future tax code."*

Find that statement in your Articles and put the page, article, and paragraph in the blank on line 1. Don't forget to check the box to the right showing you have the required clause in your organizing document.

## LINE 2A: DISSOLUTION CLAUSE

To be approved for nonprofit status by IRS, you must have a dissolution clause that basically states that if you stop being a tax-exempt organization, all your assets will be given to another nonprofit organization. Here is an example of an acceptable dissolution clause contained in the IRS instructions for completing Form 1023:

*"Upon the dissolution of this organization, assets will be distributed for one or more exempt purposes within the meaning of section 501(c) (3) of the Internal Revenue Code, or corresponding section of any future federal tax code, or shall be distributed to the federal government, or to a state or local government, for a public purpose."*

Don't forget to check the box to the right showing you have the required clause in your organizing document.

## LINE 2B: LOCATION OF DISSOLUTION CLAUSE

From your organizing document, list the page, article, and paragraph of the dissolution clause.

## LINE 2C: OPERATION OF STATE LAW

If you checked 2a, you do not check this box. Most people will not use this block of the application. If you use this block, remember to check the box and fill in the state.

In some states, you do not need specific provisions for dissolving assets in case of closing a nonprofit organization. If you live in Arkansas, California, Louisiana, Massachusetts, Minnesota, Missouri, Ohio, and Oklahoma, you do not have to specify in your organizing documents.

In testamentary charitable trust instruments from several states, no specific statement of dissolution of assets needs to be in the document. These states are: Alabama, Louisiana, Pennsylvania, South Dakota, and Virginia.

In testamentary charitable trust instruments from almost two-thirds of the states, only a general statement of intent to benefit charity upon dissolution is required. These states are: Arkansas, California, Colorado, Connecticut, Delaware, District of Columbia, Florida, Georgia, Illinois, Indiana, Iowa, Kansas, Kentucky, Maine, Maryland, Massachusetts, Michigan, Minnesota, Mississippi, Missouri, Nebraska, New Hampshire, New Jersey, North Carolina, Ohio, Oklahoma, Oregon, Rhode Island, Tennessee, Texas, Vermont, Washington, and Wisconsin.

Foreign organizations can submit their relevant laws (translated into English) with their application to eliminate or reduce the requirement to include charitable dissolution procedures. To avoid the need, just put the required statement in the organizational documents.

# CHAPTER 16

## PART IV: NARRATIVE DESCRIPTION OF YOUR ACTIVITIES

*"You have to perform at a consistently higher level than others. That's the mark of a true professional."*

—Joe Paterno

Kids Play Int'l (KPI) uses sports to educate and empower African youth. KPI develops sustainable after school programs to teach life skills and the importance of physical fitness and healthy living. This program is currently being implemented in orphanages and schools in Malawi and Rwanda, Africa. KPI also organizes volunteer service trips for people who want to travel with a purpose. Volunteers will use sports as the vehicle to teach important lessons to kids in orphanages while also seeing and experiencing the culture and countryside.

## THE HEART OF THE APPLICATION

You have come to the heart of your application and it is now time to touch the heart of the IRS agent who will be processing your package. This is your chance in a few pages, to describe the mission you are undertaking to do good things in the world. The key to getting your application approved lies in your willingness to put forth the effort to make your vision come alive. You have to answer the questions in the IRS agent's mind, not just the ones on the application, but the other ones that any interested person would want to know when finding out about your mission.

What do you tell people about your organization when you are explaining it one-on-one or in a small group? How did your organization come into existence? What was the deciding impetus that led to its creation? What excites you most about it? Who is involved? What are their qualifications? What do you want to accomplish? How are you going to accomplish it? How will you pay for it (make sure this information agrees with your financial section of the application)? How will you select the people, groups, or organizations you will help?

Remember to answer the questions asked on the application in enough detail to answer the Who, What, When, Where, How, How Much, and Why of each question.

## NO RIGHT OR WRONG WAY

There is no right or wrong way format the narrative section, but by definition, a narrative can be an essay, biographical sketch, or autobiography (in this case of the organization), usually in chronological or other logical order. Use positive, powerful terms and word choices.

Don't limit your future growth, but at the same time, do not take on the world. For example, do not say you are going to provide laptop computers to three rural schools in Alabama, because later you may want to provide iPads or work with schools in Mississippi as well.

Instead, you might say you are going to improve technology access to rural schools in the southern U.S., beginning with providing laptop computers to three rural schools in Alabama. You show a small start, and give your organization room to grow in your narrative.

## TELL YOUR STORY

Tell a story with your narrative and weave in the important points as part of the story. Be careful in this section not to refer to the organization with ownership; it is a separate entity that is not owned by anyone. Appendix A has many narratives that are well written. You may want to review several applications to get the flavor of this section. Live links to the websites in Appendix A are available at www. doyourownnonprofit.com

Another way to get your mission across is to add copies of brochures, flyers, handouts, printed copies of website pages, and any other written material that will expand the IRS agent's understanding of what you are trying to do. You can also add short biographies of the board of directors demonstrating how they are qualified to perform the organization's mission.

You might also want to justify your procedures and structure by citing IRS regulations. You can quote specific content in the instruction booklet for filling out Form 1023, recite guidance given on the IRS website for nonprofit organizations, and quote or mention passages of IRS Revenue Rulings found at: http://www.irs.gov/Charities-&-Non-Profits/Archive-of-Published-Guidance. An example of a Revenue Ruling you might use for tax deductibility of donated items would be Revenue Ruling 2002-67, which can be reviewed at http://www.irs.gov/pub/irs-drop/rr-02-67.pdf . This states that:

> *"A donor may use an established used car pricing guide to determine the fair market value of a single donated car if the guide lists a sales price for a car that is the same make, model, and year, sold in the same area, and in the same condition, as the donated car. However, a donor may not use an established used car pricing*

*guide to determine the fair market value of a single donated car if the guide does not list a sales price for a car in the same condition as the donated car. In such a case, the donor must use some other method that is reasonable under the circumstances to determine the value of the car. See Publication 561, "Determining the Value of Donated Property."*

Your narrative might read: "Donated property to this organization will be accounted for using Publication 561 and the intent of Revenue Ruling 2002-67 which held that a donor must use methods reasonable to determine the value of the donated property."

By inserting periodic Revenue Rulings and IRS published guidance into your narrative, you give credibility to your application package and show the IRS agent that you are abreast of guidelines that affect your nonprofit operation.

**NOTE:** *Every page of your application and all attachments must have the organization name and EIN on it. If you are typing your narrative, you may want to include this information in a header or footer.*

# CHAPTER 17

## PART V: COMPENSATION AND OTHER FINANCIAL ARRANGEMENTS WITH YOUR OFFICERS, DIRECTORS, TRUSTEES, EMPLOYEES, AND INDEPENDENT CONTRACTORS

*"A winner never stops trying."*
—Tom Landry

Ready, Set, Gold! tackles the epidemic problems of childhood obesity and chronic diseases by pairing Olympians and Paralympians with schools of the Los Angeles Unified School District to help promote student fitness, nutrition and healthy living habits. Each Olympian/Paralympian is matched to a specific school and meets with the PE classes five times during the school year to inspire, educate and motivate the students toward a long and healthy drug-free life through fun physical activity and good nutrition. (CA)

## POSSIBLE CONFLICTS OF INTEREST

This section of your application is designed to disclose any conflicts of interest, personal profit to organization officials (or their friends, business associates, or family members), and undue influence because of relationships, contracts, and mingled loyalties between organizations. If you are a new organization with beginning operations, this section will be easy and fast to complete because chances are you will not have any of these issues to disclose.

## LINE 1A: LIST NAME, TITLE, MAILING ADDRESS, AND COMPENSATION FOR ALL OFFICERS, DIRECTORS, AND TRUSTEES

You can use the organization's mailing address if desired. Include exact compensation if possible. Compensation includes salary or other compensation, deferred retirement, health insurance coverage paid for by the organization, value of vehicles provided, and any other compensation in kind from use of equipment, or personal items provided such as travel or memberships. Reimbursing expenses from receipts provided is not compensation as long as the reimbursement is reasonable.

If no compensation is given, enter -0-. Information given in this section must match the financial data given in Part IX. Compensation must be reasonable for the position. Compensation that is in any way linked to income or donations to the organization waves a big red abuse flag at IRS.

## LINE 1B: FIVE HIGHEST COMPENSATED EMPLOYEES OVER $50,000 A YEAR THAT ARE NOT LISTED IN LINE 1A

If you have anyone who fits this category, provide total compensation information. If not, put N/A and move on. This information must match Part IX. Compensation must be reasonable for the position.

## LINE 1C: FIVE HIGHEST COMPENSATED INDEPENDENT CONTRACTORS OVER $50,000 A YEAR

IRS publication 15 gives a general rule for independent contractors, which is:

> *"That an individual is an independent contractor if you, the person for whom the services are performed, have the right to control or direct only the result of the work and not the means and methods of accomplishing the result."*

If you do not have anyone in that category, put N/A and move on. This information must match Part IX, Financial Data.

## LINE 2A: FAMILY OR BUSINESS RELATIONSHIPS

Here is a make-or-break question on your Form 1023. If there is a husband and wife on the board, or members that are related by blood or business, take caution. The IRS is going to look hard at your organization to make sure that related parties do not make up over half the voting power of the organization. It's best to have either husband or wife, or to add board members so that the related parties (personal or business) do not have the majority of the vote. If none, check "No." If there are relationships, check "Yes."

Explain in the narrative section answering any questions about the relationship that a reasonable person would have and eliminating the concern on the part of the IRS agent that abuse may occur as a result of this relationship.

IRS instructions list the following family relationships that need to be disclosed:

- Spouses
- Ancestors
- Children
- Grandchildren

- Great grandchildren
- Siblings (whole or half-blood)
- Spouses for any of these

## LINE 2B: BUSINESS RELATIONSHIPS WITH OFFICERS, DIRECTORS, OR TRUSTEES

Another make-or-break question on Form 1023. Other than being a part of the organization as an officer, director, or trustee, does the organization have any business relationship with these members? For example, do you hire one of the board members to perform any services for the organization? If so, this must be disclosed. If none, check "No."

If there are relationships, check "Yes." Explain them in the narrative section answering any questions about the relationship that a reasonable person would have and eliminating the concern on the part of the IRS agent that abuse may occur as a result of this relationship.

## LINE 2C: RELATIONSHIPS BETWEEN BOARD MEMBERS AND HIGHEST COMPENSATED EMPLOYEES OR INDEPENDENT CONTRACTORS

You guessed it – this is yet another make-or-break question. If there are any relationships between officers, directors or trustees, and your five highest compensated employees or contractors who receive over $50,000 per year, you need to disclose it here. Explain it in the narrative section answering any questions about the relationship that a reasonable person would have and eliminating the concern on the part of the IRS agent that abuse may occur as a result of this relationship.

## LINE 3A: NAME, QUALIFICATIONS, AVERAGE HOURS WORKED AND DUTIES FOR EVERYONE LISTED IN 1A, 1B, OR 1C

In the narrative section, provide this information for everyone listed even if they are volunteers who receive no compensation. If you are not sure of some of the information, give the most accurate information you can determine. If you have included a job description in your bylaws, you can simply state the page and paragraph where the job description exists for each position. If you have already listed the qualifications of the board members in the narrative, you can refer to that section instead of giving the same information again.

## LINE 3B: COMMON CONTROL

This line is designed to disclose where control rests in an organization and if there are any other organizations exercising influence and control over your organization.

Here is an example: I am on the board of directors for *Kid Care America of Rolla, Inc.* It is a separate organization from First Assembly of God-Rolla, but the church pays part of the salary for the director and provides facilities for the after-school program for at-risk kids. This information had to be disclosed in the Form 1023.

IRS instructions for Form 1023 define common control as:

> *"you and one or more other organizations have (1) a majority of your governing boards or officers appointed or elected by the same organization(s), or (2) a majority of your governing boards or officers consist of the same individuals. Common control also occurs when you and one or more commonly controlled organizations have a majority ownership interest (I added: more than 35%) in a corporation, partnership, or trust."*

## LINE 4A, B AND C: COMPENSATION-SETTING PRACTICES

"Yes" to all three of these questions means that you are using good judgment and practices in establishing compensation for your higher level officers, and also means IRS is not concerned with these items. If you answer "No" to any of these, put an explanation in the narrative.

## LINES 4D, E, F, G: HOW DO YOU SET REASONABLE COMPENSATION AND HOW DO YOU DOCUMENT IT?

If you arrived at your compensation by doing a comparison of other nonprofit and profit companies of similar size and function, and you document how you arrived at the compensation, then you can answer "Yes." If your board is not compensated, then you have no problems with this question. If you answer "No" to any of these questions, you must include an explanation in the narrative of how you arrived at reasonable compensation for your top officials. Overcompensating can result in loss of tax exempt status.

## LINES 5A, B, C: CONFLICT OF INTEREST POLICY

If you have adopted a conflict of interest policy similar to the example given in Chapter 11, check "Yes" and move on. If you answered "No," you must answer lines 5b and 5c.

## LINES 6A AND 6B: NON-FIXED COMPENSATION FOR TOP OFFICIALS

If you answer "Yes" to either of these items, you have waved a huge red flag and your tax exempt status is not likely to be approved. If you are basing compensation on performance, percentages, revenue or bonuses, you are using non-fixed payments and IRS looks for corruption and sees this as a way to spread the profits around to insiders.

## LINES 7A AND 7B: PURCHASING GOODS, SERVICES, AND ASSETS FROM TOP OFFICIALS, EMPLOYEES, OR CONTRACTORS.

Another big red flag here if you answer "Yes." If you do purchase any goods, services, or assets from insiders, make sure you explain it well in the narrative.

## LINES 8A, 8B, 8C, 8D, 8E, 8F: LEASES, CONTRACTS, LOANS, AND AGREEMENTS WITH INSIDERS

Answering "Yes" to 8a does not necessarily throw up a red flag unless the compensation is more than is customary for the services or facilities in question. Remember to provide copies of all documents and include an in-depth explanation in the narrative section.

## LINES 9A, 9B, 9C, 9D, 9E, 9F: LEASES, CONTRACTS, LOANS, AND AGREEMENTS WITH OTHER ORGANIZATIONS IN WHICH YOUR OFFICERS, DIRECTORS, OR TRUSTEES ARE ALSO OFFICERS, DIRECTORS, OR TRUSTEES

This question looks to uncover any undue influence, or conflicts of interest, of officials who might also have influence or ownership (35% or more) in another organization you do business with. A "Yes" answer to 9a requires thorough explanation in the narrative section and copies of any documents involved.

# CHAPTER 18

## PART VI: YOUR MEMBERS AND OTHER INDIVIDUALS AND ORGANIZATIONS THAT RECEIVE BENEFITS FROM YOU

*"When you have confidence, you can have a lot of fun. And when you have fun, you can do amazing things."*

—Joe Namath

SOCCER
IN THE STREETS

Soccer in the Streets empowers kids who lack opportunity by using soccer as a medium to make them employable adults. Since 1989, the organization has served over 125,000 kids across the United States and beyond. From encouraging basic good manners, cooperation and teamwork to helping teens build their resume and find summer jobs, we intend to have a measurable impact on the life outcomes of our program participants. (GA)

## IDENTIFYING WHO WILL BENEFIT

This part of the application seeks to find out how you are selecting your target group to assist and aims to ferret out any selection process that benefits members or private interests instead of public interest. A good test is whether you know ahead of time the names of the people or organizations you will help. If so, you may not be a 501(c)(3) public charity, but a private foundation instead.

## LINE 1A: BENEFITS TO INDIVIDUALS

If your nonprofit organization will be helping individuals directly, check "Yes" and describe your programs and how you will carry them out. Make sure to emphasize that your target individuals are from a class of people (such as poor, disabled, homeless, or senior citizens), not specific individuals you can name ahead of time. It is permissible to help specific individuals as long as you do not limit your services to specific people, and leave opportunity to add others in the future whose names you do not even know yet. If you will be helping individuals indirectly through other organizations, check "No" and move on.

## LINE 1B: BENEFITS TO ORGANIZATIONS

If you provide goods and services to organizations, tell what programs you will offer and how you will carry them out. Make sure to emphasize that your target organizations are from a class of organizations (such as orphanages, hospitals, schools, senior citizen homes, etc.), not specific organizations that you can name ahead of time. It is fine to begin operations helping specific organizations, but make sure your narrative reflects the desire and opportunity to add other similar organizations at a later date. If not, IRS may declare you a private foundation instead of a 501(c)(3) organization.

## LINE 2: PROGRAM LIMITS

Answering "Yes" to this item is another big red flag for IRS. If you limit your scope to specific individuals or specific organizations, you do not meet the requirement for 501(c) (3) status. You cannot select specific people or organizations ahead of time to the exclusion of all others who might be in that class or group. If you do then you are not a true public charity. For example, you cannot start a charity to benefit one specific orphanage, one specific school, or members of one specific family. But you can start with one specific orphanage, one specific school or members of one specific family as long as you plan to add others later.

## LINE 3: SERVICES TO RELATIVES OF INSIDERS

"Yes" to this question is another red flag to IRS. If the answer is yes, you must disclose it. Give a detailed explanation in the narrative.

# CHAPTER 19

## PART VII: YOUR HISTORY

*"Aim for the sky and you'll reach the ceiling.
Aim for the ceiling and you'll stay on the floor."*

—Bill Shankly

BRIDGE II SPORTS — INCLUSIVE SPORTS CLUB — Bridge II Sports is a non-profit organization that provides opportunities for children and adults who are physically challenged to play team and individual sports. Bridge II Sports, in partnership with community partners, provides the equipment, coaching and play space, as well as develops teams. The goal of Bridge II Sports is to help individuals discover tenacity, confidence, self-esteem, and the joy of finding the player within. (NC)

This section tells whether your organization was formed from a previous organization, and whether you have filed for 501(c) (3) status within 27 months of filing your Articles of Incorporation.

### LINE 1: ARE YOU A "SUCCESSOR" TO ANOTHER ORGANIZATION?

If you answer "yes," it means that you have taken over all the assets or activities of another organization, been converted or merged from another organization, and/or have the same officials as another organization that doesn't exist anymore but served the same function. The previous organization could have been a tax exempt organization, but does not have to be.

An example that comes to mind is in my town. Twenty or so years ago, there was an organization called LOVE (Local Organization of Various Enterprises), that assisted people who had difficulty paying utility bills in winter, buying food, and paying rent. LOVE was closed, and the organization was converted to another organization called GRACE (Greater Rolla Area Charitable Enterprises). It became a one-stop facility for anyone who needs help with living expenses.

Local churches and helping organizations send everyone to GRACE first, and records are kept there of who received what help from where and when they received it. This has stopped abuse of the helping organizations in this area.

United Way lets residents contribute to GRACE, and local schools have canned food drives at holidays to assist GRACE in its mission. So GRACE was the successor of LOVE, and in this case, both were nonprofit tax exempt organizations.

If you answer "Yes," you must complete Schedule G of the application.

## LINE 2: TIME LIMIT OF 27 MONTHS TO FILE FOR TAX-EXEMPT STATUS

IRS gives you 27 months to file Form 1023 from the last day of the month in which your organization was formed, or your Articles of Incorporation were filed with the state. If you file within that time, your tax-exempt status can be effective from day one. If you miss the 27 month deadline, your application can be approved, but will only be effective from the date of the postmark on the application. This could cause a problem for your donors because their donations would not be deductible before the postmarked date. You can request a waiver but there is no guarantee you will get it.

If you did not file within 27 months, you will need to fill out and attach Schedule E to the application. You might be eligible for 501(c)(4) status for the time that does not qualify for 501(c) (3) status, but that requires you to file a Form 1024 in addition to this Form 1023. Best and easiest to file within the 27 month window.

# CHAPTER 20

## PART VIII: SPECIFIC ACTIVITIES

*"The difference between the impossible and the possible
lies in a man's determination."*

—Tommy LaSorda

The Summer and Winter Deaflympics are among the world's fastest growing sports events. More than 4,000 deaf athletes and officials from 77 nations participated in the 21st Summer Deaflympics in Taipei, Chinese Taipei, in September 2009. Over 600 athletes and officials participated in the 16th Winter Deaflympics in Salt Lake City, United States in February 2007.

## LINE 1: DO YOU SUPPORT OR OPPOSE CANDIDATES IN POLITICAL CAMPAIGNS IN ANY WAY?

If you answer this question "Yes," you just wasted a lot of time and effort, because 501(c) (3) organizations CANNOT engage in political activities that endorse or oppose candidates. Period. End of Conversation. NO EXCEPTIONS.

Involving yourself in any political activity can be hazardous to your tax-exempt status. Because rightly dividing the regulations can be tricky, it is best to call IRS and discuss any proposed activities with them before you engage in them so as not to jeopardize 501(c) (3) status eligibility.

## LINE 2A: DO YOU ATTEMPT TO INFLUENCE LEGISLATION?

This is yet another fine line to navigate. If you answer "Yes," that means you are trying to persuade people to support or oppose legislation. You must give an explanation in the narrative that spells out how much time and money you are spending on it. Tax exempt organizations are not allowed to engage in "substantial legislative activities." Although "substantial" is not well defined, case law has shown over time that 5% of time and money is NOT substantial, while 16% is.

This is a tricky area. If you answer "Yes," you may want to contact a professional to assist you with meeting the requirements of the Internal Revenue Code and applicable Treasury regulations. Failure to abide within the parameters can result in loss of tax-exempt status, not getting tax-exempt status in the first place, and excise taxes being levied against the organization. An excellent article, *Legislative and Political Campaign Activity Limitations under Internal Revenue Code Section 501(c) (3)*, by Joanna Pressman is available online at Simpson Thatcher website.

## LINE 2B: FORM 5768, ELECTION/REVOCATION OF ELECTION BY AN ELIGIBLE SECTION 501(C) (3) ORGANIZATION TO MAKE EXPENDITURES TO INFLUENCE LEGISLATION

If you answered yes to line 2a, you may elect to have your activities to influence legislation calculated by how much you spent based on section 501(h). See Publication 557 for more details on filing Form 5768. Churches and private foundations are not allowed to complete Form 5768.

## LINES 3A, 3B, 3C: BINGO

If you are going to conduct Bingo games or have them conducted on your behalf, answer these questions to fit your plans and circumstances. Provide details in the narrative. Remember that winners of high stakes Bingo games must be reported to IRS so they can collect the taxes due on the winnings. If you are not going to engage in Bingo in any facet, mark "No," and move on.

## LINES 4A, 4B, 4C, 4D, 4E: FUNDRAISING

Whatever you put here must be explained, described, and it's a good idea to include copies of any paperwork you use. If you are contemplating a certain type of fundraising but have not firmed up specifics or undertaken that mode of fundraising yet, you might want to leave it off for now. Put only what you are actually doing or will actually do in the near term.

The more you include, the more justification and paperwork you need, and the more chance that something will be questioned. I do not advocate leaving out anything material. Be honest and complete, but leave your future plans to the future, especially if you have not ironed out enough details to pass IRS scrutiny at the time of this application. Make sure this line agrees with Part IX, Financial Data.

You should be aware that IRS will look hard at any applicant who plans to use professional fundraisers. Due to frequent abuse of donor advised accounts for personal gain, IRS also looks hard at organizations who plan to use them, and you may be subject to excise tax or not be granted 501(c) (3) status. See http://www.irs.gov/Charities-&-Non-Profits/Charitable-Organizations/New-Requirements-for-Donor-Advised-Funds and http://www.irs.gov/Charities-&-Non-Profits/Charitable-Organizations/Donor-Advised-Funds for more information, or contact IRS to discuss your specific situation.

You might want to review some of the Form 1023 links in the Appendix to see how other organizations have addressed fundraising on the application and in the narrative. You do not need to reinvent the wheel.

## LINE 5: GOVERNMENT UNIT AFFILIATION

Government units are not normally eligible for 501(c) (3) status because they have power to establish, control, manage, and/or supervise legal or government issues. However, some organizations, such as municipal hospitals, are affiliated with government units or Indian Tribal Governments, and are eligible because they do not have those powers, or because they lessen the burden on the government. See http://www.irs.gov/pub/irs-tege/eotopich04.pdf for more guidance. If you answer "Yes," include an explanation in the narrative. If not, check "No" and move on.

## LINES 6A AND 6B: ECONOMIC DEVELOPMENT

Organizations created to counter deterioration of neighborhoods that have been recognized by a government agency as economically depressed, deteriorating, or blighted, qualify for 501(c) (3) status as economic development organizations. The services provided can be loans, grants, sharing knowledge and skill with business plans or other business development tasks. Services can also include creation of industrial parks as well as to aid in eliminating prejudice and discrimination, or to decrease government burdens through business development.

IRS instructions for completing Line 6a include the following guidance:

*"If your exempt purpose is to combat community deterioration, describe whether the area or areas in which you will operate have been declared blighted or economically depressed by a government finding. If the area has not been declared blighted or economically depressed, a more suitable exemption may be under sections 501(c) (4) or 501(c) (6). See Publication 557 for more information.*

*If your exempt purpose is to eliminate prejudice and discrimination, describe how your activities further this purpose.*

*If your exempt purpose is to lessen the burdens of government, describe whether the government has recognized your activities as those for which it would otherwise be responsible, and any involvement you have with governmental entities that demonstrates that you are actually lessening governmental burdens."*

For Line 6b, in the narrative, include a complete description of your target audience and how your services will fulfill exempt purposes.

## LINES 7A, 7B, 7C: DEVELOPMENT AND MANAGEMENT RELATIONSHIPS

Once again IRS is looking for abuse or situations in which insiders and their families, friends, and business associates unfairly benefit or profit from affiliation with a tax-exempt organization. If any of these apply, full disclosure is required in terms of explanation, description of services, and copies of all agreements and contracts. You must explain how compensation was arrived at and how you ensured it was reasonable for services rendered or to be completed. Expect IRS scrutiny if you answer "Yes" to these.

## LINE 8: JOINT VENTURES

This item seeks to establish whether your tax exempt organization plans to join forces with other individuals or organizations that are not 501(c) (3) approved, for profit purposes. IRS instructions for this line define a joint venture as:

*"a legal agreement in which the persons jointly undertake a transaction for mutual profit. Generally, each person contributes assets and shares risks. Like a partnership, a joint venture can involve any kind of business transaction and the persons involved can be individuals, companies, or corporations."*

A nonprofit that I founded (Pasture Valley Children Missions, EIN 35-2468924) entered a joint venture with a local pharmacy to provide a market for jewelry made by orphans in Swaziland. The agreement called for a 20% commission (the pharmacy's standard commission) on all items sold. This is the type of agreement that would need to be disclosed and explained if known or planned at the time of application. As it turned out, no commission was actually ever charged. The pharmacy donated the commission to the organization instead.

The same type of agreement was made with another organization to market the jewelry, but no disclosure was required because the second organization was also a tax exempt organization.

This is a tricky area, and I highly recommend you talk with IRS about it if you have any joint ventures in force or planned with organizations that are not tax exempt.

## LINES 9A, 9B, 9C, 9D. CHILDCARE ORGANIZATIONS

Two choices exist for tax exempt here. You can be tax exempt as a childcare facility if you are classified as a school under Internal Revenue Code 170(b)(1)(A)(ii) which reads:

> *"An educational organization which normally maintains a regular faculty and curriculum and normally has a regularly enrolled body of pupils or students in attendance at the place where its educational activities are regularly carried on."*

You must complete Schedule B of the application in addition to the Form 1023.

The second choice is a 501(k) childcare organization. You can qualify under Section 501(k) if the kids come to your location, you are allowing parents to work or seek work, and you serve the general public. If you are only serving a specific employer or group, you are not eligible for 501(c) (3) status. At least 85% of those families you serve must meet these conditions, or you must describe how you are going to meet the requirement and increase the percentage to 85% to be eligible for tax exempt status. Details are available at http://www. irs.gov/pub/irs-tege/eotopicd86.pdf

## LINE 10: INTELLECTUAL PROPERTY

IRS instructions say that intellectual property includes patents for inventions; copyrights (for literary and artistic works such as novels, poems, plays, films, musical works, drawings, paintings, photographs, sculptures, architectural designs, performances, recordings, film, and radio or television programs); trade names, trademarks, and service marks (for symbols, names, images, and designs); and formulas, know-how, and trade secrets.

Intellectual property also includes any written materials either published, printed, copied, or displayed on a website online. If you have a slogan or a logo, this is also intellectual property. If you are just starting out and have none of these yet, answer "No."

If you have developed any educational materials, brochures, or websites or any intellectual property from the ones listed above, you must answer "Yes," and give complete details on all items required for this line. Further guidance is available at http://www. irs.gov/Charities-&-Non-Profits/Form-1023:—Information-about-Ownership-of-Intellectual-Property or http://www.irs.gov/pub/irs-tege/eotopicb99.pdf

## LINE 11: CONTRIBUTIONS OF REAL PROPERTY

Although cash is real, real property is anything but cash. IRS is concerned about scams and abuse in this area. See http://www.irs.gov/Charities-&-Non-Profits/Conservation-Easements for more details. The main areas of concern are how some are overvaluing the property for tax deduction purposes, and who has actual control of the contributed item.

## LINES 12A, B, C: OPERATING IN FOREIGN COUNTRIES

If you have operations in foreign countries, you need to explain the locations, operations, and how those operations promote or advance your tax exempt purpose. You may want to read http://www.irs.gov/pub/irs-tege/eotopico83.pdf which summarizes previous revenue rulings about conducting foreign operation although you are the domestic charity. It is allowed and you can quote the revenue rulings in your narrative as support for your foreign operations.

Although tax deductions are not permitted for giving to foreign charities, people and businesses can donate to a U.S. 501(c) (3) approved organization that gives to foreign charities. Ever since the tragedy of 9/11, funneling money into terrorist activities has been a concern. You may want to explicitly state that your organization has no ties to terrorist activities and that all foreign operations are for tax exempt purposes within the letter and the intent of Section 501(c) (3) of the Internal Revenue Code.

## LINE 13A, 13B, 13C, 13D, 13E, 13F, 13G: DISTRIBUTIONS TO ORGANIZATIONS

If you make grants, loans, or distributions to organizations, you need to answer each part of this section and include copies of all forms you use in deciding who is eligible for a distribution, how much they get, and how you will monitor the funds to make sure they are being used for exempt purposes.

You also need to describe how you will keep records and reports you will require. If there is a relationship between you and the grantee, you must disclose the details in your narrative.

Here is an acceptable way to answer Line 13e (you can borrow these words if they apply):

> *(Organization) will maintain its financial records on QuickBooks software in accordance with general accounting principles for non-profit organizations. Cash received is applied*

*to Accounts Receivable Ledger and cash distributed is recorded in the Accounts Payable Ledger. Likewise, organizations that receive distributions are required to maintain general accounting records, and are required to report on a regular/monthly basis as to how, when and where funds are applied.*

## LINES 14A, 14B, 14C, 14D, 14E, 14F: DISTRIBUTIONS TO FOREIGN ORGANIZATIONS

If you distribute funds to foreign organizations, you must explain to IRS how you make sure the money is going for its tax exempt purpose. As you answer the questions in this section, you may want to include a statement in the narrative that states if the organizations you are distributing to were located in the United States, they would qualify for 501(c) (3) status because their purposes are consistent with Section 501(c) (3).

## LINE 15: DO YOU HAVE A CLOSE CONNECTION TO ANY OTHER ORGANIZATION?

Another item designed to detect undue influence or abuse. IRS instructions for this item specify that a close connection exists if:

*You control the organization or it controls you through common officers, directors, or trustees, or through authority to approve budgets or expenditures. You and the organization were created at approximately the same time and by the same persons. For example, you were formed within months of the time that a social welfare organization and a political action committee were established by the same persons who were instrumental in your formation.*

*You and the organization operate in a coordinated manner with respect to facilities, programs, employees, or other activities. For example, you share rental expenses for office space and employees with a for-profit corporation.*

*Persons who exercise substantial influence over you also exercise substantial influence over the other organization and (1) you either conduct activities in common or (2) have a financial relationship. For example, a voting member of your governing body is also a voting member of the governing body of a business league with which you intend to cooperate in planning an advertising campaign that will inform the public about the benefits of a particular program. For example, a voting member of your governing body is also a voting member of the governing body of a business league that has made a loan to you.*

A tax exempt organization (such as Kid Care America of Rolla, Inc.) can have a close connection to another tax exempt organization (such as First Assembly of God-Rolla), and this is not an issue. Both are 501(c) (3) approved, so it is fine for them to share facilities, have some of the same people involved in both organizations, and share some expenses of conducting tax exempt activities.

## LINE 16: COOPERATIVE HOSPITAL SERVICE ORGANIZATIONS

Section 501(e) lists operations that fall under the heading of cooperative hospital service organizations. They include: data processing, purchasing, warehousing, billing and collection, food, clinical, industrial engineering, laboratory, printing, communications, record center, and personnel services. Only a narrow percentage of 501(e) organizations can make the cut to get 501(c) (3) status. If you answered yes to this item, call IRS and discuss the specifics and also read http://www.irs.gov/irm/part7/irm_07-025-024.html#d0e10 before submitting your application.

## LINE 17: COOPERATIVE SERVICE ORGANIZATIONS OF OPERATING EDUCATIONAL ORGANIZATIONS

These organizations perform collective investment services for educational organizations. IRS Publication 557 advises that if you answer yes to this item, call IRS and discuss the specifics of your eligibility for 501(c) (3) status because this type of organization falls under Section 501(f) but the Form 1023 is still used to apply.

## LINE 18: CHARITABLE RISK POOL

This type of organization provides insurance. If that describes you, contact IRS and discuss the details to determine if you are eligible for tax exempt status. The IRS website lists the following criteria for exemption:

A charitable risk pool is treated as organized and operated exclusively for charitable purposes if it:

1. Is organized and operated only to pool insurable risks of its members (not including risks related to medical malpractice) and to provide information to its members about loss control and risk management,
2. Consists only of members that are section 501(c) (3) organizations exempt from tax under section 501(a)
3. Is organized under state law authorizing this type of risk pooling,
4. Is exempt from state income tax, or will be after qualifying as a Section 501(c) (3) organization,
5. Has obtained at least $1,000,000 in startup capital from nonmember charitable organizations,
6. Is controlled by a board of directors elected by its members, and
7. Is organized under documents requiring that:

    a. Each member be a section 501(c) (3) organization exempt from tax under section 501(a)
    b. Each member that receives a final determination that it no longer qualified under section 501(c) (3) notify the pool immediately, and

   c.  Each insurance policy issued by the pool provide that it will not cover events occurring after a final determination described in (b).

## LINE 19: DO YOU OR WILL YOU OPERATE A SCHOOL?

You have extra paperwork to submit if you are applying for 501(c)(3) status as a school, as well as proving you have a well-publicized nondiscrimination policy. IRS defines a school as:

> *"An educational organization whose primary function is the presentation of formal instruction and which normally maintains a regular faculty and curriculum and normally has a regularly enrolled body of pupils or students in attendance at the place where its educational activities are regularly carried on."*

This may include any level of compulsory education as well as higher education, trade and technical schools, and preschools or nurseries. In addition, schools that are part of museums, historical societies, or churches are also eligible. You will have to fill out Schedule B with your application. For specifics, read IRS Publication 557 located at http://www.irs.gov/pub/irs-pdf/p557.pdf beginning on page 27.

## LINE 20: HOSPITAL OR MEDICAL CARE

This type of organization treats medical conditions, including mental disability, either on an inpatient or outpatient basis. IRS recognizes rehab, mental health, and drug treatment centers; and medical education and research facilities as part of this category. You must complete Schedule C as part of your application. There are many rules for this category and I suggest you call IRS and discuss the specifics before filing Form 1023. In addition, read these new guidelines found at http://www.irs.gov/Charities-&-Non-

Profits/Charitable-Organizations/New-Requirements-for-501(c)
(3)-Hospitals-Under-the-Affordable-Care-Act

## LINE 21: ELDERLY OR HANDICAPPED AND LOW INCOME HOUSING

IRS instructions give the following definitions and guidance:

"Low-income housing" refers to rental or ownership housing provided to persons based on financial need.

"Elderly housing" refers to rental or ownership housing provided to persons based on age, including retirement, assisted-living, independent living, continuous care, and life care arrangements.

"Handicapped housing" refers to rental or ownership housing provided to persons based on physical or mental disabilities, including nursing homes. If you are a skilled nursing facility, you should also complete *Schedule C*.

This category has many rules to comply with, so I suggest you contact IRS and discuss your specifics before filing. You must also file Schedule F with your application. You may also want to read the revenue rulings contained in this document: http://www.irs.gov/pub/irs-tege/eotopicg04.pdf

## LINE 22: SCHOLARSHIPS, FELLOWSHIPS, LOANS, AND GRANTS

IRS instructions for this line include the following guidance:

Answer "Yes" if you pay monies to an individual as a scholarship, fellowship, or educational loan, for travel, study, or other similar purposes. Also answer "Yes" if you pay such amounts on behalf of an individual to a school or a tuition or educational savings program.

Travel, study, or other similar purposes include payments made to enhance a literary, artistic, musical, scientific, teaching or other similar capacity, skill, or talent of the individual recipient. For example amounts paid to:

- Vocational high school students to be used to purchase basic tools.
- Teachers to induce them to teach in an economically depressed public school system.
- A scientific researcher to underwrite that individual's research project.

Educational grants do not include amounts you pay to an individual as compensation, such as payments made to a consultant for personal services or to produce a report for you.

Educational grants do not include amounts paid to another organization that distributes your funds as a scholarship to an individual if you have no role in the selection process.

There is an excellent article on scholarships located at http://www.hembar.com/media/pnc/9/media.219.pdf that you may want to read. IRS has much to say about grants and scholarships as well and a summary appears at http://www.irs.gov/pub/irs-tege/eotopicn82.pdf for your review.

Robert Sumner of Sumner & Associates, P.C., posted some very clear guidance on scholarships at http://www.sumnerfirm.com/2011/06/scholarship-programs-conducted-by-association-related-501c3-foundations/ that may be helpful to you. IRS will want a copy of your scholarship application with the Form 1023, and a completed Schedule H.

# CHAPTER 21

## PART IX: FINANCIAL DATA

*"The principle is competing against yourself. It's about self-improvement, about being better than you were the day before."*

—Steve Young

The MLSE Team Up Foundation strives to improve the lives of youth by building facilities, giving to sustainable programs and empowering youth through sports and recreation. The MLSE Team Up Foundation is the charitable arm of Maple Leaf Sports & Entertainment (MLSE), combining the philanthropic efforts of all four MLSE teams – the Toronto Maple Leafs, Toronto Raptors, Toronto FC and Toronto Marlies. Launched in December 2009 and building on the past successes of the Raptors Foundation for Kids and the Leafs Fund for Kids, the MLSE Team Up Foundation is committed to making an even bigger difference for youth across Ontario.

## LOOKING AT THE FINANCES

This section may seem difficult or tricky, but it does not have to be. IRS wants to know what has occurred financially to date with your organization, and/or what you expect to happen in the near future (the next few years). If you are a brand new organization that has had nothing but minimal financial support or transactions, then this part is very easy to complete. Just remember that what you put in this section has to match the rest of the application including the narrative. Also be aware that IRS issued an update (Notice 1382 available at www.irs.gov/pub/irs-pdf/n1382.pdf requiring financial information for three years if you are less than one year old, and four years if you are more than one year old).

Bear in mind that the application filing fee is based on the actual (for organizations that have been around for a while) or projected (for new organizations just getting started) income of the organization.

If the average combined gross revenue over a four year period of time is less than $10,000 per year, the filing fee is currently $400. If it is over $10,000 a year, the fee is $850. The application says $300 and $750 because IRS did not reprint the form, they simply issued an update stating the price had gone up. If you do not know what your revenues will be, give it your best educated guess. IRS will not penalize you for being over or under if you are projecting. Do the best you can. A projection is a guess, a prediction, an estimate.

If you are using a standard financial software program like QuickBooks, you can print the required reports and attach them instead of filling out the forms in Part IX. Simply write "See Attached" and place the reports behind the appropriate page of the application so that the IRS agent won't have to look for it. The easier you make it, the less time and correspondence will be required to get your determination letter.

You will need a statement of revenue and expenses (either actual, projected, or a combination of the two), and a balance sheet. That's it. Don't let the columns and categories overwhelm you. It's possible that much of it doesn't even apply to your organization. If a line doesn't apply to you, leave it blank or put in a zero and move on.

**HINT:** Start by putting zeroes on all the lines in all the columns that do not apply. That way you can see progress immediately and only have to deal with the blanks that do not have zeroes. This can make the task seem easier and less complicated.

**October 2013 Revision** defines "Years in existence" as completed tax years. Instructions below incorporate these October 2013 changes, although they will not be on the actual forms until IRS publishes a revised form.

**If you have been in existence for five or more years,** chances are you already have financial statements for that timeframe. IRS wants to see them for the past five years or as long as you have been in business if it is less than five years. Attach them on the *Revenue and Expenses* form, include the current year and the previous up to three years financial data, and attach the rest to provide financial data for up to five years. Complete the balance sheet for the previous tax year and remember to end it on the last day of the last month of the last full tax year. For example, if your tax year ends December 31, then the balance sheet would have an ending date of December 31 last year.

**If you have been in existence for one, but less than four years,** attach your own revenue and expense statements. Or use the first column to provide revenue and expenses for this year to date (actually as of the last day of last month). Use the other columns for years you have existed prior to this year, and any leftover columns to project your income and expenses to the best of your ability for future years. This way you are providing four full years of either actual or projected income, plus information for this year to date. Be sure to put correct dates in the columns so that IRS knows what is actual and what is projected. Mark any attached financial statements clearly so there is no misinterpretation of whether you are giving past historical financial data, or projections of what you expect to happen. Remember, if you have completed one full tax year, IRS wants to see up to four years of financial statements, depending on how long you have been operating.

**If you have been in existence less than one year,** this is going to be so easy! You get to make the whole thing up for three years, giving it your best effort to determine the most likely income and expenses. So what if you don't know for sure? Give it your best shot. Start somewhere, and think it through. Don't stress out over it. Just do it! No penalty for being wrong, but be as accurate as you can, knowing full well you won't know the real numbers until after the fact. IRS knows it is not accurate, you know it is not accurate, but they make you do it anyway. So just do it.

You can do this, it is just paperwork, one line at a time, so let's get started:

## LINE 1: GIFTS, GRANTS, AND CONTRIBUTIONS RECEIVED (DO NOT INCLUDE UNUSUAL GIFTS)

Unusual grants are unexpected large sums received from a disinterested party. Because the amount is large, it can affect your organization's classification as a public charity which must be supported primarily by the general public. For this reason, grants like this are reported further down on the form on Line 12.

On line 1, you report gifts, grants, and contributions from various sources that help you accomplish your tax-exempt purpose. You also report government units helping you that provide a service or facility to the general public (as opposed to a specific group). If you receive revenue to complete a program or function for the general public (for example, hired by someone or an organization), report it on this line. If you sell tickets to the general public as opposed to being hired for a fee to perform, that income goes on Line 9, Gross Receipts. If you are not sure which line to put the income on, contact IRS and ask before filling out the form.

## LINE 2: MEMBERSHIP FEES

Most charitable nonprofits do not have membership fees because they do not have members. If you do have members and you charge a membership fee to support the organization, put the total of the fees on this line. Do not include fees charged to members for anything except membership. Any other fees paid (such as for admission, merchandise, services, or use of facilities) are gross receipts, not membership fees.

## LINE 3: GROSS INVESTMENT INCOME

Any income received from any investment (loans, rents, royalties, dividends, interest, etc.) is entered here.

## LINE 4: NET UNRELATED BUSINESS INCOME

Do you have any income from unrelated business activity? Any income of which less than 85% of the labor was not completed by volunteers? Any income that did not have anything to do with your exempt purpose? You report it on line 4. Contact IRS or see Publication 598 if you need more information on this line, specifically Chapter 4 to figure the unrelated business income. You can access it at http://www.irs.gov/publications/p598/

## LINE 5: TAXES LEVIED FOR YOUR BENEFIT

If the public paid any taxes on your behalf, include the amount collected here.

## LINE 6: VALUE OF SERVICES OR FACILITIES FURNISHED BY A GOVERNMENT UNIT WITHOUT CHARGE (NOT INCLUDING THE VALUE OF SERVICES GENERALLY FURNISHED TO THE PUBLIC WITHOUT CHARGE)

Use the fair market value that would be charged for an organization that is not tax exempt.

## LINE 7: ANY REVENUE NOT OTHERWISE LISTED ABOVE OR ON LINES 9–12 BELOW.

(Attach an itemized list) In my opinion, this line should have come AFTER line 12 because you have to complete lines 9–12 before you can answer this one. If you have other forms of income that do not fit into one of the other categories, put them here. Itemize them, and give a brief description (less brief if you think IRS needs more details to avoid sending you a letter asking for more information). If in doubt, contact IRS and ask before entering it here.

## LINE 8: TOTAL LINES 1 – 7

Use a calculator and add every column, as well as a total of all columns in the far right column.

## LINE 9: GROSS RECEIPTS FROM ADMISSIONS, MERCHANDISE SOLD, OR SERVICES PERFORMED, OR FURNISHING OF FACILITIES IN ANY ACTIVITY THAT IS RELATED TO YOUR EXEMPT PURPOSES

(Attach itemized list) Do not include amounts you have already included on other lines of this form. You only want to count the amounts once. If you received funds for use of facilities that was not for the direct benefit of the general public, list it here. You must itemize and include what government agency paid you, purpose of the payment, and the amount. If in doubt, contact IRS and see Publication 598 before filling out this line. You can access this publication at http://www.irs.gov/publications/p598/

## LINE 10: TOTAL OF LINES 8 AND 9

Enter the total of both lines in each column and combine the totals in the far right column.

## LINE 11: NET GAIN OR LOSS ON THE SALE OF CAPITAL ASSETS

(Attach the following schedule and see instructions) This is the format for the schedule referred to in this question (from the IRS website):

## FIGURE 2. PART IX-A. STATEMENT OF REVENUES AND EXPENSES LINE 11. NET GAIN OR (LOSS)

| | | Categories | | |
|---|---|---|---|---|
| | | (A) Real Estate | (B) Securities | (C) Other |
| 1. | Gross sales price of assets (other than inventory) by category. | | | |
| 2. | **Less:** Cost or other basis and sales expenses. | | | |
| 3. | Gain or (loss). Subtract line 2 from line 1. | | | |
| 4. | Net gain or (loss)–Add line 3 of columns (A), (B), and (C). Enter here and on Form 1023, *Part IX–A. Statement of Revenues and Expenses*, line 11. | | | |

If this line applies to your organization, put the total amounts for each category (not an itemized list). Create this format as best you can to include all required information, as an actual form does not exist.

## LINE 12: UNUSUAL GRANTS

Did you unexpectedly receive a large grant from an disinterested party? This is where you record it. You must also completely describe your unusual grant in Part X, line 7. More information is available in Publication 557 which can be accessed at http://www.irs.gov/uac/Publication-557,-Tax-Exempt-Status-for-Your-Organization-1

## LINE 13: TOTAL REVENUE. (ADD LINES 10-12)

Add each column, put in the total, and also the cumulative total in the far right column.

## LINE 14: FUNDRAISING EXPENSES

What are you spending (or plan to spend) for fundraising? If you hire a professional fundraiser, you must disclose the amount paid here as well. The income for fundraising should be on line 1, and this line has to do with any expenses incurred to make the fundraising revenue reported in line 1.

## LINE 15: CONTRIBUTIONS, GIFTS, GRANTS, AND SIMILAR AMOUNTS PAID OUT

(Attach itemized list). Who received it? How much? What for? If disclosing the name of the individual receiving the payout violates privacy provisions (such as names of those who receive scholarships), then lump the totals together and list them by program or category instead of by person.

## LINE 16: DISBURSEMENTS TO OR FOR THE BENEFIT OF MEMBERS

(Attach an itemized list) If you disbursed funds to members of your organization, full disclosure of who, how much, and why is required. IRS instructions for this form say not to include any amount already included in line 15. Make sure to explain this item completely. Exempt organizations under Section 501(c) (3) exist to benefit the public, not their members, so this area can be a little tricky. If in doubt, contact

IRS and talk with them about your specifics before filling out this line.

## LINE 17: COMPENSATION OF OFFICERS, DIRECTORS, AND TRUSTEES

In Part V of the application, you were asked to list the officers, directors, and trustees and their compensation. Make sure the information provided here matches the information given there. Enter the totals for all columns.

## LINE 18: OTHER SALARY AND WAGES

Do you have any employees who are not officers, directors, and trustees? Enter the totals paid to them in all columns.

## LINE 19: INTEREST EXPENSE

How much interest did you pay, if any? Do not include mortgage interest if it is being reported as part of an occupancy expense on line 20.

## LINE 20: OCCUPANCY

Utilities, mortgage interest, real estate taxes, janitorial services, rent, electricity, heat, etc. This includes all facilities for which you pay these expenses to complete your exempt purpose. Enter the total for all columns.

## LINE 21: DEPRECIATION AND DEPLETION

These are calculated the same way they would be in a for-profit organization, the same rules apply. If in doubt, contact IRS and ask before filling in this line.

## LINE 22: PROFESSIONAL FEES

Accounting, consulting, legal counsel, contract management, and other fees paid to people or organizations who are not your employees. Do not include professional fundraising fees here that you have already reported on line 14. Independent contractor fees would be reported on this line.

## LINE 23: ANY EXPENSE NOT OTHERWISE CLASSIFIED, SUCH AS PROGRAM SERVICES

(Attach itemized list) If you have expenses you have not included above, combine the totals here and make an itemized list. Examples of expenses that may not be included above could be the filing fee for this application and the cost of this book, postage, telephone service (if not included in occupancy above), vehicle expenses, insurance payments, website fees, even bank charges can be included here. This is the catch-all line very much like the one at the end of Schedule C of Form 1040 for business owners.

## LINE 24: TOTAL EXPENSES. (ADD LINES 14 -23)

Total the expenses in all columns.

### Balance Sheet

A balance sheet is a financial statement that ascertains the net worth of a business on a specific date. It includes the assets and the liabilities. If your financial software has a balance sheet program, you can print it and attach it behind this section. Just be sure to write "See Attached" on this section of application. If not, use the form in the application.

IRS wants to know the net worth as of the last day of the most recently completed tax year. If your tax year ends in December, then the date would be December 31 of last year. This is great news for a new nonprofit that did not exist on December 31 last year. Every line gets a zero and you are ready to move on.

If your organization did exist as of the last day of your most recent tax year, then the information you provide should reflect the status as of that date.

## Assets

### LINE 1: CASH

Combine all short term assets (less than one year until maturity) and put the total in. This includes, cash, petty cash, money in checking and savings accounts, money markets, certificates of deposit, treasury bills, etc.

### LINE 2: ACCOUNTS RECEIVABLE, NET

Unpaid accounts that you expect to collect from sales or services, minus any reserve for bad debts.

### LINE 3: INVENTORIES

What do you have on hand that you bought, or made, and are either going to use or sell in the future? What is the inventory worth after you subtract the cost to produce or acquire it?

### LINE 4. BONDS AND NOTES RECEIVABLE

(Attach an itemized list) This item is for bonds or notes your organization issued that you expect to be repaid to you. The itemized list needs to include the borrower's name, what the form of the obligation is and a description, the rate of return, when it is due and how much is due.

## LINE 5: CORPORATE STOCKS

(Attach an itemized list) What is the fair market value of stocks your organization holds? The itemized list should include any stocks from closely-held corporations (those companies in which although the public owns some stock, most of it is held by a few people who have no plans to sell it). Include the name of the company, its capital structure, how many shares are held, and the fair market value. For stock listed on an exchange or sold in sufficient quantities OTC to make it liquid, you must include the name of the company, the exchange, identify the stock and number of shares, and the fair market value.

## LINE 6: LOANS RECEIVABLE

(Attach an itemized list) If your organization made loans, either uncollateralized or mortgage loans, you must list each loan separately and who the loans were made to, the amount, the purpose, what interest rate, and terms for how the loan is being paid back. Total all the loans and put that amount on line 6.

## LINE 7: OTHER INVESTMENTS

(Attach an itemized list) This is where you list items, government securities, or properties held for investment. List them separately on an attached sheet and give the value of each.

## LINE 8: DEPRECIABLE AND DEPLETABLE ASSETS

(Attach an itemized list) This is where you list items, equipment, or buildings not held for investment. Be sure to include the cost basis of the item in the itemized list. The cost basis is the original cost minus depreciation.

## LINE 9: LAND

This is where you list land that the organization owns that is not for investment.

## LINE 10: OTHER ASSETS

(Attach an itemized list) Anything else the organization owns, including patents and intellectual property gets a book value assigned and is listed here.

## LINE 11: TOTAL ASSETS (ADD LINES 1 THROUGH 10)

Add them all up and put in the total.

### Liabilities

## LINE 12: ACCOUNTS PAYABLE

Include bills that need to be paid or are payable but not yet due. For example, suppliers, salaries, accumulated payroll taxes, and interest.

## LINE 13: CONTRIBUTIONS, GIFTS, GRANTS, ETC. PAYABLE

What commitments have you made that you have not yet paid for? For example, are you obligated to a scholarship but have not written the check? This category includes individuals and organizations you have made commitments to.

## LINE 14: MORTGAGES AND NOTES PAYABLE

(Attach an itemized list) What is the balance due for notes and mortgages at the end of the current tax year/period? On the itemized list, show each note or mortgage, the lender, purpose, repayment terms, interest rate, and the original amount of the loan.

## LINE 15: OTHER LIABILITIES

(Attach an itemized list) If you owe anything else, put it here and list it on the attachment with enough details to satisfy the IRS agent's curiosity.

## LINE 16: TOTAL LIABILITIES

Add lines 12 through 15. Put the total in on this line.

### Fund Balances or Net Assets

## LINE 17: TOTAL FUND BALANCES OR NET ASSETS

Assets minus liabilities equals fund balances and may also be called net assets. For purposes here, if your software program uses fund accounting, report it. Otherwise, use only net assets which include capital stock, paid-in capital, retained earnings or accumulated income, and endowment funds. More details are available at http://www.irs.gov/instructions/i990/ch02.html#d0e10850

## LINE 18: TOTAL LIABILITIES AND FUND BALANCES OR NET ASSETS (ADD LINES 16 AND 17)

Put the total on this line.

## LINE 19: HAVE THERE BEEN ANY SUBSTANTIAL CHANGES IN ASSETS OR LIABILITIES SINCE THE END OF THE PERIOD SHOWN ABOVE?

If "Yes," explain. Don't forget to explain why the change occurred.

# CHAPTER 22

## PART X: PUBLIC CHARITY STATUS

*"Set your goals high, and don't stop till you get there."*

—Bo Jackson

**NOMAD SPORTS ACADEMY FOR ORPHANS AND UNDERPRIVILEGED YOUTH** is a unique community of orphans and marginalized young people of Zambia who train to become professional athletes. The Academy was founded by John Nomad and his wife, Carmen, a Canadian couple that spent most of the last 20 years in Africa working with affected people in several countries.

### WHY YOU ARE A PUBLIC CHARITY

Part X is where you establish yourself as a public charity, which is eligible for 501(c) (3), instead of a private foundation. If it is the latter, donations may not be completely deductible (often limited to 30%–50%). It is not the intent of this book to cover private foundations. If you are a private foundation, I suggest you consult IRS about your requirements.

In the beginning of this book, we looked at why you would be a public charity instead of a private foundation. In brief, your source of income in a private foundation does not come from the public, while a public charity's revenues do. To be a public charity, you must be a church, school, hospital, government unit, be testing for public safety, receive most of your support from the general public, or support other organizations that are public charities. Otherwise, you are a private foundation.

## LINE 1A: ARE YOU A PRIVATE FOUNDATION?

If you can answer "No" because you are a public charity, go to Line 5. A private foundation is one in which most of the support comes from predetermined sources such as a specific company or family. Private foundations pay some taxes on their investment income and cannot do as they want or invest where they want to. There are some restrictions that affect your operation.

## LINE 1B: MANDATORY PROVISIONS

If you answer "Yes," to Line 1a, your organizing documents must contain the required language for tax exempt eligibility, and you must include an explanation giving the location of these provisions in your documents.

Well over half the states require the mandatory provisions be included in the foundation's governing instruments. Details can be found in the following revenue ruling: http://www.irs.gov/pub/irs-tege/rr75-038.pdf You can also see *Publication 557, Chapter 3, Section 501(c) (3) Organizations, Private Foundations* for examples of required wording in organizing documents. You can access this publication http://www.irs.gov/publications/p557/ch03.html#en_US_2011_publink1000200115 and then find section 508(e) by scrolling about a third of the way down the webpage.

## LINE 2: DIRECT INVOLVEMENT FOR THE ACTIVE CONDUCT OF TAX EXEMPT PURPOSES

If your foundation actually runs its own programs instead of contributes money to other organizations running tax exempt programs, then you check "Yes," continue the application. If "No," sign the application at the end of Part XI.

## LINE 3: HAVE YOU EXISTED FOR ONE OR MORE YEARS?

If "Yes," attach financial statements and sign Part XI. If no, continue.

## LINE 4: ATTACHMENTS

If you have been around for less than a year, then you need proof or at least verification from an attorney of what your operations are and how you will fund them, and that they satisfy the requirements to be categorized as a private foundation. If you do not have opinion of counsel, you can provide a statement giving the required information.

## LINE 5: TYPE OF PUBLIC CHARITY.

Somewhere in the list for line 5, you will find the type that fits your charity. If unsure, contact IRS and ask them to help you decide. Many organizations select 5g because they rely on the public for much of their support and they do not fall into some other category such as a church, school, a hospital, or exist to support another tax exempt organization.

If you select 5a, 5b, 5c, or 5d, you have an additional schedule to complete. Instructions for these schedules are contained in the next chapter.

If you select 5e, 5f, 5g, 5h, or 5i, you do not have any additional schedules to complete. You can select 5i and let IRS decide what type of public charity you are. This will delay approval of tax exempt status if they determine you are one of the categories that need to fill out an additional schedule.

For public charity status, there is a one-third public support test you must meet or a 10% facts and circumstance test. It's not that complicated. If at least one third of your support comes from the public, you can have public charity status. If between 10% and 33% comes from the public, but there are circumstances to be considered, then you may qualify under the facts and circumstances test. For more information, see IRS Basic Determination Rules at http://www.irs.gov/pub/irs-tege/eotopicj93.pdf

## LINE 6A: ADVANCED RULING

This section no longer applies and should not be filled out. DO NOT SIGN IT. IRS did not reprint the form to eliminate it, they simply issued an update (Notice 1382 saying not to fill it out anymore). A copy of Notice 1382 is located at http://www.irs.gov/pub/irs-pdf/n1382.pdf

## LINE 6B: DEFINITIVE RULING

If you are less than five years old, you get a pass on this question as well. Notice 1382 says not to complete it unless your organization is at least five years old. A copy of Notice 1382 is available at http://www.irs.gov/pub/irs-pdf/n1382.pdf

If you are more than five years old, you have already completed the financial data so that you can answer the questions in Line 6b.

## LINE 7: UNUSUAL GRANTS

Once again, Notice 1382 http://www.irs.gov/pub/irs-pdf/n1382.pdf made this line to only apply to organizations that have been operating for five or more years.

# CHAPTER 23

## PART X: SCHEDULES A, B, C, D

*"The key to winning is poise under stress."*

—Paul Brown

 Progression Athletics International (PAI) is a nonprofit 501(c) (3) organization. We use athletics as a platform to positively influence at-risk youth in our community and around the world by teaching life skills, accountability, leadership, importance of education, healthy lifestyle choices and cultural diversity. One thing that makes PAI unique is the fact we are 100% volunteer based from our C.E.O. and all the way down to our volunteers. EVERY penny donated to the organization is used for the youth we serve and does not go to any compensation. (CA)

## SCHEDULE A: CHURCHES

If it looks like a church, acts like a church, and functions like a church, it is probably a church. This classification includes mosques, temples, synagogues, etc. There must be a congregation or other membership. IRS has some specific attributes it wants to know about. You do not need to have them all, but if some are missing that are typical for a church, or if the congregation is very small, it may create some thought of fraud or misrepresentation in the IRS agent's mind. Here is the list of attributes according to IRS:

- A distinct legal existence
- A recognized creed and form of worship
- A definite and distinct ecclesiastical government
- A formal code of doctrine and discipline
- A distinct religious history
- A membership not associated with any other church or denomination
- Ordained ministers ministering to the congregation
- Ordained ministers selected after completing prescribed courses of study
- A literature of its own
- Established places of worship
- Regular congregations
- Regular religious services
- Sunday schools for the religious instruction of the young
- Schools for the preparation of ministers

## LINE 1A: WRITTEN STATEMENT OF FAITH

Your written creed, statement of faith, or summary of beliefs must be attached.

## LINE 1B: FORM OF WORSHIP

What are the practices of your church that show your dedication to your beliefs?

## LINE 2A: CODE OF DOCTRINE AND DISCIPLINE

What laws or rules do you function under?

## LINE 2B: RELIGIOUS HISTORY

Give an overview of how you came into being, tell your history and milestones.

## LINE 2C: LITERATURE

Any writings containing any of the above items: practices, rules, laws, doctrines, history.

## LINE 3: RELIGIOUS HIERARCHY OR ECCLESIASTICAL GOVERNMENT

What is the chain of command?

## LINE 4A: REGULARLY SCHEDULED RELIGIOUS SERVICES

Give days of the week and times, order of events, and an explanation of how these activities further your religious purpose. Include copies of church bulletins, pamphlets, or other printed material handed out to members or the public.

## LINE 4B: AVERAGE ATTENDANCE

If the congregation numbers are small, IRS is suspicious.

## LINE 5A AND 5B: ESTABLISHED PLACE OF WORSHIP AND OWNERSHIP

You do not need to own the location which you use to conduct services. You can rent it or it can be provided to you for no charge. If you do not have a location, where are you meeting?

## LINE 6: ESTABLISHED CONGREGATION

This means an established membership that includes people from more than one family. If you do not have an established membership yet, you can wait to file the application until you do, or choose another public charity type on Part X, Line 5 of Form 1023. If in doubt, contact IRS and discuss your circumstances. Very small congregations are suspect to IRS.

## LINE 7: NUMBER OF MEMBERS

Enter number of members or if none, enter zero.

## LINE 8A, 8B, 8C, AND 8D: PROCESS TO BECOME A MEMBER

Answer "Yes" if you keep records of who is currently a member. If all your members are from the same family, you are not classified as a church. Give IRS the details requested to determine how a person would become a member of your church and what the benefits of that membership are. Attach a copy of an application if one exists.

## LINE 9: CHURCH RITES AND RITUALS PERFORMED

These include weddings, baptisms, funerals, and other rites.

## LINE 10: RELIGIOUS INSTRUCTION

Do you have regularly scheduled youth or children's educational activities such as Sunday school?

## LINE 11A AND 11B: PRESCRIBED COURSE OF STUDY

What training has your minister or religious leader completed? Self-ordination, self-study, or methods that did not include a formal course of instruction and learning do not qualify as a prescribed course of study.

## LINE 12: IS YOUR RELIGIOUS LEADER AN OFFICIAL IN YOUR CHURCH?

If the minister or other religious leader is listed in Part V, Line 1a, check "Yes."

## LINE 13: DO YOU ORDAIN, COMMISSION, OR LICENSE MINISTERS?

If so, include an explanation of the requirements to be ordained, commissioned, or licensed.

## LINE 14: ARE YOU PART OF A GROUP OF CHURCHES WITH SIMILAR BELIEFS AND STRUCTURES?

Are you part of a convention, association, or union of churches? Include the name of the group you are part of.

## LINE 15: DO YOU ISSUE CHURCH CHARTERS?

If so, what are the requirements for issuing a charter?

## LINE 16: FEE FOR CHARTER

If you paid a fee for a church charter, include a copy of the charter. Be sure to tell which organization provided the charter and their requirements. Do not include organizational charters from the Secretary of State, Franchise Tax Board, or other governmental administrative function.

### LINE 17: ADDITIONAL INFORMATION

Is there anything else you want IRS to know to decide if you qualify for tax exemption as a church? Attach it to the package or include it in the narrative.

# SCHEDULE B: SCHOOLS, COLLEGES, AND UNIVERSITIES

Not all schools are created equal and not all schools qualify for tax exempt status. Your organization is only qualified if your main activity is conducting formal instruction, if you have scheduled habitual customary curriculum, qualified teachers, an identifiable student body who take classes on a regular basis, and there is an identifiable location for these classes and students to meet to conduct this formal, habitual, scheduled curricular instruction. Sounds like a mouthful, but it is the IRS making sure you actually are conducting instruction, not running a diploma mill.

IRS definition of school includes "primary, secondary, preparatory, high schools, colleges, and universities." Home schools do not qualify for tax exempt status.

## Section I: Operational Information

### LINES 1A AND 1B: DO YOU QUALIFY AS A SCHOOL?

If you can answer "Yes" to both questions, provide requested descriptions in the narrative and move on. If not, you are NOT a school for tax exempt purposes.

### LINES 2A AND 2B: ARE YOU A PUBLIC SCHOOL?

If you can answer "Yes" to both questions, provide requested descriptions in the narrative and move on. If not, do not fill out the rest of Schedule B.

## LINE 3: YOUR LOCATION

What is the name of the public school district, and county where you conduct instruction?

## LINES 4, 5, AND 6: DISCRIMINATORY PRACTICES

These questions seek to determine if you discriminate based on race, color, and national or ethnic origin. If you do, you do not qualify for tax exempt status. Include a copy of your bylaws containing your nondiscrimination policy. If it is not included in your formal organizing or operating documents, include a copy of your signed resolution approving a nondiscrimination policy.

## LINE 7: FAIR MARKET VALUE OF SERVICES

It is possible that if this applies to your school, you have already answered this question back in Part VIII, question 7. If so, you can reference that answer, but be sure and include any additional information requested that is not included in Part VIII.

## LINE 8: WHO WILL MANAGE YOUR ACTIVITIES?

If you select "No" be sure to include all required documentation. You can reference Part VIII if you have already provided this information.

### Section II: Establishment of Racially Nondiscriminatory Policy

Revenue Procedure 75-50 located at http://www.irs.gov/pub/irs-tege/rp1975-50.pdf requires that you not only have a racial nondiscrimination policy, but that you also publicize it. The statement that must be used is included in quotes in the next paragraph.

Revenue Ruling 71-447 located at http://www.irs.gov/pub/irs-tege/rr71-447.pdf clarifies what nondiscrimination means in terms of tax exempt status,

*"The _____ School admits the students of any race to all the rights, privileges, programs, and activities generally accorded or made available to students at that school and that the school does not discriminate on the basis of race in administration of its educational policies, admissions policies, scholarship and loan programs, and athletic and other school-administered programs."*

In addition, nondiscrimination statements must be included in all brochures, advertisements, catalogs, and other printed materials given to the public and the student body. Don't forget to include it on internet pages. The exact wording IRS likes to see is:

*"The _____ School admits students of any race, color, and national or ethnic origin."*

## LINE 1: DO YOU HAVE A NONDISCRIMINATORY POLICY IN EFFECT?

If you do not, you must approve a resolution implementing one and attach evidence to this application that you have one in place or you will be denied tax exempt status.

## LINE 2: IS THE NONDISCRIMINATORY POLICY PUBLICIZED IN YOUR DOCUMENTS?

If "Yes," attach a copy of one of your documents like a brochure or catalog that shows how you are marking your documents. If "No," that means you agree to put the policy in all future documents for the public or student body.

## LINE 3: PUBLICATION IN A GENERAL CIRCULATION NEWSPAPER

You have to prove to IRS that the public knows you do not discriminate. The easiest way to meet this requirement is to publish the following statement in the newspaper annually. If you have done so, send the entire newspaper page with the application. No partial pages or copies from a copying machine are acceptable. The newspaper disclosure should read:

"The _____ School admits the students of any race to all the rights, privileges, programs, and activities generally accorded or made available to students at that school and that the school does not discriminate on the basis of race in administration of its educational policies, admissions policies, scholarship and loan programs, and athletic and other school-administered programs."

Specific guidance is available in Revenue Ruling 75-50, located at http://www.irs.gov/pub/irs-tege/rp1975-50.pdf

## LINE 5: RACIAL COMPOSITION

IRS wants numbers of students, not percentages. Do not include names of staff, faculty, or students, just the actual number (or projected number if you are just starting out) in each category. If you are estimating, you have to submit information explaining to IRS how you came up with the estimates. You can use census data for your area and estimate based on percentages from the census. If your numbers differ significantly from the census data submitted, you have to explain why.

## LINE 6: RACIAL COMPOSITION FOR LOANS AND SCHOLARSHIPS

Use current year actual numbers and projected numbers for next academic year.

## LINE 7A AND 7B: LIST OF THOSE WHO WERE INSTRUMENTAL IN STARTING THE SCHOOL AND WHETHER THEY WANT TO SEGREGATE

For 7a, provide a list of all incorporators, founders, board members, donors of land, and donors of buildings. Then in 7b, explain any circumstance in which any of those listed in 7a have an objective to keep public or private education segregated by race. Schools who promote segregation are not eligible for tax exempt status.

## LINE 8: RECORDS FOR THREE YEARS

Revenue Ruling 75-50 requires you to keep specific records if you want to get and keep tax exempt status. You need to maintain records for a minimum of three years showing your school's racial composition, evidence that your scholarships and loans are awarded without discrimination, copies of solicitation materials for contributions, copies of brochures, advertisements, application forms, catalogs, etc. If you plan to do that or are already doing it, answer "Yes." If "No" you must explain how you plan to meet these requirements.

# SCHEDULE C: HOSPITALS AND MEDICAL RESEARCH ORGANIZATIONS

If you are a cooperative hospital service organization, you do not need to fill out Schedule C. It is only used if you are a hospital or medical research organization operated in combination with a hospital. If the main function of an organization is medical treatment services, it qualifies as a medical care facility even though it may be operating on an outpatient basis. Treatment can be for physical or mental conditions and includes drug treatment centers.

The definition of hospital does not include convalescent homes, children or elderly homes, or institutions providing job training for the handicapped.

According to IRS guidelines, a medical research organization is one whose "principal purpose or function is the direct, continuous, and active conduct of medical research in conjunction with a hospital." In addition, IRS requires that "the research must be to discover, develop, or verify knowledge relating to the causes, diagnosis, treatment, prevention, or control of human physical or mental diseases and impairments."

Hospitals complete Section I of Schedule C. Medical Research Organizations complete Section II.

## Section I: Hospitals

### LINE 1: WHO HAS STAFF PRIVILEGES?

If all doctors in your area have staff privileges or are only restricted due to capacity, then mark "Yes." If "No," describe how you determine which courtesy staff has privileges at your facility and the exact criteria and selection procedures used.

### LINES 2A, B, C: INSURANCE, SELF-PAY, MEDICARE, AND MEDICAID

If you restrict admission in any of these categories, you must provide an explanation of how and why you restrict patient admittance to exclude any of these categories.

### LINE 3A AND 3B: MEDICARE/MEDICAID DEPOSITS

If you require a deposit, how do you determine the amount, and why do you require it? Is a similar deposit required of patients who do not have Medicare or Medicaid? If not, why not? Describe in detail.

### LINES 4A, 4B, AND 4C: EMERGENCY SERVICES

What provisions do you have to treat emergencies when someone cannot pay? Do you have a written policy? Do you have written or verbal agreements with first responders concerning emergency services? Describe them and include copies of written policies and agreements. If you have verbal agreements, explain them in detail to include how and when the agreement was made.

## LINES 5A, 5B, 5C, 5D, 5E: PROVISIONS FOR CHARITY PATIENTS

Describe in detail how you handle charity patients.

## LINES 6A AND 6B: MEDICAL TRAINING AND COMMUNITY EDUCATION

Include details of how your program works and any organizational affiliations.

## LINE 7: OFFICE SPACE TO PHYSICIANS

If you lease to physicians, you must show IRS that you are getting fair market value for the space and provide representative copies of leases.

## LINE 8: GOVERNING BOARDS

This question seeks to ascertain whether your board of directors is representative of the community where you are located. IRS instructions for this item give this exact guidance:

Answer "Yes" if you have a board of directors that is representative of the community you serve. Include a list of each board member with the individual's name and employment affiliation. Also, for each board member, describe how that individual represents the community. Generally, hospital employees and staff physicians are not individuals considered to be community representatives.

Answer "Yes" if an organization described in section 501(c) (3) with a community board exercises rights or powers over you, such as the right to appoint members to your governing board of directors and the power to approve certain transactions. Describe these rights and powers. In addition, describe how each of that organization's board of directors represents the community.

Answer "Yes" if you are subject to a state corporate practice of medicine law that requires your governing board to be composed solely of physicians licensed to practice medicine in the state. If you answer "Yes" on this basis, also provide the following information:

Describe whether a hospital described in section 501(c) (3) exercises any rights or powers over you.

Identify the corporate practice of medicine law under which you operate.

Explain how the section 501(c) (3) hospital exercises any rights or powers over you, such as the right to appoint members to your governing board of directors and the right to approve certain transactions.

Explain what services you provide to the section 501(c) (3) hospital.

## LINE 9: JOINT VENTURES

Make sure that if you participate in joint ventures, you answer each part of this question and your answers match Part VIII, Line 8.

## LINE 10: MANAGING YOUR PROGRAMS

If you contract the management of your programs, provide all requested information and make sure your answers match Part VIII, Line 7b.

## LINE 11: PHYSICIAN RECRUITMENT INCENTIVES

It is okay to offer incentives to recruit physicians, especially in shortage areas. Disclose all incentives in detail.

## LINE 12: DO YOU LEASE FROM PHYSICIANS WHO HAVE A FINANCIAL OR PROFESSIONAL RELATIONSHIP WITH YOUR HOSPITAL?

This question includes any physician you have a business relationship with: employees, staff physicians, those who are in a joint venture with you, or those you have service contracts with. How did you establish fair market value?

## LINE 13: PURCHASE FROM BUSINESS COLLEAGUES

If you purchased an existing medical practice, supplies, equipment, or any other business asset from anyone you had a business relationship with, you must disclose it, and how you established fair market value. Include copies of sales contracts and appraisals.

## LINE 14: CONFLICT OF INTEREST POLICY

If you do not have one in place, how do you avoid conflicts in business dealings? If you do have one, does it meet or exceed the IRS example? How did you adopt it: bylaws, resolution, etc.? You can review the example available at http://www.irs.gov/instructions/i1023/ar03.html

Having a conflict of interest policy is not required by tax law, but IRS looks at it as one more step to ensure that you are operating to benefit the community and not for private advantage or gain.

### Section II: Medical Research Organizations

## LINE 1: RELATIONSHIPS WITH HOSPITALS

Provide a list of all hospitals you work with, describe the nature of the interaction and relationships, and attach copies of all agreements.

## LINE 2: SCHEDULE OF ACTIVITIES

Whether actual or proposed, provide a schedule of your activities that directly support your medical research. Include the characteristics and features of the activities and how much money you are spending or will spend on each activity. According to IRS, making grants to other organizations is not an activity of your research.

## LINE 3: ASSETS

List your assets, their fair market value, and what percentage of each asset is being used for research.

# SCHEDULE D: SECTION 509(A) (3) SUPPORTING ORGANIZATION

If you chose Part IX, line 5d, you have to complete Schedule D because you said you are an organization that only gives money to other nonprofit organizations. This is common when you are a supporting arm of an established tax exempt organization that doesn't want to detract from its nonprofit mission to raise funds. So you are the fundraising body that supports the other organization. This is permissible as long as you maintain control, but several possibilities exist that you may be controlled (in the eyes of IRS) by "disqualified persons."

Electing this schedule has many technical applications, and I strongly suggest you seek the help of a tax professional before filing to eliminate months of follow up paperwork to meet the intent and letter of the law for IRS. The technicalities are beyond the scope of this book. It is a book in itself, and is worth every cent you spend to get a professional to complete this schedule. You may want to go back and see if this is the best selection under Part IX. If another less complicated selection is possible, you may want to choose it.

However, if you are still sure you want to file Schedule D, here is some basic guidance and resources to figure out the technicalities.

If in doubt, contact IRS and talk with them about your specific circumstances before filing.

First of all, you can qualify as a public charity under Section 509(a) (3) if you operate entirely to benefit, perform the functions of, or carry out the purposes of one or more public charities listed in Section 509 (a) (1). This will include organizations who get their funding from a wide range of sources, such as churches, schools, hospitals, etc. You can also qualify as a public charity if you exclusively benefit Section 509(a) (2) organizations, which include organizations that get their funds from grants, donations, or fees for their nonprofit purpose.

You can also qualify as a supporting organization if you are supporting the charitable purposes of 501(c) (4) organizations (civil leagues, social welfare organizations, local associations of employees), 501(c) (5) organizations (labor, agriculture, and horticultural organizations), or 501(c) (6) organizations (business leagues, chambers of commerce, and real estate boards).

You also must meet a relationship test, and not be controlled directly or indirectly by "disqualified persons" which are defined at http://www.irs.gov/irm/part7/irm_07-027-020.html

An IRS guidance sheet is available at http://www.irs.gov/pub/irs-tege/509a3_typeiandii_guidesheet.pdf to help you determine if you qualify.

## Section 1: Identifying Information about Supporting Organizations

### LINE 1: ORGANIZATIONS YOU SUPPORT

Write the name, address, and employer identification number of every organization you support. Attach another sheet of paper if you have more than will fit in the blanks.

### LINE 2: ARE YOU SUPPORTING ORGANIZATIONS UNDER SECTION 509(A) (1) OR 509(A) (2)?

If "Yes" go to Section II, Line 1. If "No," continue this section.

## LINE 3: ARE SUPPORTING ORGANIZATIONS UNDER SECTION 501(C) (4), 501(C) (5), OR 501(C) (6)?

These organizations include: Civil leagues, social welfare organizations, local associations of employees. These are 501(c) (4) organizations; Labor, agriculture, and horticultural organizations. These are 501(c) (5) organizations; and Business leagues, chambers of commerce, and real estate boards. These are 501(c) (6) organizations. If so, you need to provide the financial data requested or otherwise explain how they are a public charity under Section 509(a) (1) or 509(a) (2).

### Section II: Relationship with Supported Organization(s)—Three Tests

According to IRS, a supporting organization must meet at least one of these three tests:

- Test 1: "Operated, supervised, or controlled by" one or more publicly supported organizations, or
- Test 2: "Supervised or controlled in connection with" one or more publicly supported organizations, or
- Test 3: "Operated in connection with" one or more publicly supported organizations.

## LINE 1: GOVERNING BOARD OR OFFICERS

Test 1 ascertains whether most of the governing board or officers are elected or appointed by the supported organization(s). If "Yes," you must give an explanation of how they are appointed or elected. If "No," go on to the next question.

## LINE 2: SERVING ON MORE THAN ONE GOVERNING BOARD

Test 2 ascertains whether most of the governing board members also serve on the governing board(s) of the supported organization(s). If

"Yes," you must give an explanation of how they are appointed or elected. If "No," go to the next question.

## LINE 3: RESPONSIVENESS TEST.

Test 3 ascertains whether you are a trust in which the supported organization(s) can force you to give an accounting under state law. If "Yes," explain and provide written proof that the supported organization(s) know they can make you give them an accounting. Then go to line 5. If "No," go on to the next question.

## LINES 4A, 4B, 4C, 4D, 4E: ALTERNATE WAYS TO MEET TEST 3

These five items are designed to provide an alternate method of qualifying under test 3. Basically, IRS wants to know the nature and extent of working relationships you maintain with supported organization(s), and how much input they have into your grand procedures, investment decisions, and use of funds. All "Yes" answers require documentation to substantiate.

## LINE 5: ACTIVITIES

This line ascertains whether you are operated in connection with supported organization(s). If you conduct activities that would otherwise be carried out by the supported organizations if you did not do them, answer "Yes" and give an explanation and skip the rest of Section II. If "No," continue with Section II.

## LINES 6A, 6B, 6C, 6D: NET INCOME DISTRIBUTION

This item provides an alternate way to meet the integral part criteria of test 3. If you distribute at least 85% of your annual net income to supported organization(s), you may qualify for public charity status. Provide requested explanations and lists. If you answer "No" to 6a, and to line 5, you do not qualify for public charity status. Go back and rethink the status you selected in Part X of Form 1023 to see if another selection is more appropriate.

## LINES 7A AND 7B: SPECIFYING SUPPORTED ORGANIZATION(S)

Look at your organizational document (Articles of Incorporation for example). Did you name the supported organization(s) in it? If "Yes," give the article and paragraph number and go to Section III. Include requested explanation of relationship(s).

If you cannot answer "Yes," you may want to amend your organizing document unless you can provide evidence of historical or continuing relationship between your organization and the supported organization(s). If you cannot do either, you do not qualify as a public charity. Go back to Part X of Form 1023 and rethink your selection to see if another selection is more appropriate.

### Section III: Organizational Test

## LINES 1A AND 1B: SUPPORTED ORGANIZATION(S) BY NAME

If you cannot answer "Yes," you do not qualify for public charity status. If you answered "No," you can go back and change your organizing documents. Otherwise, you do not meet the organizational test. You can still go back and change Part X of Form 1023 and select a different choice for public charity status eliminating the need to do Schedule D.

### Section IV: Disqualified Person Test

## LINES 1A, 1B, AND 1C: DISQUALIFIED PERSONS

Organizations controlled directly or indirectly by disqualified people make the organization ineligible for public charity status. Section

4946 of the IRS code gives the following guidelines on who is a disqualified person:

- Substantial Contributor (normally more than $5,000 a year if that is more than 2% of the total contributions of the previous year)
- Foundation manager (includes officers, directors, and trustees)
- Owner of more than 20% interest in an organization that is a substantial contributor
- Family members. IRS defines family members to include "an individual's spouse, ancestors, lineal descendants, and the spouses of his or her lineal descendants. Also, the legally adopted child of an individual is his or her child within the meaning of this regulation. Internal Revenue Code (IRC) 4946(d) provides that the family of any individual shall include only his spouse, ancestors, children, grandchildren, great grandchildren, and the spouses of children, grandchildren, and great grandchildren… The surviving spouse of a child, grandchild, or great grandchild of a substantial contributor (until remarriage).
- Persons who hold more than a 35% interest
- Government official

# CHAPTER 24

## PART X:
## SCHEDULE E: ORGANIZATIONS NOT FILING FORM 1023 WITHIN 27 MONTHS OF FORMATION

*"I want to build a team that's invincible, so that they have to send a team from bloody Mars to beat us."*

—Bill Shankly

Rising Stars of America was founded in 2004 by Baron Davis, point guard for the Los Angeles Clippers, as a way for him to give back to the community. RSOA's mission is to utilize athletics as a means of teaching ethical, social values and life skills through mentorship and positive role modeling to today's youth. (CA)

If you have been in existence for more than 27 months, you have some special filing rules as far as effective date of your organization. File

Schedule E to determine effective date if you want the effective date to be more than 27 months prior to the application date.

Does the date on Form 1023 meet your organization's needs? If so, do not complete Schedule E. If you need to seek a date prior to 27 months, (for example, you have a donor who needs the tax deduction), then you have to fill out Schedule E and prove to IRS that you meet one of the exceptions to the 27 month filing rules.

Here are the exceptions: churches, gross revenue under $5,000 a year, formed before 1969, or if you can prove you acted in good faith and that if IRS granted the earlier date, it would not prejudice the interests of the government. One way you used to be able to prove good faith was to file the Form 1023 before IRS told you to, although it does not always work anymore.

If it is determined that you do not qualify for 501(c) (3) status from date of formation, you may still qualify for 501(c) (4) status for the dates between formation and filing the Form 1023. Normally donations are not deductible for periods covered under 501(c) (4) status.

## LINE 1: CHURCHES

You only have to fill out Schedule A. Do not complete Schedule E.

## LINE 2: GROSS RECEIPTS

If your gross receipts are under $5,000 or if you are filing within 90 days of the tax year in which your receipts went over $5,000, you get to stop here and not complete the rest of Schedule E.

## LINES 3A, 3B, 3C: GROUP EXEMPTION

If you answer "No," go to line 4. If you answer "Yes," it means you were part of a group exemption application or an actual subordinate of another group that has notified you that you will no longer be part of that group. If this applies, IRS wants to know if you are applying within 27 months of either being turned down or 27 months from no longer being part of the group. If you answer "Yes," you get to stop filing out this form, you are done.

## LINE 4: CREATED BEFORE OCTOBER 9, 1969?

If yes, you get to stop. You are done filling out Schedule E.

## LINE 5: WHY DIDN'T YOU FILE WITHIN 27 MONTHS?

If you answered "No" to lines 1 – 4, answer "yes" to this questions. You are not eligible for an earlier 501(c) (3) status effective date unless you can provide an explanation to IRS why you did not file, why you did not file in good faith, and how approving the earlier date does not compromise the best interest of the government. This can include relying on a tax professional's advice, IRS guidance given in error, complexities in your circumstances making it difficult to ascertain whether to file, etc. You get to stop on this question.

## LINE 6A: ADVANCED RULING

Notice 1382 eliminated advance ruling. Do not answer.

## LINE 6B: CHANGES IN SOURCE OF SUPPORT

If you anticipate changes in sources of support, mark "Yes" and fill out line 7.

## LINE 7: TWO YEARS PROJECTED INCOME

If you anticipate changes in your source(s) of support, fill out two year's projected income using this table.

## LINE 8: EXEMPTION UNDER 501(C) (4) FOR PERIODS OF OPERATION PRIOR TO POSTMARK OF THIS APPLICATION

If you want to apply for Section 501(c) (4) status for the times of operation prior to the postmark of this application, fill out page 1 of IRS Form 1024 and attach to the application. Although donations will not normally be tax deductible, there will be no IRS taxes due from the organization for the periods covered under Section 501(c) (4).

# CHAPTER 25

## PART X: SCHEDULES F, G, AND H

*"Winners never quit and quitters never win."*
—Vince Lombardi

SportsChallenge Leadership Academy is the nation's leading youth-serving leadership and sports nonprofit. SportsChallenge was founded in 1996 by career educators who believed there was an opportunity within the culture of youth sports to inspire student-athletes to be more open, confident and broader minded. Over time, SportsChallenge evolved into something more dynamic, teaching young men and women to see themselves as difference makers not only in the athletic arena but also in the world around them.

## SCHEDULE F: HOMES FOR THE ELDERLY OR HANDICAPPED AND LOW-INCOME HOUSING

Homes for elderly and low income must provide affordable housing to a "significant segment" of elderly, handicapped or low income individuals in the community.

## Section 1: General Information

### LINE 1: TYPE OF HOUSING

Describe the type of housing you are providing (i.e.–apartment, condo, co-op, private residence).

### LINE 2: APPLICATION

Provide a copy of the application you use to select tenants.

### LINE 3: PUBLIC AWARENESS

Explain how you advertise your facilities.

### LINES 4A, 4B, 4C, AND 4D:

Describe each facility, how many people each accommodates, and whether they are renting or purchasing.

### LINE 5: CONTRACTS AND AGREEMENTS

Attach samples of documents used for occupancy.

### LINE 6: JOINT VENTURES

Provide details of any joint ventures. Make sure the details agree with Part VIII, line 8.

### LINE 7: FAIR MARKET VALUE OF SERVICES CONTRACTED

Are you contracting with other organizations for services on these properties? If so, how are you arriving at a fair market value for services? Your answer here must agree with Part VIII, line 7a.

## LINE 8: MANAGEMENT

Elect whether you will manage your facilities in-house, with volunteers, or with independent contractor(s). Make sure your answer agrees with Part VIII, line 7b.

## LINE 9: GOVERNMENT HOUSING PROGRAMS

Describe any involvement in state, local, and federal government housing programs.

## LINE 10: OWNERSHIP

Do you own or lease? How did you acquire the property? Copies of all applicable documents need to be attached to the application.

### Section II: Homes for the Elderly or Handicapped

## LINES 1A AND 1B: WHO DO YOU PROVIDE HOMES FOR?

Select which class of individuals (elderly or handicapped or both) you provide housing for. Describe how they qualify and how you select applicants.

## LINES 2A, 2B, AND 2C: FEES AND AFFORDABILITY

Explain the financial requirements and provide documentation.

## LINES 3A AND 3B: WHEN SOMEONE CANNOT PAY.

What do you do when someone cannot pay?

## LINE 4: HEALTH CARE

Do you have health care arrangements for residents? If so, describe them.

## LINE 5: NEEDS OF ELDERLY AND HANDICAPPED

Describe how your facilities meet physical (such as grab bars in bathrooms, wide doorways for wheelchairs, etc.), emotional, recreational, social, religious and other needs of the elderly and handicapped.

## Section III: Low Income Housing

## LINE 1: LOW INCOME HOUSING

If you provide low income housing, what is the criteria to qualify and how do you make the final selection?

## LINE 2: FEES IN ADDITION TO RENT OR MORTGAGE

Are there any other fees? How are they determined? Give detailed explanation.

## LINES 3A AND 3B: IS YOUR HOUSING AFFORDABLE TO LOW INCOME INDIVIDUALS?

Give details and explain restrictions to ensure low income.

IRS gives guidance at http://www.irs.gov/pub/irs-tege/rp_1996-32.pdf

Revenue Procedure 96-32, 1996-1 C.B. 717, provides guidelines for providing low-income housing that will be treated as charitable. (At least 75% of the units are occupied by low-income tenants or 40% are occupied by tenants earning not more than 120% of the very low-income levels for the area.)

### LINE 4: SOCIAL SERVICES

Do you provide social services to residents? If so, describe the services provided.

# SCHEDULE G: SUCCESSORS TO OTHER ORGANIZATIONS

The main reason for this schedule is to make sure that no private benefit to shareholders or individuals occurs when one organization (the predecessor) is taken over by or converted to another organization, even if the predecessor was not a tax exempt organization.

### LINES 1A AND 1B: PREVIOUS ORGANIZATION FOR-PROFIT

Was the previous organization a for-profit organization? If so, give the details of how you came to take it over.

### LINES 2A, 2B, 2C, 2D, AND 2E: PREVIOUS ORGANIZATION NOT-FOR-PROFIT

Provide all requested details about previous organization, 501(c) (3) status, and why you took over the organization and its assets. Be detailed and specific.

### LINE 3: NAME, ADDRESS, EIN OF PREVIOUS ORGANIZATION

Self-explanatory.

## LINE 4: WHO RAN THE PREVIOUS ORGANIZATION?

Provide requested information in the table provided. Attach a sheet if necessary to provide complete information.

## LINE 5: WILL ANYONE FROM PREVIOUS ORGANIZATION BE INVOLVED IN NEW ORGANIZATION?

Provide complete details.

## LINES 6A, 6B, AND 6C: ASSETS

If any assets were transferred to the new organization, what were they, how was their worth established, and were there any restrictions on the sale or use of these assets? Include copies of all agreements made.

## LINE 7: DEBT TRANSFER

Did the new organization take on any debts from the previous organization? If so, give full details.

## LINE 8: LEASES

Provide full disclosure of any lease arrangements the new organization will have for previously-owned equipment with the previous for-profit organization or any of its members, officers, trustees, or directors.

## LINE 9: LEASES

Will the new organization lease any equipment to the previous organization or any of its members, officers, trustees, or directors? Provide full disclosure.

# SCHEDULE H: ORGANIZATIONS PROVIDING SCHOLARSHIPS, FELLOWSHIPS, EDUCATIONAL LOANS, OR OTHER EDUCATIONAL GRANTS TO INDIVIDUALS AND PRIVATE FOUNDATIONS REQUESTING ADVANCE APPROVAL OF INDIVIDUAL GRANT PROCEDURES

IRS wants to make sure that any scholarships you give as a tax exempt organization are fair in terms of nondiscrimination, merit or need, and available to an open-ended group instead of a preselected group. The scholarship is tax free to the recipient if he or she is a degree-seeking candidate, and uses the funds for educational expenses that include tuition, fees, books, supplies, and equipment for courses. Acceptable educational expenses do not include room, board, travel, research, clerical help, and equipment not required for a course.

### Section 1: Public Charities and Private Foundations

### LINES 1A, 1B, 1C, 1D, 1E, AND 1F: TYPES OF GRANTS AND LOANS

Provide full explanation of grants, loans, scholarships, etc. provided. Although several items are requested, the most important is the application form for your loan or grant. If you do not have one yet, you can find copies online to use as examples to draft one. Answer each part of this question completely.

### LINE 2: CASE HISTORIES

Do you keep complete records of who got scholarships, grants, loans, etc.? Describe the records you keep. More information is found in

Revenue Ruling 56-304, 1956-2 C.B. 306 as well as Revenue Ruling 77-380, 1977-2. You can review Revenue Ruling 56-304 at http://www.irs.gov/pub/irs-tege/rr56_304.pdf If you do not keep records, you must explain how you will make sure your program meets exempt purposes.

## LINE 3: SPECIFIC CRITERIA FOR ELIGIBILITY

Who is eligible? What is your criteria?

## LINE 4A, 4B, 4C, AND 4D: SPECIFIC CRITERIA TO SELECT RECIPIENTS

How will you select recipients, number of recipients, amount for each recipient, and any requirements (such as grade point average) the recipients must meet.

## LINE 5: PROCEDURES

How will you award the grant and make sure the requirements have been met?

## LINE 6: SELECTION COMMITTEE

Who is on the current selection committee, what are the requirements, how do you replace selection committee members?

## LINE 7: REMAINING UNBIASED

Are family members of your selection committee eligible? If so, how do you remain unbiased in selection? Private foundations are not allowed to award to disqualified persons.

### Section II: Private Foundations only

Public charities do not fill out this section. You are done!

# CHAPTER 26

## PART XI: USER FEE INFORMATION

*"Behind every kick of the ball there has to be a thought."*
—Dennis Bergkamp

Formula Smiles uses sports as a tool to improve the quality of life of Colombian children. With the help of sports, we strive to improve their education, teach them to have a healthier lifestyle and help them become part of a community after years of being victims of Colombian's social conflict. Formula Smiles Foundation is a non-profit organization founded in 2003 by Colombian race car driver Juan Pablo Montoya and his wife Connie Freydell. Its goal is to improve the lives of thousands of children burdened by poverty and violence in their daily lives, teaching them how they can dream about being better persons and having a more promising future through sports, highlighting commonalities and bridging cultural or ethnic divides. (FL)

If your financials reflect more than $10,000 average gross receipts per year for four years, the user fee is $850. If the average is less than $10,000, the fee is $400. (See Notice 1382 at www.irs.gov/pub/irs-pdf/n1382.pdf).

When you (meaning an officer, director, or trustee) sign the application, you are certifying that everything you are sending is true, correct and complete to the best of your knowledge.

Note: At the end of the application is Form 1023 Checklist. Fill out the Checklist and put it on top of the application, then put the check on top of the cover sheet. DO NOT STAPLE the check to the application. It makes the folks at IRS upset with you.

# PART III

## SPECIAL CIRCUMSTANCES

# CHAPTER 27

## AUTOMATIC REVOCATION OF 501(C) (3) STATUS

*"Confidence doesn't come out of nowhere. It's a result of something… hours and days and weeks and years of constant work and dedication."*

— Roger Staubach

The mission of the NCAS is to use the power of sport to affect positive social change. We educate and empower individuals and organizations by inspiring values-based thinking leading to actions that promote social responsibility and equality. The NCAS evolved in response to the need to "keep the student in the student-athlete." Since its inception in 1985, NCAS member institutions have proven to be effective advocates for balancing academics and athletics. The NCAS is an ever-growing organization of colleges and universities that provides opportunities for current and former student-athletes to continue their pursuit of higher education, while working in the community addressing social issues.

Most tax exempt organizations have to file an annual report with IRS. This report is some version of the Form 990, and can be:

- Form 990, Return of Organization Exempt From Income Tax
- Form 990-EZ, Short Return of Organization Exempt From Income Tax
- Form 990-PF, Return of Private Foundation
- Form 990-N, (information e-Postcard)

If you fail to file this return for three consecutive years, on the anniversary of the third due date, IRS takes away or revokes your tax exempt status. This is called Automatic Revocation because the computer does it automatically and you are put on a list of organizations that are no longer tax exempt. That list can be found at http://www.irs.gov/Charities-&-Non-Profits/ Automatic-Revocation-of-Exemption-List

If you have been automatically revoked, you must resubmit (including the required fee) your entire application and ask IRS to reinstate your tax exempt status.

BE SURE TO WRITE *"AUTOMATICALLY REVOKED"* AT THE TOP OF THE APPLICATION AND ON THE ENVELOPE.

Details of the reinstatement process are contained in IRS Notice 2011-44 located at http://www.irs.gov/irb/2011-25_IRB/ar10.html

Normally the reinstatement date is the date of the new application to IRS, but there are some exceptions. For the date to be retroactive back to the date of revocation, you must file your application for reinstatement within 15 months of whichever is later:

- The date on the revocation letter from IRS
- The date IRS posted the revocation on their website

In addition, you have to jump through some hoops to get the retroactive date. For example, IRS requires you to submit a request for retroactive reinstatement attached to the Form 1023 that includes:

- A detailed statement of all the facts surrounding repeated failure to file, for the entire three year period as well as for each individual year.
- What circumstances led to continual failure, discovery of failure, and what you did to stop or lessen the consequences of the failure to file.
- You must address what you are doing now to keep this from happening again (you can add the task of filing the appropriate return to the job description of one of the board positions such as secretary or treasurer to make sure it gets done so that there is a responsible person to carry out the task or follow up with a bookkeeper or accountant to see that it is done on time).
- Documentation and evidence of the explanations you gave to get retroactive reinstatement.
- All the missing returns for all the years a return was due (some form of Form 990), including the three years not filed and the current year if applicable. If in doubt, contact IRS and ask them specifically what returns are due.
- A signed and dated statement from an authorized official (trustee, officer, or director) that says:

*I, (Name), (Title) declare, under penalties of perjury, that I am authorized to sign this request for retroactive reinstatement on behalf of [Name of Organization], and I further declare that I have examined this request for retroactive reinstatement, including the written explanation of all the facts and information pertaining to the claim for reasonable cause and the evidence to substantiate the claim for reasonable cause, and to the best of my knowledge and belief, this request is true, correct, and complete.*

- You must provide proof that you "exercised ordinary business care and prudence in determining and attempting to comply with…reporting requirements under section 6033 for each of the three years, and over the entire three-year period." IRS will consider all your evidence and determine if you meet the Reasonable Cause Standard. Here are some things they consider to give a decision in your favor:

    - If you relied on written information from IRS that was in error
    - Events beyond your control that caused you not be able to file for each of the three years and the three year period as a whole
    - Acting responsibly by taking steps to avoid the failure to file and to keep it from happening in the future by trying to prevent the failure if it was foreseen; removing the problem that caused you not to file as soon as you became aware of the failure to file; putting policies and safeguards in place to make sure it doesn't happen in the future
    - A history of complying with filing and other requirements before and after the three year period
    - How heavily you rely on volunteers to perform organizational activities also plays a part in the decision making process. The more, the better.

If you want retroactive coverage of tax exempt status, you need to be very thorough in your explanation of what happened and make sure you let IRS know that you did not fail to comply as rebellion against the tax system. You may even want to start your explanation with that statement so IRS gets the idea immediately that you were not being rebellious. You must provide evidence of everything you say to justify the problem, and you must make sure you have instituted safeguards to make sure it never happens again. If your request for retroactive status is turned down, the date of your new Form 1023 filing will be the effective date for tax exempt status.

You will not be revoked a second time unless you fail to file for three years AFTER receiving the new determination letter reinstating your tax exempt status.

# CHAPTER 28

## INTERACTIVE ONLINE FORM i1023

*"Life is ten percent what happens to you and ninety percent how you respond to it."*

—Lou Holtz

**THE AUSTEN EVERETT FOUNDATION** The Austen Everett Foundation works to inspire, empower, and improve the lives of children faced with cancer by matching and integrating these special individuals with professional and intercollegiate athletic organizations. Through our mission, the Austen Everett Foundation hopes to liberate children from their illness while raising awareness and funds to fight the battle against cancer. We here at AEF will coordinate with the child's favorite sport team or athlete and give them a once-in-a-lifetime experience to become a professional or intercollegiate athlete for that specific sport and game. If we can offer the opportunity for a child to share moments of laughter, happiness and gain an everlasting bond with an athlete, then we have achieved Austen's dream of showing kids firsthand that Cancer should not define who you are.

Over the past several years, articles have appeared on the internet purporting that when the interactive IRS Form i1023 becomes a reality, the process of getting approved for tax-exempt status would be simplified and would require much less work. In September, 2013, the Form i1023 was available for review, although the application could not actually be used to file with IRS. I was able to test drive the form and give feedback to IRS. This is what I found.

The form was pretty much exactly like the paper form and the form available as a fillable form online. IRS put pop-up information boxes throughout the form. The information in the boxes was, in most cases, word-for-word out of the instruction manual for filling out the Form 1023. The only other additions were occasional links to certain IRS publications that give definitions and time saving access to publications.

Unfortunately, the interactive form, which is now available at http://www.stayexempt.irs.gov/StartingOut.aspx does not lessen the requirements or speed up processing of the application. At one time, IRS was developing a "Cyber Assistant" in which you would be able to actually apply online. When they were talking of that idea (for about a decade), the application fee was going to be highly reduced. No such discount has been whispered or breathed about with this new online form. In essence, the interactive online form i1023 will be about the same as the fillable form currently available, except for the pop-up boxes with instructions and the links to other publications and parts of the IRS website.

# PART IV

## OPTIONAL FOLLOW UP TASKS

# CHAPTER 29

## REGISTER FOR CHARITABLE FUNDRAISING AND SOLICITATION

*"If you do not believe you can do it then you have no chance at all."*

—Arsene Wenger

The California State Soccer Association–South (Cal South) is a 501(c) (3) California public benefit corporation and is the official youth and adult state soccer association of the United States Soccer Federation, the United States Youth Soccer, and the United States Adult Soccer Association. Cal South represents over 280 Affiliate Member Leagues and Clubs comprising our membership of more than 195,000 registered players, coaches, referees and league administrators. The organization, with a service area that extends from San Luis Obispo to San Diego, provides rewarding recreational and competitive opportunities for players of all ages, genders and skill levels.

## UNIFIED REGISTRATION STATEMENT (URS)

Consumer protection laws exist to ensure that citizens of a state do not fall prey to false charity solicitations. It's so they do not get suckered into parting with their hard-earned money to causes that are not really tax exempt. Many states require nonprofits to register before they are allowed to raise funds in that state. The paperwork, fees, and time frames vary depending on the state, but the Unified Registration Statement (URS) simplifies the process.

The URS is a multi-state registration form that allows your organization to fill it out once, then file it with many states instead of filling out a different form for every state you plan to do fundraising in. Not all states accept the URS (Arizona, Colorado, District of Columbia, Florida, Maine, Ohio, Oklahoma, and South Carolina). But many do, either for initial registration, renewal, or both. You can access the form at http://www.multistatefiling.org/ or http://www.multistatefiling.org/urs_webv401.pdf

As of 2013, the following states do not require you to register for fundraising:

| |
|---|
| Delaware |
| Idaho |
| Indiana |
| Iowa |
| Montana |
| Nebraska |
| Nevada |
| South Dakota |
| Texas* (see note below) |
| Vermont |
| Wyoming |

\*    Texas requires registration for law enforcement, public safety, and veteran causes only.

As of 2013, the following states require your organization to register before you are permitted to raise funds in that state:

| | |
|---|---|
| Alabama | Mississippi |
| Alaska | Missouri |
| Arizona | New Hampshire |
| Arkansas | New Jersey |
| California | New Mexico |
| Colorado | New York |
| Connecticut | North Carolina |
| District of Columbia | North Dakota |
| Florida | Ohio |
| Georgia | Oklahoma |
| Hawaii | Oregon |
| Illinois | Pennsylvania |
| Kansas | Rhode Island |
| Kentucky | South Carolina |
| Louisiana | Tennessee |
| Maine | Utah |
| Maryland | Virginia |
| Massachusetts | Washington |
| Michigan | West Virginia |
| Minnesota | Wisconsin |

Each state has its own requirements, fees, and filing procedures. Many adhere to the Charleston Principles to determine if a tax exempt organization should file if they have only minimal financial dealings within a state or may access donors by internet only. States are not bound by these principles and set their own rules of who has to register. The Charleston Principles can be viewed at http://www.afpnet.org/ResourceCenter/ArticleDetail.cfm?ItemNumber=3309

The following table addresses charity solicitations.

| ST | Contact Info | URS Initial/ Renew | Fee Initial/ Renewal | Comments: |
|---|---|---|---|---|
| AL | Office of the Alabama Attorney General Consumer Protection Attn: Charitable Organization Registration, P.O. Box 300152, Montgomery, AL 36130 1-800-392-5658 or 334-242-7335 http://www.ago.state.al.us/Page-Consumer-Protection-Consumer-Charities | Yes/ Yes | $25/ $25 | Must renew within 90 days from the end of the fiscal year. |
| AK | State of Alaska Department of Law Attorney General's Office 1031 W. 4th Ave., Suite 200, Anchorage, AK 99501 907-269-5200 http://www.law.state.ak.us/department/civil/consumer/charityreg.html | Yes/ Yes | $40/ $40 | Renew by Sep 1 |

| | | | | |
|---|---|---|---|---|
| **AZ** | Arizona Secretary of State Attn: Business Services, Charities Division 400 West Congress 2nd Floor Room 252 Tucson, AZ 85701  602-542-6187 or 800-458-5842 http://www.azsos. gov/business_ser- vices/Charities/ Default.htm | No/ No | None/ None but late fee $25 | Renew between Sep 1 and Sep 30 |
| **AR** | Office of the At- torney General ATTN: Charitable Registration 323 Center Street, Suite 200 Little Rock, AR 72201 501-682-2007/1- 800-482-8982  http://arkansasag. gov/programs/ arkansas-lawyer/ charities-registra- tion | *Yes/ Yes | None/ None  Fund- raising counsel and paid solicitors must pay fees | *Must file sup- plemental form http://www. multistatefiling. org/F_Ark_Supp. pdf  Renew by anni- versary of initial registration  Annual financial report due by May 15 or 6 months from end of fiscal year. |
| **CA** | California At- torney General's Office | Yes/ No | $25 paid to Dept of Justice/ | Renew within 4 months and 15 days from end of fiscal year. |

| | | | | |
|---|---|---|---|---|
| | Registry of Charitable Trusts P.O. Box 903447 Sacramento, CA 94203-4470 916-445-2021 rct@doj.ca.gov http://oag.ca.gov/charities | | Depends on annual gross revenue | Must use renewal form RRF-1 http://oag.ca.gov/sites/all/files/agweb/pdfs/charities/charitable/rrf1_form.pdf? |
| CO | Charitable Solicitations Program Office of the Secretary of State 1700 Broadway, Suite 200 Denver, CO 80290 303-894-2200, option 2 charitable@sos.state.co.us http://www.sos.state.co.us/pubs/charities/charitableHome.html | No/ No | $1/ $1 $300 fine for soliciting without registration | Registration done online only. No mailed applications. Renewal dates same as IRS Form 990 due dates. |
| CT | Public Charities Department of Consumer Protection 165 Capitol Avenue Hartford, CT 06106-1630 860-713-6170, 800-842-2649; | Yes/ No | $50/ $50 Payable to Treasurer, State of Connecticut | Renewal form by mail: http://www.ct.gov/dcp/lib/dcp/pdf/applications_added_2013/chr_website_renewal_form.pdf |

| | | | | |
|---|---|---|---|---|
| | ctcharityhelp@ ct.gov http://www.ct. gov/dcp/cwp/ view.asp?a= 1654&q=459952 | | | |
| **DC** | Department of Consumer & Regulatory Affairs 1100 4th Street SW Washington, DC 20024 (Not the mailing address for applications) 02-442-4400 http://dcra.dc.gov/ service/general-business-and-charitable-solicitation-licenses | No/ No | $412.50/ $412.50 2 year registration | Must renew within 30 days of expiration. $250-500 late fee. https://cpms.dcra. dc.gov/osr/SimpleRenewal.aspx |
| **FL** | Florida Department of Agriculture & Consumer Services Solicitation of Contributions P.O. Box 6700 Tallahassee, FL 32314-6700 800-435-7352 in Florida 850-410-3800 | No /No | Fees based on last year's financials | Forms located at: http://www.fresh-fromflorida.com/ Divisions-Offices/ Consumer-Services/Business-Services/Charitable-Organizations Renewal due on anniversary of initial registration date. |

| | | | | |
|---|---|---|---|---|
| | cswebmaster@ freshfromflorida. com; http:// www.800helpfla. com/socbus. html#forms | | | |
| **GA** | Securities and Business Regulation<br><br>2 Martin Luther King, Jr. Dr. #802 W. Tower<br><br>Atlanta, GA 30303-9000<br><br>404-656-3920<br><br>http://sos.georgia. gov/securities/ charitable_organi- zation.htm | Yes/ Yes | $35 for 2 years/ $20 | State renewal form is easier that URS<br><br>Renewal form using URS must contain Georgia Supplement form:<br><br>http://www.multi- statefiling.org/I_ Georgia_Supp.pdf |
| **HI** | Department of the Attorney General<br><br>Tax & Charities Division<br><br>425 Queen Street<br><br>Honolulu, HI 96813-2903<br><br>808-586-1480; Marlene.Baba@ hawaii.gov http:// hawaii.gov/ag/ charities | *Yes / **No | None/ De- pends on revenues | Annual Financial Statement link:<br><br>http://efile. form990.org/frm- NPParticipating- StateSCOHI.asp<br><br>*Must use online registration.<br><br>**Renewal not re- quired, but annual financial state- ment is. |

| | | | | |
|---|---|---|---|---|
| **IL** | Office of the Illinois Attorney General Charitable Trust Bureau 100 W. Randolph St. 11th Floor Chicago, IL 60601 312-814-2595 http://www.illinoisattorneygeneral.gov/charities/file_require.html | Yes/ Renewal Not Required | $15 Payable to Illinois Charity Bureau Fund/ None but $200 late fee for soliciting before registering | Annual report due 6 months from end of fiscal year: $15* fee plus late fees if applicable, *depending on income and assets |
| **KS** | Kansas Secretary of State Memorial Hall, 1st Floor 120 S.W. 10th Avenue Topeka, KS 66612-1594 785-296-4564 kssos@sos.ks.gov http://www.kssos.org/forms/forms_results.asp?division=BS# Charitable Organizations | Yes/ Yes | $35/ $35 | Renewal due by last day of 6th month following end of fiscal year |
| **KY** | Office of the Attorney General 1024 Capital Center Drive, Suite 200 Frankfort, KY | Yes/No* | $0/ $0 | Must attach Form 990 with renewal. |

| | | | | |
|---|---|---|---|---|
| | 40601<br>Attn: Charity Registration<br>502-696-5300<br>http://ag.ky.gov/civil/consumer-protection/charity/Pages/registration.aspx | | | |
| **LA** | Public Protection Division<br>1885 N. 3rd St., 4th Floor<br>Baton Rouge, LA 70802-5146<br><br>225-326-6400 or 1-800-351-4889<br>http://www.ag.state.la.us/Article.aspx?articleID=291&catID=0 | Required/<br>Required | $25/<br>$25<br>Payable to Louisiana Department of Justice | Required attachments to application included here:<br><br>http://www.ag.state.la.us/Shared/ViewDoc.aspx?Type=3&Doc=213<br><br>Renewal by Oct 1 |
| **ME** | State of Maine Department of Professional & Financial Regulations<br>Office of Professional & Occupational Regulation<br>35 State House Station<br>Augusta, ME 04333 | No/<br>No | $50/<br>$25 | http://www.state.me.us/pfr/professionallicensing/professions/charitable/pdf/Initial%20App-Charitable%20Organization.pdf<br><br>Renewal by Nov 30 |

| | | | | |
|---|---|---|---|---|
| | 207-624-8603 charitable.sol@ maine.gov<br><br>http://www.state. me.us/pfr/profes- sionallicensing/ professions/chari- table/index.htm | | | |
| **MD** | Office of the Secretary of State Charitable Organizations Division State House Annapolis, MD 21401-1547<br><br>410-974-5534 http://www.sos. state.md.us/Char- ity/RegisterChar- ity.aspx | Yes/ No | Depends on income/ Depends on income | Renewal within 6 months of end of fiscal year using this form:<br><br>http://www.sos. state.md.us/char- ity/AnnualUp- date.pdf |
| **MA** | Office of the Attorney General Non-Profit Organizations/Public Charities Division One Ashburton Place Boston, MA 02108 617-727-2200, ext. 2101 | Yes/ No | Sliding scale depending on income | 2 step process: Initial costs $100; Long form fee is a sliding scale from $35 - $2,000<br><br>Renewal due within 4 1/2 months of end of fiscal year |

| | | | | |
|---|---|---|---|---|
| | http://www. mass.gov/ago/ doing-business-in-massachusetts/ public-charities-or-not-for-profits/ soliciting-funds/ overview-of-solici-tation.html | | | |
| **MI** | Department of Attorney General Charitable Trust Section P.O. Box 30214 Lansing, MI 48909-7714  517-373-1152 ct_email@michigan.gov  http://www. michigan.gov/ ag/0,4534,7-164-17337_18095---,00.html | Yes/ Yes | None/ None unless revenues over $100K | Renewal 7 months after end of fiscal year  There may be a supplemental form if income over $100K and organization files Form 990-EZ: Michigan Statement of Functional Expenses |
| **MN** | Office of the Attorney General 1200 Bremer Tower 445 Minnesota Street St. Paul, MN 55101-2130 | Yes/ Yes | $25/ $25 | Need supplement for initial and renewal to use URS:  http://www. ag.state.mn.us/ Charities/Forms/ MinnesotaURS. pdf |

| | | | | |
|---|---|---|---|---|
| | ATTN: Charities/ Civil Division<br><br>651-757-1311<br>http://www. ag.state.mn.us/ Charities/ | | | Renewal due 15th day of the 7th month following fiscal year end. |
| **MS** | Mississippi Secretary of State's Office Charities Registration P.O. Box 136 Jackson, MS 39205-0136<br><br>601-359-1371 or 888-236-6167;<br><br>http://www.sos. ms.gov/securities_and_charities_charities.aspx | Required/ Required | $50/ $50 | Supplement required:<br><br>http://www.sos. ms.gov/links/ sec_char/FORM_ FS_FinalReport. pdf<br><br>Renewals before expiration date of current registration |
| **MO** | Missouri Attorney General's Office Attn: Registration Specialist P.O. Box 899 Jefferson City, MO 65102-0899<br><br>573-751-3321 http://ago.mo.gov/ checkacharity/ charityregistration. htm | Yes/ Yes | $15/ $15 | Renewal Within 75 days of fiscal year end. |

| | | | | |
|---|---|---|---|---|
| **MT** | Montana Secretary of State P.O. Box 202801 Helena, MT 59620-2801  406-444-5522 AnnualReports@ mt.gov  http://sos.mt.gov/ Business/Forms/ index.asp  https://doj. mt.gov/consumer/ for-nonprofits-2/ | | N/A / $15 an-nual re-port fee | No registration required, but must file an annual re-port by April 15. |
| **NH** | Office of the New Hampshire Attor-ney General Charitable Trusts Unit 33 Capitol Street Concord, NH 03301-6397  603-271-3591 charitabletrusts2@ doj.nh.gov www.doj.nh.gov/ charitable-trusts/ | Yes/ No | $25/ $75 | Must attach a Conflict of Inter-est Policy to URS  Renewal due 4 months and 15 days after fiscal year end. |
| **NJ** | NJ Division of Consumer Affairs Charities Registra-tion Section P.O. Box 45021 | Yes/ Yes | $30 - 250/ $30 - 250 | Renewals due 6 months after fiscal year ends. |

| | | | | |
|---|---|---|---|---|
| | Newark, NJ 07101-8002 973-504-6215 AskConsumerAffairs@lps.state.nj.us http://www.njconsumeraffairs.gov/ocp/charities.htm | | Depends on revenue | |
| NM | Charities Unit New Mexico Attorney General 111 Lomas Blvd NW, Suite 300 Albuquerque, NM 87102-2368 505-827-6000 charity.registrar@nmag.gov http://www.nmag.gov/the_office/Communications-Division/consumer-protection/charities | No with rare exceptions/ No | $0/ $0 | Electronic registration required. Renewals also online. |
| NY | New York State Department of Law Office of the Attorney General Charities Bureau – Registration Section 120 Broadway, | Yes/ No | $25/ $10 - 25 Depending on revenue | Renewal due 15th day of the 5th month after fiscal year. |

| | | | | |
|---|---|---|---|---|
| | New York, NY 10271<br><br>212-416-8401<br>charities.bureau@ag.ny.gov www.charitiesnys.com | | | |
| **NC** | North Carolina Department of the Secretary of State Charitable Solicitation Licensing Division P.O. Box 29622 Raleigh, NC 27626<br><br>919-807-2214<br>csl@sosnc.com<br>http://www.secretary.state.nc.us/csl/ThePage.aspx | Yes/ Yes | $0 - 200/ $0 - 200<br><br>Depending on revenue | Must file supplemental form with URS:<br><br>http://www.multistatefiling.org/M2_%20NC_Fundraising_Disclosure.pdf<br><br>Renewal due 65 days before expiration |
| **ND** | Secretary of State State of North Dakota 600 E. Boulevard Ave. Dept. 108 Bismarck, ND 58505-0500<br><br>701-328-3665 or 800-352-0867 ext. 83665;<br><br>sosadlic@nd.gov | Yes/ No | $25/ $10 | Must file 2 supplemental forms if URS used:<br><br>http://www.multistatefiling.org/N2_NDak_Supp.pdf and<br><br>http://www.multistatefiling.org/N1_NDak_Supp.pdf |

| | | | | |
|---|---|---|---|---|
| | http://www. nd.gov/sos/non-profit/charitable-org/index.html | | | |
| **OH** | Ohio Attorney General Charitable Law Section 150 E. Gay St., 23rd Floor Columbus, OH 43215-3130 1-800-282-0515 CharitableRegis-tration@OhioAt-torneyGeneral.gov http://www.ohio-attorneygeneral. gov/Business-and-Non-Profits/Char-ity/Charitable-Registration.aspx | No/ No | $0/ $0-200 Depend-ing on revenue | Everything is online |
| **OK** | Office of the Sec-retary of State 2300 N. Lincoln Blvd, Suite 101 Oklahoma City, OK 73105-4897 405-521-3912 https://www.sos. ok.gov/charity/De-fault.aspx | No/ No | $15 or 65/ $15 or 65 Depend-ing on revenue | State filing form: https://www.sos. ok.gov/forms/ FM0101.PDF |

| | | | | |
|---|---|---|---|---|
| **OR** | Charitable Activities Section Oregon Department of Justice 1515 SW 5th Ave., Suite 410 Portland, OR 97201-5451<br><br>971-673-1880 charitable.activities@doj.state.or.us<br><br>http://www.doj.state.or.us/charigroup/pages/howtoreg.aspx | Yes/ No renewal required | $0/ No renewal required, but annual report fees are based on revenues and run from $10 – 200 | Checks payable to Oregon Department of Jusice |
| **PA** | Pennsylvania Dept. of State Bureau of Charitable Organizations 207 N. Office Building, Harrisburg, PA 17120 717-783-1720 or 1-800-732-0999 ST-CHARITY@ pa.gov<br><br>http://www.portal.state.pa.us/portal/server.pt/community/charities/12444 | Yes/ Yes | $15 - 250/ $15 - 250<br><br>Depending on revenue | Renewal reminders ARE NOT mailed. |
| **RI** | State of Rhode Island | Yes/ Yes | $90/ $90 | Renewal due no later than 30 days |

| | | | | |
|---|---|---|---|---|
| | Department of Business Regulation, Securities Division Charitable Organization Section 1511 Pontiac Avenue John O. Pastore Complex Bldg. 69-1 Cranston, RI 02920-4407

401-462-9583 www.dbr.state.ri.us/divisions/securities/charitable.php | | | prior to expiration. **Must** be submitted on CD-rom. |
| **SC** | South Carolina Secretary of State Attn: Public Charities 1205 Pendleton St., Suite 525 Columbia, SC 29201

803-734-1790 charities@sos.sc.gov www.scsos.com/Public_Charities | No/ No | $50/ $50 | Registration form:

http://www.sos.sc.gov/forms/Charities/ChariesRegistrationForm.pdf

Renewal due 3 to 4 and 1/2 months after fiscal year ends. |
| **TN** | Division of Charitable Solicitations and Gaming | Yes/ Yes | $50/ $100 - 300 | If using URS, must file supplement: |

| | | | | |
|---|---|---|---|---|
| | 312 Rosa L. Parks Avenue Snodgrass Tower, 8th Floor Nashville, TN 37243 615-741-2555 charitable.solicitations@tn.gov www.state.tn.us/ sos/charity.htm | | Depending on revenues | http://www.state. tn.us/sos/forms/ SS-6002_new.pdf |
| **TX** | https://www.oag. state.tx.us/consumer/nonprofits. shtml | | | Law enforcement, public safety, and veterans organizations only |
| **UT** | Department of Commerce Division of Consumer Protection 160 East 300 South, 2nd Floor Box 146704 Salt Lake City, UT 84114-6704<br><br>801-530-6601 http://consumerprotection.utah. gov/registrations/ charities.html | Yes/ Yes | $100/ $100 | If URS used, must file supplements:<br><br>http://consumerprotection.utah. gov/downloads/ urs-supplement. pdf and<br><br>http://consumerprotection.utah. gov/downloads/ statement-of-functional-expenses.pdf<br><br>Renewal annually on Jan 1, Apr 1, Jul 1, or Oct 1, whichever comes first after initial registration expires. |

| VA | Virginia Department of Agriculture & Consumer Services Office of Charitable and Regulatory Programs PO Box 526 Richmond, VA 23218-0526 804-786-1343; http://www. vdacs.virginia. gov/allforms. shtml#charitable | Yes/ Yes | $100/ $30 - 325 Depending on revenue | Renewal due 4 and 1/2 months after fiscal year end. |
|----|------|------|------|------|
| WA | Secretary of State Charities Program P.O. Box 40234 801 Capitol Way South Olympia, WA 98504-0234 Phone: 800-332-4483 in state or 360-725-0378 charities@sos. wa.gov http://www.sos. wa.gov/charities/ Charitable-Organizations.aspx | Yes/ Yes | $60/ $40 $50 expedite fee | Must file supplement if using URS: http://www.sos. wa.gov/_assets/ corps/URS-Addendum.pdf Renewals due before expiration date. |
| WV | Charities Division, Secretary of State, 1900 | Yes/ Yes | $15 - 50/ $15 - 50 | Renewal due on anniversary of registration |

| | | | | |
|---|---|---|---|---|
| | Kanawha Blvd East Bldg. 1, Suite 157-K Charleston, WV 25305-0770<br><br>304-558-6000 http://www.sos. wv.gov/business-licensing/charities/ Pages/default.aspx | | Depend-ing on revenue | |
| **WI** | Department of Regulation & Li-censing Charitable Organi-zations P.O. Box 8935 Madison, WI 53708-8935 608-266-5511 DSPS@wisconsin. gov<br><br>http://ww2.wis-consin.gov/state/ license/ app? COMMAND= gov.wi.state.cpp. license.command. ShowPermit-Types& selectedLicense= 200110160909 412872058 | Yes/ No | $15/ $54 | Supplement re-quired when using URS:<br><br>http://dsps. wi.gov/Docu-ments/Credential-ing%20Forms/ Business%20 Application%20 Forms/fm1952. pdf<br><br>Renewal by Jul 31. |

# CHAPTER 30

## ANNUAL FILING REQUIREMENTS WITH IRS

*"It's not the size of the dog in the fight, but the size of the fight in the dog."*

—Archie Griffin

The Mia Hamm Foundation is a reflection of my life experiences. I created this foundation to benefit important issues that have directly affected me throughout my life. The foundation is focused on providing support for two important causes: raising funds and awareness for families needing marrow or cord blood transplants and continuing the growth in opportunities for young women in sports.

### REPORTS TO FILE

The IRS gives you tax exempt status, but with conditions. You must report to them annually (with very limited exceptions) about the income and expenses of the nonprofit organization. The form used to report depends on the status of the organization in terms of revenue, assets, and/or type of nonprofit. The smaller you are, the less you have to report. In most cases, if your income is less than $50,000, you do not even have to give an exact amount.

If you are a church or subordinate auxiliary of a church, you have no reporting requirements. However, many churches choose to report voluntarily to create transparency and keep everything on the up and up. Other organizations that do not have to file annual reports include state institutions and organizations that fall under parent organizations and qualify as auxiliary organizations of the parent, as well as nonprofit organizations that have not been officially approved by IRS for tax exempt status yet. When in doubt, call IRS and ask. The number is 877-829-5500.

If you fail to file the required form for three years, your tax exempt status will be automatically revoked on the due date of the report for the third year. At that time, you must reapply for tax exempt status and pay the fee all over again, except that you must justify the reason for not filing (for each year you didn't file and for the entire time of failure to file). Consider assigning the responsibility of completing the required returns to a specific position on the board of directors or board of trustees so that it gets done on time every year. The person holding the assigned position should be responsible to report the progress, the completion, or problems to the board concerning the required filings.

The reports you file with IRS are public record except that the name of the donors and the amount of their contributions is not public record. When filing, leave off social security numbers and other identifying information for the officers, directors, trustees and other officials because the information given in the return is public.

Filing consists of completing some version of the IRS Form 990. The versions are similar to the Form 1040 taxpayers file in that there is a long form (Form 1040), short form (Form 1040A), and the simple uncomplicated form (Form 1040EZ). You can look at a copy of the various Forms 990 and review the required information at http://www. irs.gov/uac/Current-Form-990-Series-Forms-and-Instructions.

The available versions for tax exempt organizations are:

## Form 990
## Return of Organization Exempt
## from Income Tax

This is the long form that must be filed if an organization's assets are over $500,000 or their income is over $200,000. It applies to all Section 501(c), 527, or 4947(a) (1) organizations except black lung benefit trusts and private foundations. The long form is similar to a tax return for an individual with a business. Just like an individual tax return, not everything on the form applies to everyone filing a return. Also, depending on the nature of the business, extra schedules may be required to be included with the return. A nonprofit organization may be required to file extra schedules depending on the nature of the nonprofit endeavors, interaction with other organizations, types of fundraising, political activity, compensation, operations outside the United States, etc.

## Form 990-EZ
## Short Form Return of Organization Exempt from
## Income Tax

This is the short form that may be filed if an organization's assets are under $500,000 and their income is less than $200,000. The exceptions are sponsoring organizations of donor-advised funds, organizations that operate one or more hospital facilities, and certain controlling organizations defined in Section 512(b) (13). They must file Form 990.

## Form 990-N
## E-Postcard

Many smaller organizations with tax exempt status and income under $50,000 can file the Form 990-N, but can also file the Form 990-EZ or Form 990 if desired. IRS contracts with Urban Institute to process electronic e-postcard information returns. To file, go to http://

epostcard.form990.org/ and set up an account online. This return is very easy to complete and requires only a few pieces of information: legal name (and any other names used) and address of organization, employer ID number, tax year, name and address of a principal officer, website address if you have one, confirmation that income is less than $50,000, and notification in the case that an organization is going out of business. This return does not require divulging the income of the organization, except that it is under $50,000. The e-postcard can be completed and filing done in less than 10 minutes per year. With such a minimal effort required for small organizations to stay IRS-compliant, there are few good reasons to be revoked for not filing every year.

## Form 990-PF
## Return of Private Foundation

Section 4947(a) (1) trusts are treated as a private foundations. Private foundations are not the focus of this book.

If you need help with filling out the forms or figuring out which form to file, you can call IRS at 1-877-829-5500, or the Help Desk if you are filing electronically at 1-866-255-0654. IRS has provided Urban Institute as their agent for online processing of Form 990-N at no charge to you. If you want to file electronically and cannot or do not choose to file Form 990-N (e-postcard), you can hire an IRS approved firm to file on your behalf. A list of authorized e-file providers is located at http://www.irs.gov/uac/Exempt-Organizations-electronic-filings-(returns-and-notices)

## WHERE TO SEND TAX EXEMPT RETURNS

For organizations within the United States, returns are normally sent to:

Department of the Treasury
Internal Revenue Service Center
Ogden, UT 84201-0027

For organizations with principal business office outside the United States, returns are normally sent to:

Internal Revenue Service Center
P.O. Box 409101 Ogden, UT 84409

## WHEN TO FILE TAX EXEMPT RETURN

The filing deadline with IRS depends on the fiscal year of the organization. Filing is required by the 15th day of the 5th month after the end of the fiscal year. There are two extensions possible, just like for individual income tax returns, except that the nonprofit extensions are 90 days each.

If an organization's fiscal year ends December 31, their Form 990, 990-EZ, 990-PF, or 990-N is due by May 15th of the following year. The first extension for Form 990, 990-EZ, or 990-PF is until August 15, and the second extension is until November 15th. No extensions are given for Form 990-N. To get an extension, you must file IRS Form 8868, Request for Extension of Time to File an Exempt Organization Return. The form is located at http://www.irs.gov/uac/Form-8868,-Application-for-Extension-of-Time-To-File-an-Exempt-Organization-Return

# CHAPTER 31

## APPLY FOR NONPROFIT STANDARD MAIL RATES

*"To succeed you need to find something to hold on to, something to motivate you, something to inspire you."*

—Tony Dorsett

O.J. Brigance is one of the few professional football players to win both a Canadian Football League and National Football League championship, and the only one to do it in the same city, Baltimore, MD. Brigance joined the Ravens in 2000, helped the team claim a Super Bowl victory, and now works as Senior Advisor to Player Development. In 2007, Brigance was diagnosed with amyotrophic lateral sclerosis (ALS) also known as Lou Gehrig's disease, a motor neuron disease and is determined to win his fight against it. Following his diagnosis with ALS, O.J. and his wife Chanda created the Brigance Brigade Foundation.

Once you have nonprofit status with IRS, you may be able to get a nonprofit standard mail rate with the United States Postal Service.

Eligible nonprofit organizations include: religious, educational, scientific, philanthropic (charitable), agricultural, labor, veterans, and fraternal.

A responsible official from your organization must fill out United States Postal Service (USPS) PS Form 3624, Application to Mail at Nonprofit Standard Mailing Rates. You can get the form online or you can get a copy of it at the post office. There will be some documents required to submit with the application.

More information is contained in USPS Publication 417. You can view a copy online at http://pe.usps.gov/text/pub417/welcome.htm

Taking the time to get approved for nonprofit mailings can save a bunch on postage. The post office will weigh one item in your bundle of exact mailings and multiply by the number of items you are mailing. The rate is lower if you use a barcode on your mailing pieces and if they can be processed by machine instead of by hand. Talk with the post office about how to secure your newsletters or other mail pieces.

If you use staples to close a newsletter, your newsletters get torn in processing, and can prohibit machining the mailing. Tape and postal seals work better and save on postage because they can be processed as machinable mail, saving significantly on every item.

It's best to talk with the postal workers who will actually process your nonprofit mailings before you send any out. They can give you all the discount information and all the requirements so you get your mailing ready correctly the first time, and show you examples of properly prepared bulk nonprofit mailings.

# CHAPTER 32

## GET SALES TAX EXEMPTION

*"Win or lose, do it fairly."*

—Knute Rockne

Doc Wayne is a Boston based non-profit with a mission of offering youth an innovative group experience delivered through the medium of team sports stressing positive youth development. We utilize coaches trained on our "do the good" sports based-therapeutic curriculum to connect with youth. Our program has had success working with a variety of youth, many of whom have faced several challenges in their young lives.

If you will be purchasing or selling goods for nonprofit purposes, you may want to apply for sales tax exemption in your state. Every state is different in their requirements and you will need to fill out the forms for your state to get approved. Below you will find the information to apply for sales tax exemption. This information is subject to change at any time, so it is advisable to contact the sales tax branch of your state government for latest information.

| ST | Purchases Exempt? | Sales by Organization Exempt? |
|---|---|---|
| AL | Limited | No |
| AK | No Sales Tax | No Sales Tax |
| AZ | Limited | Yes |
| AR | Limited | Churches and Charitable Organizations |
| CA | Limited | Limited |
| CO | Yes | For Fundraising 12 days or less and under $25,000 |
| CT | Yes | Five 1 day fundraising events/year |
| DE | No Sales Tax | No Sales Tax |
| DC | Yes | Limited and Charity Auctions, no more than three per year |
| FL | Yes | Limited to donated property to benefit minors and churches |
| GA | Yes | Fundraisers for libraries, churches, and Boys and Girl Scouts |
| HI | No | No |
| ID | Limited | No |
| IL | Yes | Very limited exemptions |
| IN | Yes | Fundraising not more than 20 days and limited exemptions |
| IA | Limited | Yes if used for exempt purposes |

| KS | Limited | No |
|---|---|---|
| KY | Yes | First $1,000 of sales |
| LA | Limited | Events when applied for in advance |
| MN | Limited | Fundraisers only within limits |
| MD | Yes | Religious organizations, certain food sales, and hospital thrift shops |
| MA | Yes | Isolated fundraising |
| MI | Yes | If less than $5,000 a year total, or else all is taxable |
| MN | Yes | Fundraising up to 24 days/year |
| MS | Limited | Girl Scout cookies, nonprofit, and schools |
| MO | Yes | Yes |
| MT | No Sales Tax | No Sales Tax |
| NE | Limited | 1 annual sale of meal by religious organization |
| NV | Yes | Yes |
| NH | No Sales Tax | No Sales Tax |
| NJ | Yes | Occasional fundraising and thrift stores |
| NM | Yes | Yes |
| NY | Yes | Exempt with a few exceptions |
| NC | Limited | 1 fundraiser per year and food sales by religious organizations |

| ND | Limited | No exemption for ongoing sales if competing with for-profit businesses. Exempts many other types of sales |
|---|---|---|
| OH | Yes | Up to six calendar days per month |
| OK | Limited | Churches and listed organizations only |
| OR | No Sales Tax | No Sales Tax |
| PA | Yes | Isolated food and beverage sales by churches only |
| RI | Yes | Items under $20 and sales that support youth activities |
| SC | No | Churches, charitable, education, literacy and listed organizations |
| SD | Yes | No except for certain admissions |
| TN | Yes | Used clothing and two sales per year up to 30 days. Otherwise, can either pay sales tax upon purchase, or charge sales tax. |
| TX | Yes | No general exemption, but several limited exemptions |
| UT | Yes | Religious and charitable only |
| VT | Yes | If less than $5,000 total for year |
| VA | Yes | Fairs, flea markets, festivals and carnivals are ALWAYS TAXABLE. Can have up to three occasional sales per year ending within 30 days |
| WA | No | Fundraising |

| WV | Limited | Fundraising for churches and nonprofits, no more than six events not to exceed 84 hours/year |
| --- | --- | --- |
| WI | Yes | Nonprofits, 20 days or less, raising under $25,000/year |
| WY | Yes | No more than four occasional sales per year for religious and charitable organizations |

# SUMMARY

Having interacted with a number of groups and individuals who are either involved in nonprofits, or who are seriously considering starting one, I have learned that we are all a hardy lot. That's why I'm confident that your tenacity has helped you navigate the ins and outs of this book.

Throughout the book I have likened this journey to that of being on a football team and all the aspects of that all-American game.

I'm often amazed at just how many hard knocks those football players can take and still jump right back up and get right back into the game. That's how I see you. You aren't afraid of a few hard knocks; otherwise you never would have chosen this book in the first place. And for that I heartily commend you. You have an idea, a dream, a vision for a nonprofit that could in some way make this old world a better place. Now it's up to you, and those on your team, to make this a winning game-play with a winning attitude.

I trust and pray that this book has been of immense value to you as you get out there on the gridiron and make it all happen. I wish you well and hope that you will stay in contact with me. I would love to shout and celebrate with you when you receive notice that your tax exempt status has been granted! When you get your determination letter, email me at support@doyourownnonprofit.com and let's get you featured as a new success story on our website.

May God Bless all your endeavors!

# APPENDIX A

## ACTUAL APPROVED NONPROFIT APPLICATIONS

### NO NEED TO REINVENT THE WHEEL

One of the best parts of starting a nonprofit corporation is that you do not have to reinvent the wheel. If you know of a similar organization, you can request a copy of their Form 1023 with narrative. Wording on applications is not copyrighted and if you see something you can use, tweak it to fit your organization instead of starting from scratch. Don't make it any harder than necessary.

I have included many links to actual approved nonprofit applications to help you get through the process. If you see one in this list that's similar to your organization, go to the website and review the application. All links worked at the time of publication. The links are also live at www.doyourownnonprofit.com

Some packages given are Form 1023 prior to the June, 2006 revision of the form, but the information is similar and those that contain the narratives are very helpful in understanding the kinds of information IRS wants to know to approve your application. I attempted to include a variety of nonprofits including religious, historical, medical, educational, and sports organizations, charitable trusts, and animal shelters. I also included an older Form 1023 for a farmer's market that failed the first attempt with IRS but includes some helpful insight into the process of how to fix applications if they are not correct the first time.

The budget information ranges from $0 for brand new nonprofits just starting, up to budgets of hundreds of thousands of dollars. These are included to give you a broad range of examples. In addition, many also include their organizing documents and bylaws. Those Form 1023s that contain the determination letter or other correspondence from IRS have been added after IRS completed their application. Your paperwork will not have those until IRS sends them after the fact.

● ● ●

A Great Example of a 2004 Completed Application with Narrative Sections particularly well done for Trolleyride.org (Minnesota Streetcar Museum):

*Minnesota Street Car Museum, Inc.:*

http://y.trolleyride.org/Member_stuff1/IRS_Documents/1023/IRS_Form_1023.pdf

http://www.trolleyride.org/Member_stuff1/IRS_Documents/1023/Narrative.pdf

http://www.trolleyride.org/Member_stuff1/IRS_Documents/1023/Attachment_D.pdf

http://www.trolleyride.org/Member_stuff1/IRS_Documents/1023/Attachment_B.pdf

http://www.trolleyride.org/Member_stuff1/IRS_Documents/1023/Attachment_C.pdf

## SOME APPLICATIONS THAT CONTAIN GREAT NARRATIVES:

*New Hampshire Supreme Court Society:*

http://www.nhsupremecourtsociety.org/1023.pdf

*Friends of the Trumbull High School Choir, Inc.:*

http://www.fothsci.org/uploads/5/2/4/9/5249683/fothsci_
form_1023_application_for_recognition_of_exemption_-_501c3.
pdf

*The HAMS Harm Reduction Network, Incorporated:*

http://hamsnetwork.org/corporate/f1023.pdf

*Friends of Niger:*

http://www.friendsofniger.org/pdf/FONTaxExemptApp.pdf

*Beaumont Charitable Foundation:*

http://www.ci.beaumont.ca.us/DocumentCenter/Home/
View/3076

*Cape Elizabeth Education Foundation:*

http://www.ceef.us/storage/downloadable-docs/01%2005%20
17%20501c3%20Application%20-%20IRS%20Form%201023.pdf

*Global Literacy Project, Inc.:*

http://www.glpinc.org/IRS_Filings/GLP_501(c) (3)_
Application-IRS_Form_1023.pdf

*LegalCORPS:*

http://legalcorps.org/wp-content/uploads/2012/01/1023-PubInspCopy.pdf

*Sandasarana Children's Educational Fund, c/o Saint Philip the Apostle Church:*

http://www.sceflanka.org/pdfs/notification/Form%201023%20petition.pdf

*Minnesota Groundwater Association Foundation:*

http://www.mgwa.org/foundation/documents/mgwaf-irs-1023.pdf

*United Way of Metropolitan Chicago:*

http://uw-mc.org/wp-content/uploads/2008/11/UWMC-IRS-Exemption-Application-1023.pdf

*Statement Arts, Inc.:*

http://statementarts.org/files/Statement_Arts_1023.pdf

*The Clear Fund:*

http://www.givewell.org/files/ClearFund/Clear%20Fund%20Form%201023.pdf

*Denver Early Childhood Council:*

http://www.denverearlychildhood.org/pdf/1023%20FINAL%20without%20addendums.pdf

*Miller & Zois Kids Foundation, Inc.:*

http://www.millerzoiskidsfoundation.com/PDF/MillerZoisKids.pdf

*Equipped to Survive Foundation, Inc.:*

http://www.equipped.com/etsfi_form1023.pdf

*The Light Millennium, Inc.:*

http://www.lightmillennium.org/501_c_3/lmtv_form_1023.pdf

*Television, Internet, & Video Association of DC, Inc.:*

http://www.tivadc.org/Resources/Documents/TIVA_Form_1023_final_093009forweb.pdf

*USA Projects:*

http://www.unitedstatesartists.org/pdf/USA_Projects_Form_1023.pdf

*Wycliffe Bible Translators International, Inc.:*

http://resources.wycliffe.net/financials/WBTI_1023_Application.PDF

*Software Freedom Conservancy, Inc.:*

http://sfconservancy.org/docs/conservancy_Form-1023.pdf

*Fort Bend County Sheriffs Employees Charitable Foundation:*

http://www.behindthebadgecharities.org/IRS%20Application%20for%20Exemption%20complete%20file.pdf

*Rocky Mountain Foundation of Hope:*

  http://www.rockymountainhope.org/_wp/wp-content/
  uploads/2010/01/RMFH%20Form%201023.pdf

*The Seniors Intervention Group Inc.:*

  http://seniorsinterventiongroup.org/app/SIG-501-c-3-Final-
  Signed.pdf

*Arizona Center for Investigative Journalism, Inc.:*

  http://arizonawatch.org/wp-content/uploads/2012/08/Final-
  1023.pdf

*Prairie Gold Homes, Inc.:*

  http://www.prairiegoldhomes.org/downloads/IRSApplication.pdf

*1by1 International, Inc.:*

  http://static.squarespace.com/static/51da06bfe4b0108eefe2761b/
  t/51f79c54e4b0dcb625417bec/1375181908106/1023.pdf

*DuPont Circle Village, Inc.:*

  http://www.dupontcirclevillage.org/Documents/
  DupontVillageForm1023-Final.pdf

*A Grain of Hope Foundation, Inc.:*

  http://www.agrainofhope.org/form1023.shtml

*Maryland Association of Non-Profit Organizations, Inc.:*

http://www.marylandnonprofits.org/dnn/Portals/0/Documents/About/Form%201023%20MDNP.pdf

*Your Town Alabama, Inc.:*

http://www.yourtownalabama.com/wp-content/uploads/2013/07/IRS-1023-Application-for-Recognition-of-Exemption.pdf

*Playa del Fuego, Inc.:*

http://playadelfuego.org/sites/default/files/boddocs/IRS-1023-complete.pdf

A few Medical 1023s:

*Maine General (several Form 1023 organizations):*

http://www.mainegeneral.org/body.cfm?id=1557

*San Francisco Free Clinic:*

http://www.sffc.org/SFFC_Form_1023_09_09_93.PDF

## OTHER APPLICATIONS THAT GIVE A WIDER RANGE OF NONPROFIT EXAMPLES:

*The Creek Bed Foundation, a Charitable Trust:*

http://thecreekbedfoundation.org/CreekBed1023.pdf

*San Diego Speculative Fiction Society, Inc.:*

http://www.sansfis.org/corporate_documents/IRS-1023/sansfis_irs1023.pdf

*National Consortium for College Completion, Inc.:*

http://www.completecollege.org/docs/Form%201023.pdf

*New Mexico GLBTQ Centers:*

https://secure.nmag.gov/coros/Documents/26-2022345%5CIRS
TaxExemptApplication(Form1023).pdf

*Hands N Feet Foundation:*

http://www.handsnfeetfoundation.org/wp-content/
uploads/2012/08/form1023.pdf

*Husky Swimming Foundation (Also shows good wording to expedite application):*

http://www.huskyswimmingfoundation.com/wp-content/HSF_
Form1023.pdf

*Shoe Giver of Tampa, Inc.:*

http://shoegiveroftampa.org/pdfs/Shoe-Giver-Application.pdf

*The Cordoba Initiative:*

http://www.investigativeproject.org/documents/misc/435.pdf

*Blount County Humane Society:*

http://www.blountcountyhumanesociety.org/PDFs/BCHS%20
1023.pdf

*Gaskov Clerge Foundation (GCF):*

http://www.gaskov.org/Documents/Completed%20990%20
Forms/GCF501C3%20%20%20501c3.pdf

*Society of King Charles the Martyr, Inc.:*

http://www.skcm-usa.org/Legal/SKCMForm1023asFiled.pdf

*One with Christ Ministries, Inc.:*

http://www.onewithchristministries.org/tax-exempt-501-c-3/
irs-form-1023/

*Shenango Chapter NAVHDA, Inc.:*

http://www.shenangonavhda.com/501_c__3__Application.pdf

*Vial of Life Project:*

http://www.vialoflife.com/images/Application%20for%20501-
c-3.pdf

*Grandfather Mountain Stewardship Foundation, Inc.:*

http://www.grandfather.com/wp-content/uploads/2011/06/
Application-for-Recognition-of-Exemption-Under-Section-
501c3.pdf

*Continuation Fund, Inc.:*

http://antiochcollege.org/sites/default/files/docs/Continuation_
Fund-1023_Applicatio.pdf

*Rural Investment Corporation:*

http://www.cfra.org/sites/www.cfra.org/files/RIC_Application_
for_Recognition_of_Exemption_1023.pdf

*Mozilla Foundation:*

> http://static.mozilla.com/foundation/documents/mf-irs-501c3-application-form-1023.pdf

*National Council of Young Men's Christian Associations of the United States of America (the original application for YMCA from 1982):*

> http://www.ymca.net/sites/default/files/organizational-profile/form_1023.pdf

*National Council of Nonprofit Association:*

> http://www.councilofnonprofits.org/files/Form%201023.pdf

*The Jackson Foundation:*

> http://www.thejacksonfoundation.org/Form1023.pdf

*Cadasil Together We Have Hope Non-Profit Organization:*

> http://cadasilfoundation.net/1023%20Original%20%20Application%20for%20Website.pdf

*Dianetics Foundation International:*

> http://www.xenu-directory.net/documents/corporate/irs/1993-1023-dfi.pdf

*Wayland Public Schools Parent Teacher Organization, Inc.:*

> http://waylandpto.org/wp-content/uploads/2012/08/Form-1023.pdf

*Multiple Sclerosis Foundation, Inc.:*

http://990online.com/docs/5/592792934_87_1023.pdf

*CAIRN Rescue USA:*

http://www.cairnrescueusa.com/docs/CRUSA_1023.pdf

*Servicemembers Legal Defense Network:*

http://sldn.3cdn.net/dd620a17021183177b_jem6iv9px.pdf

*Thunderridge Grizzly Bear Backer Club:*

http://thunderridge.coloradosportscastnetwork.com/GBBC/forms/1023%20Application%20for%20Exemption%20smaller%20file.pdf

*Saint Martin's Hospitality Center:*

http://www.smhc-nm.org/wp-content/uploads/2012/05/Form-1023.pdf

*The Seti League, Inc.:*

http://www.setileague.org/finances/1023.pdf

*Napa Emergency Women's Services:*

http://www.napanews.org/assets/upload/Form_1023.pdf

*The Putnam County Foundation, Inc.:*

http://www.pcfoundation.org/documents/PCCFForm1023.pdf

*National Foundation for the Centers for Disease Control and Prevention, Inc.:*

http://www.cdcfoundation.org/sites/default/files/upload/pdf/Form1023.pdf

*Partner in Health, Inc.:*

http://partnerforsurgery.org/wp-content/uploads/2013/03/Form-1023.pdf

*The Endeavor Initiative, Inc.:*

http://share.endeavor.org/financial/1023%20Form.pdf

*Quixote Humane Incorporated:*

http://www.quixotehumane.org/501c3/Quixote_Humane_Form_1023.pdf

*The Marie A. Dornhecker Charitable Trust:*

http://www.dornheckerfoundation.org/Documents/ct_1023.pdf

*United States Australian Football League, Inc.:*

https://usafl.com/files/USAFL%20Form%201023%20Exemption%20Application.PDF

*The Columbia Historical Foundation:*

http://www.columbiahistoricalsociety.org/chs_irs_1023_form_093084.pdf

*Internet Corporation for Assigned Names and Numbers:*

http://archive.icann.org/en/financials/tax/us/form1023.htm

*Stegall Charitable Educational Foundation* (also includes Form 990s)*:*

http://foundationcenter.org/grantmaker/stegall/appexempt.pdf

*Investigative Project on Terrorism Foundation:*

http://www.tennessean.com/assets/pdf/DN1658741022.PDF

*Malin Bergquist Charities Inc.:*

http://www.mbcharities.org/documents/IRSForm1023-Filed2010.pdf

*Longer Life Foundation:*

http://www.longerlife.org/form_1023.pdf

*The Doris M. Carter Family Foundation:*

http://carterfamilyfoundation.org/home/images/stories/Treasury-Form-1023.pdf

*TALX Charitable Foundation:*

http://www.talx.com/aboutus/1023.pdf

*Austin Browncoats:*

http://www.austinbrowncoats.com/docs/ABC_1023.pdf

*The CarMax Foundation:*

> http://www.carmax.com/assets/
> xckxeqcxxizfediqz5c5e5lav5ewx5of/form%20
> 1023-application%20for%20recognition%20of%20
> exemption-090308.pdf

*Trinity Mission Works, Inc.:*

> http://www.trinitymissionworks.org/Documents/IRS%20
> 1023%20ap.pdf

> *United Way of Southwest Louisiana Community Foundation:* https://
> www.foundationswla.org/swla/Portals/12/docs/Financial/IRS%20
> 1023%20Application.pdf

*Louisiana Hiking Trails, Inc.:*

> http://louisianahikingtrails.org/about/tax-exempt/1023.pdf

*Friendship Academy of Fine Arts Charter School:*

> http://www.friendshipacademy.org/wp-content/uploads/2012/12/
> form_1023_.pdf

*Maplewood Memorial Library Foundation:*

> http://maplewoodlibraryfoundation.files.wordpress.com/2013/07/
> application-for-501c3-status.pdf

*Moldova Mosaic Foundation:*

> http://moldovamosaic.org/mmorg/wp-content/uploads/2011/02/
> Form-1023-web.pdf

## OLDER BUT GOOD FUNDRAISING EXPLANATION:

*Nautilus of America, Inc.:*

http://oldsite.nautilus.org/admin/taxform-1023.PDF

## OLDER BUT GOOD WORDING TO SUPPORT THEIR FUNCTION:

*Southwestern Foundation:*

http://www.southwestern.edu/live/files/1234-irs-form-1023

## NO FORM 1023, BUT GOOD NARRATIVE SECTION WORTHY OF INCLUDING:

*Angels Above Foundation:*

http://www.aaf-epmo.org/AngelsAbove/Assets/aaf-documents/501C3_Appl_Narative.pdf

*Greater Tulsa Health Access Network*:

http://greaterthan.securespsites.com/Shared%20Documents/Governing%20Documents/Form%201023%20Attachments.pdf

*San Francisco-Krakow Cities Association:*

http://www.polishclubsf.org/Summary.pdf

*Friends of Olympia Farmer's Market (turned down the first attempt, but fixed the application and then approved. Shows application and IRS correspondence):*

http://www.farmers-market.org/wp-content/uploads/2012/10/Application-of-Exemption.pdf

# JOINT VENTURE FUNDRAISING

If your organization needs to raise money and you are tired of car washes and bake sales, consider holding a joint fundraiser with Pasture Valley Children Missions.

We purchase handmade jewelry from the Bambanani Project in Nhlangano, Swaziland, made by older orphans at Pasture Valley Children's Home, and women in the community. The necklaces, bracelets, and earrings are made from paper beads that have been rolled tightly and varnished. Some are also made of seeds. I have worn the same favorite necklaces for several years and they have held up perfectly as they are made with great pride and quality.

*Marielle DeJong (right) and friend at Pasture Valley Children's Home*

In addition, you can order laminated bookmarks made from local plants in Swaziland, decorated by hand, with your organization info and logo on the back. Very impressive but very reasonable. Buy for $1, sell for $2.50, or give away to your supporters.

## HOW IT WORKS

You tell us how many necklaces you want and what sizes (short fits most people), medium, long, and extra-long (wraps at least twice around the neck). We also have bracelets and earrings and can get matching sets in requested colors. There are other crafts available as well: purses, passport bags, etc.

You deposit half the retail cost of the jewelry plus shipping, either by check from you or your organization. Then you hold your sale. It is an easy way to raise $500-$1,500 quickly. We suggest a price of double the wholesale price you purchase for, but you can charge whatever you wish at your sale. Small group sales where people have time to try on the jewelry with no pressure produces great sales.

If you sell it all, you keep what you collected, we keep the deposit. If you do not sell it all, we will refund the portion of your deposit for the amount of jewelry you return to us in the same condition you received it.

The half we collect goes right back into the Bambanani Project so that we have funds available to purchase more jewelry. We offer this joint fundraiser as a convenience, not to make money. We have worked with several organizations and all have been happy: Tri-County Independent Living, Phelps R-III school district in Salem, Missouri to help fund space camp for 10 of their students, USA Athletes International to name just a few. These items sell well to church groups, women's clubs, and in schools.

You can also purchase directly from the Bambanani Project by going to http://pasturevalley.com/the-bambanani-project/

Contact us at: support@pasturevalleychildren.com
or visit www.pasturevalleychildren.com

# ORDER FORM

## Attorney-Prepared
## Fill-in-the-Blank Templates
## For Required State Documents

Name _____

Address _____

City _____ St _____ Zip_____

Phone _____

Email my order to:

_____

Fill out reverse side and mail payment to:

Chalfant Eckert Publishing
1028 S. Bishop Avenue, Dept. 178
Rolla, MO 65401

For Credit Card Orders with immediate email delivery:

www.doyourownnonprofit.com

I would like to order documents for _____ (state or DC)

_____ Articles of Incorporation in Word format     $9.95
_____ Bylaws in Word format     $9.95
_____ Articles and Bylaws with FREE BONUSES     $19.95
           Includes these 3 FREE Templates:
           Conflict of Interest Policy
           Annual Conflict Statement
           Initial Board Meeting Minutes

           Total enclosed            _____

*Thank you for your order.  We hope it saves you much time and effort in getting 501(c) (3) status.*

*Note: If you need a different format, please email us at support@doyourownnonprofit.com and we will try to accommodate your request.*

www.ingramcontent.com/pod-product-compliance
Lightning Source LLC
Chambersburg PA
CBHW060318200326
41519CB00011BA/1770